BLOOD & GUTS

BLOOD & GUTS

DISPATCHES FROM THE WHALE WARS

SAM VINCENT

Black Inc.

Published by Black Inc.,
an imprint of Schwartz Publishing Pty Ltd
37–39 Langridge Street
Collingwood Vic 3066 Australia
email: enquiries@blackincbooks.com
www.blackincbooks.com

The National Library of Australia Cataloguing-in-Publication entry:

    Vincent, Sam, author.
    Blood & guts : dispatches from the whale wars / Sam Vincent.
    9781863956826 (paperback)
    9781922231659 (ebook)
    Sea Shepherd (Ship)—Anecdotes. Animal rights activists—Anecdotes. Whaling—
    Law and legislation. Whaling—Economic aspects. Whaling—Political aspects.
    Whaling—Japan.
    338.372950952

Cover design by Peter Long
Cover photograph by Michael Nichols, *National Geographic*
Text design by Thomas Deverall

I.M.
Bob Balderstone

CONTENTS

AUTHOR'S NOTE

Japan's scientific whaling establishment is made up of several instruments. To avoid confusion, I explain them briefly here. The Fisheries Agency is the government department that finances the hunting of whales under research pretensions. Kyodo Senpaku is the company it employs to catch these whales and to sell the 'by-product' as meat. The Institute of Cetacean Research is the body that purports to analyse the catch scientifically.

The ICR's JARPA, which stands for the Japanese Whale Research Program under Special Permit in the Antarctic, ran from 1987/88 to 2004/05; the second phase of the program (JARPA II) began in 2005/06 and ended in 2013/14. Its domestic equivalent is JARPN, or the Japanese Whale Research Program under Special Permit in the North Pacific, which ran from 1994 to 1999; JARPN II began in 2000 and is ongoing.

Except where stated, money amounts in this book are given in Australian dollars. Finally, the names of certain people have been changed for privacy reasons.

PROLOGUE

S niffing my armpits, I realise I stink. I'm FOB – Fresh Off the Boat – but my leaky junk arrived from the south, not the north. Last night I saw my first house in three months, glinting on a headland like a castaway with a mirror; this morning I woke among skyscrapers and cranes, with ten lanes of traffic slowly bridging the mouth of the Yarra.

Into port and onto land, and I'm noticing everything for the first time again: the way strangers look down when you smile at them; the tram riders, plugged in and zoned out; a ground that stays still underfoot; the rush to your head of sun on bare skin; and rules, rules, everywhere rules. It's rare to be an observer of the world to which you belong, and it's important, I think, to appreciate such moments.

The long-awaited hiss and rat-a-tat-tat of an espresso machine make me grin like a stoner. If my editor wishes I'd showered more than five times this summer, he doesn't show it, plying me with coffees as I excitedly recount the voyage. It's only when I wipe my moustache from a second flat white that he cuts to the chase.

'So what's this conflict *actually* about?'

I carefully place my cup well away from the table's edge, a habit I won't lose for weeks. And then I'm speechless. I'm nervous, sure: this is the first time I've met my editor, the man whose laconic email and parcel of paperwork prompted a frenzy of flight-booking, job-quitting, subletting and bag-packing so I could drop everything and hitch a ride to Antarctica with the closest thing the environmental movement has to pop stars. But that's not why I can't answer his question.

What's this conflict actually about? Would the builder I once worked with who sported a Sea Shepherd sticker on his ute – and told me climate change was bullshit – be able to answer that? Or the two Japanese cops I met last year in the whaling town? They wanted to know if I was an eco-terrorist when they saw the crest on my passport. How about the crowd waiting on the dock today at Williamstown with their pirate merchandise and totes of donations? Perhaps my editor should ask them.

But the truth is I don't think any of them would fare any better. I mumble something about the oceans that we both know isn't right. Perhaps if he reframed the question I could begin to give him an answer. What this conflict's about is much harder to explain than what it's not about. Because it sure as hell isn't about whales.

WHALE HUGGERS

NEPTUNE'S NAVY

The Salvation Army band is playing 'Jingle Bells' when the *Brigitte Bardot*, looking like a floating fighter jet, opens its hatch. Auckland is unusual in that its harbour is located downtown; eco-pirates are more interesting than the Salvos, so the *Bardot* soon attracts a small crowd of onlookers.

Named for the French actress turned animal rights activist, the *Bardot* is a high-speed trimaran belonging to the Sea Shepherd Conservation Society, a vigilante marine-protection group whose members are considered eco-terrorists by the Japanese government. Captained by the Canadian Paul Watson, Sea Shepherd's vegan fleet, Neptune's Navy, espouses nonviolent direct action in a bid to stop whalers, sealers and illegal tuna and shark-fin fishermen. After clashing with a Norwegian Coast Guard vessel during an anti-whaling campaign off that country's north coast in 1994, Watson was labelled a pirate by the local press; ever since, Neptune's Navy has proudly sailed under a modified Jolly Roger, with a skull resting not on crossbones but on a trident crossed with a shepherd's crook.

The *Bardot* displays two such flags: one rippling above its stern, the other painted in a mural on its bow, clasped by a young Bardot herself, arms outstretched like Superwoman as she flies across the water's surface. In her spare hand Bardot holds a trident; two daggers are stuffed down her knickers.

I pick up my duffel bag and push through the throng of kids with scooters and their intrigued parents. The *Bardot* is in Auckland to ferry newly recruited volunteers to a secret location in international waters, where Watson, in hiding since he fled house arrest in Germany four months earlier, has recently emerged to take the helm of Sea Shepherd's flagship, the *Steve Irwin*.

I've arranged to live with the crew of the *Steve* for three months, as they embark on what has become an annual game of cat and mouse with Japan's government-run Antarctic whaling fleet. For the past seven summers Sea Shepherd has brought its unique brand of coercive conservation to Antarctica, ramming Japanese whaling vessels with its own, deploying 'prop foulers' to entangle and disable these ships' propellers, and responding to drenchings from the whalers' water cannons with volleys of paint bombs and verbal abuse (and even, at one time, canisters of butyric acid: stink bombs likened to rancid butter). Sea Shepherd claims the whalers are poachers of the Southern Ocean Whale Sanctuary, a 50-million-square-kilometre protected area; the Japanese government doesn't recognise the sanctuary and claims to be legally whaling for scientific research under the auspices of the International Whaling Commission (IWC), the global body that regulates the killing of whales.

For Australians, media coverage of the 'whale wars' evokes summer as much as leftover turkey sandwiches and Christmas cake. It's a familiar story of the struggle between good and evil: NGO 'eco-warriors' pitted against the might of the Japanese state; 'majestic giants of the deep' pursued by industrial weaponry; the pristine Southern Ocean running red with blood.

But beyond this simplistic version of events, I want to know who these self-mythologising pirates are, and what motivates them to pursue what is, environmentally, a relatively low-impact hunt in some of the most perilous waters on Earth; why Japan's government doggedly continues to bankroll a highly unprofitable program; and how Australia became the most vocal anti-whaling nation of all. In a theatre rarely seen by objective eyewitnesses, I want to know exactly what happens when the two fleets engage in their much-hyped naval jousts. Most of all, I want to know why whales have become a flashpoint for diplomatic, cultural, economic and environmental tension.

With four ships, five inflatable boats, one helicopter, two drones and 120 crew – representing twenty-four nationalities – Operation Zero Tolerance is to be the biggest campaign of Sea Shepherd's thirty-five-year history. 'The campaign's objective,' an email informed me before I left Australia, 'will be to intercept and intervene against the intent of the Japanese whaling fleet to murder 1035 whales in the Southern Ocean Whale Sanctuary.'

Fellow newcomers to the campaign embarking in Auckland are Tod, a nerdy Asian-American computer programmer from New York; Olav, a German father of three who wears a whale-fluke pendant around his neck; Bruce, the *Steve*'s Seniors Card–carrying third mate; Gav, an acne-scarred animal rights activist from Phillip Island; and Giacomo, a Berlin-based Italian photographer on assignment for a Manhattan PR agency (whose brief is to 'make Paul Watson appear like a superhero').

With his short-back-and-sides haircut and grey nomad uniform of jeans, polo shirt and gleaming white sneakers, Bruce doesn't fit my vegan vigilante stereotype for Sea Shepherd converts. While the crew of the *Bardot* takes on food supplies, I ask him why he signed up.

'I've always been interested in conservation, so given my skill set [10,000 nautical miles of racing yacht navigation], this was a natural progression,' he says. 'Paul needed a new third mate; I'm retired and the kids have left home, so I thought: *Bugger it, why not?*' When I mention I'm not a volunteer but a writer, Bruce's wrinkles scrunch into a smile. 'Aha, so you're here to win us the war!'

Sea Shepherd has been criticised for feeding the media misinformation and for dramatising accounts of clashes on the high seas to further its cause. Watson is infamous for embellishment; he once wrote: 'Surviving in a media culture meant developing the skills to understand and manipulate media to achieve strategic objectives. The issue of whaling is purely academic unless high drama is introduced to make it newsworthy.'

I'm to be the only journalist embedded for the entire campaign, and Neptune's Navy has obviously been briefed on this. Bruce leans close to me and conceals his words with the palm of his hand, as if Paul Watson himself has his ear cupped to the ceiling of the hold below us. 'Before coming here, I agreed not to talk Sea Shepherd strategy or tactics with the media, so I'm going to be careful what I say to you.'

I ask Bruce whether he thinks media manipulation is justified if it results in fewer whales being killed. 'Absolutely. This is a war we're fighting, and you've got to think of it in those terms. Any military operations HQ wouldn't want loose-lipped soldiers leaking secrets.'

We leave Auckland behind, its footpaths stained scarlet with pohutukawa stamens, and press out into the calm waters of the Hauraki Gulf. The gentrified island of Waiheke slips by, where marijuana plantations were replaced by vineyards when the yuppies usurped the hippies in the 1990s. Beside it sits Rangitoto Island with its candy-cane lighthouse, and beyond, the nature reserve island of Tiritiri Matangi.

It's a nine-hour journey to our rendezvous point with the *Steve*, so I descend into the hold to look around. The *Bardot* is Sea

Shepherd's smallest and fastest ship, mainly used as a scout. Skippered by the French adventurer and yacht racer Jean-Yves Terlain, the *Bardot*'s eight crewmembers are rumoured to be the most eccentric of Neptune's Navy, products of long Antarctic campaigns spent in close quarters.

'Welcome to the madhouse,' giggles 'Chili', a wisp of a woman kneading a blob of dough while watching a Disney cartoon on a laptop balanced atop a microwave. The kitchen around her is neat and compact, all hanging pots and bespoke plate enclosures. On the fridge a sticker declares: 'The Revolution Starts in *Your* Kitchen'; the adjoining photo depicts a bandanna-clad man doing his best to look like a revolutionary while julienning a carrot.

The floor of the *Bardot*'s tiny mess is packed with suitcases and boxes of fresh produce. One wall is covered with framed and signed black-and-white photos of the vessel's patron saint. In one, Brigitte pouts on a Harley-Davidson. In black texta, she's written: '*Pour mes pirates avec tout mon cœur.*'

A voice interrupts my perving. It's Heino, a barefoot German deckhand, brandishing a baking tray of biscuits. His pot belly, faded truckie's tatts and long grey hair evoke an aging rocker – or an aging rocker's roadie. 'Hey, Mr Writer, you want a cookie? I can't promise they're vegan, though. Some ants were crawling around the kitchen when I was cooking.'

I oblige, then follow Heino and his ant-tainted cookies to the bridge. Outside, Auckland's silhouetted skyline has disappeared, and with it, the clouds. The sun's appearance transforms the Pacific from dirty snow to Polynesian aquamarine; terns and gannets jink in the thermals to port side.

On the bow I run into Tod, who is basking in the sun and grinning widely. 'It's good to be home,' he tells me. For many, Operation

Zero Tolerance will be just one in a long series of Sea Shepherd campaigns that has come to consume – and define – their lives. This is only Tod's second campaign to the Antarctic, but he has also been involved in several Sea Shepherd campaigns to combat illegal shark-fin fishing in the Galápagos, and he would happily volunteer for the organisation full-time if life commitments back home didn't get in the way.

Tod was seven years old when he first saw a whale harpooned. A PBS TV broadcast had him captivated: 'I'd never seen a whale – so big, so beautiful, *and* they sang!' This was before the moratorium on commercial whaling came into force; it wasn't a nature documentary but a news piece. 'I thought, *As soon as I am old enough, I will protect you.* As an intelligent creature with the capability and desire to protect an innocent creature, I would do it.

'So, how about you?' Tod asks me. 'When did you have *that* moment?' I blush and clutch at words. I say something wet about being a storyteller, not an activist, that I'm here not to protect the whales but to chronicle their protectors. I'm worried I've said the wrong thing, but Tod is forgiving. 'Hey, well, that's important too. Without you, we wouldn't be able to tell our story.'

A half-moon's reflection is bobbing on the water when we finally reach the *Steve*. An inflatable boat is dispatched, and passengers, luggage and supplies are transferred via a rope ladder and a crane.

Once aboard, I'm led down the prow past an overwhelming array of new faces; names are given and forgotten immediately. The ship seems infinite: a Minotaur's labyrinth of dead ends and companionways, garlanded with whale-saving paraphernalia. It's past midnight when I fall asleep in my man-cot aboard my new home for the next few months, the *Steve*'s engine humming like a washing machine on spin cycle.

THE RUNAWAY CAPTAIN

'What the hell am I gonna do with a diamond-encrusted trident?' demands Captain Paul Watson. I feel like one of the three wise men visiting a fat, loud baby Jesus as I take my place in Watson's office behind two other gift-bearers. Once the trident donor is dismissed from His Holiness's court, Giacomo hands over a bag of goodies from Sea Shepherd volunteers in Berlin: herbal tea, Christmas biscuits, a teach-yourself book of German verbs. Watson raises his eyebrows as he inspects the book.

When I present my own gift – a bottle of Jamaican spiced rum – Watson adds it to a liquor cabinet groaning with bottles of Patrón tequila. 'John Paul DeJoria is a huge fan of Sea Shepherd,' he says by way of explanation. Watson, I will learn, is better than Phillip Adams at name-dropping.

*

If you were casting the role of a net-slipping international fugitive, Paul Franklin Watson wouldn't even get an audition. For starters, he's not very mobile: at sixty-two, he is an overweight, pear-shaped man. When he shuffles across the room in his black tracksuit pants and tatty espadrilles to meet me, I think of a male emperor penguin trying not to dislodge an egg that it's precariously incubating atop its feet. Far from the threatening outlaw I'd read about, Watson looks tired – pathetic, even – with puffy eyes, a double chin and an unkempt beard that's been white since his forties.

Then there's the poetry. Watson seems to spend more time bashing out verse on his laptop than eco-terrorising, with day-to-day management of the *Steve* deferred to first mate Sid Chakravarty. The poems – mainly about whales – end up as gifts or even books. Watson tells me he has no literary influences (he's reading *Game of Thrones* for fun), though he does recite poems by heart during mealtimes in the mess (those of Dante, Robert W. Service or his own – especially his own). He loves working a crowd.

Prolific in his output, Watson has authored several books on conservation; during Operation Zero Tolerance he'll be simultaneously working on three others that illustrate his passion for history: one on the Confederate naval raiders who attacked Yankee merchant shipping – and whaling – during the American Civil War, and another two on Christianity: 'Initially, it was one book, but my chapter about all the bad shit the popes have done grew into a book in itself. I'm gonna call it *All the Dope on the Popes*.' Stiff, sluggish, bookish: this is not an activist who evades the cops by jumping razor-wire fences and legging it. But evade them he has.

Sea Shepherd has long enjoyed the tacit approval of the governments of the United States (where the organisation is based), Australia (where most of its crew is from) and New Zealand (whose ports are crucial to its Antarctic campaigns), despite those governments officially denouncing Sea Shepherd's actions as reckless and irresponsible. Moreover, Paul Watson is not naive: he harasses the Japanese whaling fleet only in the international waters of the Southern Ocean – opaque not only in water colour but also in legal status, where responsibility for law enforcement is ambiguous, and prosecution difficult to pursue.

While Watson is no stranger to the police lock-up, he has not served a term of imprisonment since 1980, when he was fined c$8000 and ordered to serve ten days in a prison for disrupting Newfoundland's annual seal hunt. The closest he's come since was in 1997, when he was convicted in absentia by a Norwegian court for attempting to sink the whaler *Nybrænna* in that country's Lofoten archipelago five years earlier and sentenced to 120 days in prison. Watson was in the Netherlands at the time of the ruling, and was detained for eighty days in a local prison before the Dutch government decided not to extradite him to Norway.

But on the afternoon of Saturday 12 May 2012, Watson's luck appeared to have run out. Arriving at Frankfurt Airport in transit on his way to the Cannes Film Festival, Sea Shepherd's commander-in-chief was detained by German authorities in relation to an incident involving a Costa Rican shark-finning boat in Guatemalan waters in 2002. After facing court the following Tuesday, he was placed under house arrest on €250,000 bail and awaited a decision on his extradition to Costa Rica to face charges of endangering the boat and its crew – essentially, reckless navigation.

Two months later, a sympathetic insider from Germany's Defence Ministry informed Watson that he would be extradited within days – not to Costa Rica, but to Japan to face charges relating to a 2010 Sea Shepherd confrontation with Japanese whalers in the Antarctic. He disappeared overnight. On 4 December – seven months after his arrest and four months after fleeing – Watson publicly emerged from hiding on board the *Steve Irwin* in international waters off the coast of American Samoa. Two Interpol Red Notices, branding him as an internationally wanted person, hung over his head.

'I can't go into details of my travels over the last four months,' Watson wrote on the Sea Shepherd website upon his return. 'I may have to do it again sometime in the future.'

*

To use Tod's term, Paul Watson's 'moment' came when he was twenty-four years old. It was the summer of 1975, four years after a small group of like-minded Vancouver-based environmental activists had founded Greenpeace, an NGO aimed at peacefully highlighting and opposing what they saw as the rapacious consumption and destruction of the Earth for the sole benefit of humans. Watson claims to have been a founding member; Greenpeace claims he became active on its second expedition against nuclear weapons testing in Alaska.

In the 1970s, the most active whaling nation was the Soviet Union, hunting whales for oil, meat and bone meal to be used as fertiliser. Watson successfully argued that Greenpeace should adopt a more aggressive tone and directly combat the Soviets, who in the summer of 1975 had a fleet operating off the coast of California. Greenpeace activists would stop short of physical violence, but would make sure the Soviet fleet did too: they planned to put themselves, on two Zodiac boats, between the whalers and the whales.

According to Watson, the approach initially worked: he manned a Zodiac with Greenpeace cameraman Fred Easton, sufficiently delaying the Soviet gunner to allow eight sperm whales to swim to safety. But then a female whale was struck, and her enraged mate charged the bow of the whaler – and the Zodiac in front of it.

What happened next could have been cribbed from the pages of *Moby-Dick*. A Soviet harpoon whizzed over the activists' heads and struck the bull before it could use its own massive head as a battering ram. Time froze as the leviathan, convulsing in its death throes, reared out of the water and traded stares with Watson and Easton, narrowly – and, according to Watson, deliberately – avoiding crushing the duo on its way back down, an action which Watson says demonstrated comprehension of what the activists were trying to achieve.

In an open letter to the Icelandic nation eleven years later, after ordering the scuttling of two of its harpoon vessels, Watson explained the significance of the moment: 'The gaze of the whale seized control of my soul and I saw my own image reflected back at me. I was overcome with pity, not for the whale but for ourselves. Waves of shame crashed down upon me and I wept. Overwhelmed with horror at this revelation of the cruel blasphemy of my species, I realised then and there that my allegiance lay with this dying child of the sea and his kind. On that day, I left the comfortable realm of human self-importance to forever embrace the soulful satisfaction of lifelong service to the citizens of the sea.'

Watson still frequently retells the story of this epiphany; during my stay on the *Steve* I would hear it repeated in the mess nearly as often as his favourite smutty joke (*What's the difference between a Catholic priest and acne? Acne waits until you're thirteen before it comes on your face*).

Watson's failure to save the bull sperm whale convinced him of the limits of peaceful activism and galvanised his will to directly intervene using 'nonviolent aggression'. This was a step too far for Greenpeace: in 1977 the hot-headed young Watson was expelled from the organisation after yanking a club from a Canadian sealer and throwing it in the ocean along with a pile of pelts. Watson tells me he didn't hurt the sealer, but for Greenpeace, the activist had demonstrated that he was no pacifist.

Greenpeace co-founder Bob Hunter, who remained a close friend of Watson's until his death in 2005 and whose portrait now hangs in the *Steve*'s mess, summarised the episode in his history of the group, *Warriors of the Rainbow*: 'We all felt we'd gotten trapped in a web no one wanted to see develop, yet now that it had, there was nothing to do but bring down the axe, even if it meant bringing it down on the neck of our brother.'

To this day, Watson believes his expulsion from Greenpeace was politically motivated; the run-in with the sealer, he claims, was an excuse for the ambitious Patrick Moore to purge himself of his only rival for the group's presidency. Moore would go on to lead Greenpeace Canada for nine years and serve as a director of Greenpeace International for six.

Whether or not that's true, Watson says that parting ways with Greenpeace was the best thing that ever happened to him: he was freed from the constraints of an organisation he saw as growing too bureaucratic and ultimately toothless. 'I didn't want to protest,' he tells me, 'I wanted to *intervene*.' In mid 1977, Watson and a few friends founded Earthforce, a militant band of skinny-jeaned scallywags who aimed to physically sabotage whaling infrastructure. Their first ship, a sixty-metre ex-trawler, was named the *Sea Shepherd*.

By 1979, the IWC had reduced the annual global quota for killing whales from 46,000 seven years earlier to less than 20,000, but several privateers continued to operate outside the regulations, selling their contraband catch to Norway and Japan. The most notorious of these 'pirate whalers' was the *Sierra*, a Cypriot-flagged floating abattoir rumoured to have killed 25,000 cetaceans during its thirty-year operation in the whaling grounds of the Atlantic.

The *Sierra* was Watson's first scalp: he rammed it off the north coast of Portugal on a broiling July day. The *Sea Shepherd* was smaller than the *Sierra*, but Watson had fortified its bow with 100 tonnes of concrete; the whaler was hit at a speed of twelve knots and opened up like a can of (dolphin-friendly) tuna, a two-metre hole gashed in its bow before a second strike staved in much of its starboard side. The *Sierra* limped into the harbour of Leixões, where it was soon joined by the *Sea Shepherd*; Watson had attempted to flee to Spanish waters but was apprehended by a Portuguese naval destroyer and forcibly escorted to port.

The clash created a quandary for the authorities onshore: as the *Sierra* was a pirate ship, its ownership was hidden behind a series of front companies, preventing the Portuguese police from locating anyone to assume responsibility for the vessel. The port captain of Leixões decided not to charge Watson with gross criminal negligence. The *Sea Shepherd* was impounded but Watson was allowed to leave Portugal. He did not pay the US$750,000 in fines and damages ordered for the return of his ship, but on New Year's Eve 1979, Watson, along with *Sea Shepherd* chief engineer Peter Woof, returned to Portugal and scuttled the *Sea Shepherd* under the cover of darkness to prevent it from being forfeited to the Liberian-registered Sierra Trading Company, one of the ownership fronts.

One month later, the newly refitted *Sierra* was sunk by a solitary limpet mine in Lisbon's harbour. The perpetrators were never caught and Watson had the alibi of being across the Atlantic. But the next morning an anonymous caller to the offices of United Press International said: 'The *Sierra* will kill no more whales! We did it for the *Sea Shepherd*.'

The brazenness of the *Sierra* episode brought Watson instant fame – and notoriety. Overall, though, the media's reaction was positive: even *Time* magazine, not known for its environmentalist credentials, celebrated the end of the 'loathed' *Sierra* under the headline 'Victory at Sea'.

Financial backers began to appear, allowing Earthforce – now renamed Sea Shepherd – to spend the 1980s and '90s taking its tactics to the ends of the Earth: sinking harpoon vessels in Spain; ramming longliners in Mexico; cutting driftnets in Taiwan; de-clubbing seal clubbers in Quebec; and, from 2002, chasing the Japanese whaling fleet around the Antarctic.

By 2013, Sea Shepherd had 48,000 financial donors worldwide, 400,000 Facebook supporters, an annual income of more than US$12 million and a fleet of four modern ships. Watson had become a brilliant marketer, turning a once-fringe organisation into a globally recognised brand with mainstream appeal, promoting a message that was both anti-authoritarian and morally enlightened. These were bad-ass do-gooders, rebels with a cause.

Sea Shepherd has famous friends, as Watson is fond of telling you ('Sean Penn and I are good buddies'; 'Hunter S. loved us'; 'Aerosmith are generous guys'). Steve Wynn, the Las Vegas casino magnate and one of America's 500 richest men, is believed to be Watson's most generous backer; John Paul DeJoria, the billionaire hair-care-products mogul and liquor baron, also pours money (and tequila) into Sea Shepherd. The organisation's board of advisers reads like my dad's dream dinner party guest list: Pierce Brosnan, Martin Sheen, Sean Connery, Kelly Slater, Jacques Perrin, Sam Simon, Stephanie Gilmore, Brigitte Bardot, MacGyver. But given his aggressive tactics, self-acknowledged arrogance and Gaddafi-grade ego, it's no surprise that Watson has also won himself many enemies.

*

The footage is deliberately overexposed, a style familiar to viewers of Brazilian *telenovelas*. A clean-shaven Watson paces the deck of the Sea Shepherd ship *Farley Mowat*, dressed like a Rhodesian tobacco farmer in matching khaki vest and shorts, with sandals completing the look. Behind him, under leaden skies, a grotty white boat finished with royal-blue trim bobs about on the angry Pacific. This is the *Varadero*, a Costa Rican longliner sprung by the *Farley* illegally fishing for sharks in Guatemalan waters in May 2002.

Watson was empowered by the Guatemalan authorities to detain the *Varadero* and escort it to shore. The subsequent footage, used in the documentary *Sharkwater*, shows the Sea Shepherds hosing the shark-finners with a water cannon before Watson says to his crew: 'Okay, let's get ready.' Moments later, the *Farley* hits the *Varadero* at slow speed, prompting the fishermen to agree to be escorted to shore.

Three hours from port, the *Farley* received a radio message that a Guatemalan gunboat was on its way to arrest *them*; they headed south and docked in Puntarenas, Costa Rica, only to be arrested upon arrival. Watson believes the Costa Rican and Guatemalan governments were paid off by the powerful Taiwanese shark-finning mafia, principal beneficiaries of a billion-dollar global industry.

'It's all politics, of course,' Watson tells me in his office below the bridge of the *Steve*, its walls covered with a peculiar combination of scantily clad women and whale flukes. 'There's some sort of deal between Japan and Costa Rica going on here, and obviously Germany's involved with it too.

'Basically, all we did [to the *Varadero*] was use water cannons and intimidate them and cut their nets and cut their lines and ordered them out of there. Anyway, we went on down to Costa Rica and found out that these guys came in a day later and filed charges for attempted murder against me, saying *I* tried to kill them! Our crew went in to testify, showed them our video footage and they tossed the whole thing out.

'Ten years later, they resurrect the whole thing, even though the statute of limitations has passed. Their argument now is: "Well, that was an act of terrorism so there is no statute of limitations." Suddenly, the allegation of eight fishermen without any evidence to back it up is now an act of terrorism!'

Costa Rica later downgraded the charge to 'causing a danger of drowning or of an air disaster', but Watson is convinced that, should he return to Puntarenas to face the charge, he would immediately be extradited to Japan. For its part, the Japanese-requested Interpol Red Notice relates to the 2010 high-seas boarding of a whaling vessel by former Sea Shepherd activist Pete Bethune, allegedly on Watson's instruction. Given Watson's decade-long history of embarrassing Japan's Antarctic whaling fleet, and by his account costing them in excess of US$100 million during that time, Watson is sceptical of receiving a fair trial there.

Both Japan and Costa Rica had previously attempted to have Watson placed on the Red List, but each time the request was dismissed by Interpol as being politically motivated. When Germany detained Watson, it did so without Interpol's assistance; it was only when Watson had fled Germany that Berlin made its own complaint to the international policing organisation, which then issued the two Red Notices requested by Japan and Costa Rica, asking any country whose territory Watson enters to arrest him.

'Knowing that if I got sent to Japan I'd never get out of there, I decided the best thing would be to leave Germany,' he tells me. 'It cost me €250,000 to do it, but there's no other choice, because if I was sent to Japan I'd probably never get out.'

Watson grows angry for the first time during our interview.

He runs five pudgy fingers through his lank hair and slowly shakes his head. 'We've got a lot of sympathy in Germany, you know. The courts, the prosecutor, the judges were all very apologetic; the police, the prison guards are all very supportive. It's that goddamned minister of justice [then Sabine Leutheusser-Schnarrenberger] – I don't know what her problem is. She got over a hundred thousand letters on this and she didn't answer a single one of 'em! There are 80,000 gangsters in Japan who aren't on the Red List, but for some reason she thinks I should be.'

Love him or loathe him, Watson has a point: Interpol Red Notices are not usually issued for dangerous driving and trespassing.

*

The reason Japan is so desperate to apprehend Watson was succinctly written on the faces – or face, as the case was and the point is – of many of the thousands of Sea Shepherd volunteers who protested his detention outside German embassies and consulates worldwide in the days following his arrest. As part of the 'Save Our Skipper' (SOS) campaign, Watson acolytes from Paris to Hong Kong held cardboard cut-outs of their hero's face, which, together with their matching Jolly Roger T-shirts, created the mass visual effect that Sea Shepherd *is* Paul Watson.

Charismatic, domineering and difficult to shut up, Watson has built Sea Shepherd in his own image, personally leading all its major voyages and near singlehandedly maintaining the organisation's media presence. Watson tells me he has dedicated his life to 'my clients, the whales and dolphins', and it is hard to fault his commitment: in the last five years, he has barely been home to Friday Harbor, Washington State. Cut off Sea Shepherd's head and would the body die?

'Sea Shepherd is Paul Watson,' Peter Hammarstedt, the captain of the *Bob Barker*, concedes to me by email, 'but Sea Shepherd is also every single one of us inspired by Paul's vision. If the whalers believed that they could stop Sea Shepherd by targeting Paul, then it was a miscalculation and strategic blunder on their part.'

In Watson's absence post-arrest, Hammarstedt was asked to take over his boss's speaking schedule, a gruelling itinerary of after-dinner speeches, public rallies and celebrity fundraising drives. When I later ask the *Bob*'s skipper if it was difficult to maintain Sea Shepherd's impressive media exposure and fundraising clout without Watson, Hammarstedt says it wasn't easy, but that the outpouring of public support he received was proof that Sea Shepherd is no longer one man's organisation – it is a movement.

'Peter Hammarstedt said that to you because you're a journo!' a bemused deckhand on the *Steve* tells me when I mention Hammarstedt's nonchalance. 'That topic came up in the car while we were [docked] in Williamstown. "It's been a tough year," Hammar said.'

It doesn't take long to see why Hammarstedt would be privately daunted by the task of filling Watson's espadrilles: the first few times I ascend to the office of the *Steve*'s skipper, I am met by a locked door and the muffled sound of Skype interviews; the first time I see him on the bridge he's giving a laptop interview to the Seven Network's *Sunrise* program. Nor would Hammarstedt or another understudy likely be able to command the unconditional loyalty that Watson does, which creates an atmosphere on board that one former Sea Shepherd member described as 'chaos run by God'.

When Watson descends to the mess, he is treated as a kind of anti-Ahab, both feared and revered by his crew. Not long after boarding the *Steve*, I notice several wide-eyed crewmembers consistently volunteering their place in the meal queue to Watson. It is hard not to think of him in divine terms the night Tod awkwardly tells me I am sitting in 'Paul's chair', leaving the statement hanging like water vapour until I shift to an identical chair beside it.

Watson denies that he is the focus of a cult of personality, contending that any maritime captain is treated with respect by his subordinates. Perhaps, but does pelagic protocol extend to signed photos of appreciation by *Playboy* playmates (one of whom, Lisa DiStefano, was once his wife), corny paintings by adoring fans and that home-made diamond-encrusted trident (which would eventually find a home above the *Steve*'s compass)? Does it extend to quaffing bottles of San Pellegrino mineral water while the rest of the crew drinks desalinated seawater?

Watson doesn't seem to actively encourage this behaviour: when on New Year's Eve a drunk engineer earnestly thanks him for 'doing more for the planet than anyone in the history of the planet', Watson seems both baffled and embarrassed; he tells me later that he is annoyed when crewmembers are too overawed to speak to him, and he appears most comfortable at the times when he's discussing not activism but politics, history or poetry. Nor, though, does he shy away from the limelight when doting crewmembers gather around 'his chair' to hear recycled anecdotes with the goggle-eyed excitement of children on the lap of a shopping-mall Santa.

Dissent does exist within Sea Shepherd, but the prevailing atmosphere is one of zealous loyalty to St Paul. When I ask a crewmember if she will be returning to Antarctica in 2013–14 on board the *Steve*, she says there won't be a next year, 'because Paul said so'.

'What if Paul's wrong?' I venture.

The crewmember is incredulous. 'Paul Watson is never wrong.'

THE *STEVE*

'Attention all crew, attention all crew: there is some kind of whale breaching on the starboard side of the vessel. It looks real neat.'

The Canadian voice booming over the *Steve*'s PA system jolts me awake, and I bounce upright like Dracula at dusk, smashing my head against the low ceiling of my cabin. I hear the squeak of ugg boots slipping around linoleum corners. Upstairs on deck, crew-members in penguin pajamas and polar-bear boxer shorts crane their necks and squint to starboard. A faint lump a mile away slips beneath the morning swell. It looks like a dull grey rock. 'Amazing, hey?' the bloke next to me says, shaking his head in wonder.

I'm getting used to this. After two weeks on the *Steve* I've heard PA announcements for a shark (which turned out to be a sunfish), a seal, an albatross and several distant spumes of mist supposedly emanating from whales. Each announcement has prompted man-overboard-style hysteria as everyone drops what they're doing to rush outside for a look.

Excitable naturalists are apt, given the name of the ship. The trademark behaviour of the late Steve Irwin, the mulleted, ocker TV presenter, was chasing startled wildlife, tackling it to the ground then panting to the camera: 'Crikey, that was a close call!' Among the international conservation community, Irwin was highly

24

regarded for his fundraising work and for acquiring large tracts of threatened wilderness in Melanesia, Australia and the United States. In 2006 Irwin, another of Watson's famous mates, expressed a desire to one day crew for Sea Shepherd in Antarctica aboard the organisation's flagship, the *Robert Hunter*. He would never get the chance, killed in a freak accident when he was barbed by a stingray off the Great Barrier Reef in September that year. Soon after, the *Hunter* was renamed in Irwin's honour.

Originally a Scottish Fisheries patrol vessel, the *Steve* was built in Aberdeen in 1975 and for twenty-eight years chased illegal cod trawlers through the North Sea as the *Westra*. Now Dutch-flagged and Melbourne-based, at fifty-nine metres it's the biggest of Operation Zero Tolerance's four vessels and, though currently drifting with its engines off, the first to start the journey south. While the *Bardot* remains floating off Auckland, the *Bob Barker*, named for the game-show host who donated US$5 million to buy it, is moored in Wellington. Sea Shepherd's newest addition, the *Sam Simon* – audaciously bought from the Japanese whalers themselves by a shell corporation with money donated by its eponymous *Simpsons* producer – has just been unveiled to the public in Hobart.

On board the *Steve*, what was at first a confusing and massive liner is soon a familiar and cosy tub. The hold comprises two levels running the length of the ship, which house the cabins, mess, galley and bathrooms, and a third, smaller level for Watson's office, a media room and the helicopter deck. The cluttered bridge commands spectacular views and, as well as being the ship's nerve centre, serves as a shrine to Steve: tacky *Crocodile Hunter* memorabilia lines the walls, and a figurine key ring hanging from a lamp depicts Irwin clutching a man-eating saltwater crocodile as if it were a box of groceries.

Outside, the *Steve*'s steel hull is painted in urban camouflage: huge grey, black and blue splodges are interrupted only by a giant Sea Shepherd Jolly Roger on the superstructure, the skull's two eye sockets circling portholes. The *Steve*'s port and starboard decks are narrow and floored by well-scrubbed wood, while the stern or aft deck is covered with gym gear and drums of helicopter fuel. The forward deck is home to the *Steve*'s three smaller boats, which are used in 'actions', and the bow is mainly reserved for wildlife watching and – weather permitting – birthday parties.

My tiny cabin, shared with the photographer Giacomo, is below the bow of the *Steve* in the 'Zero Gravity' sector, so-called because of its legendary turbulence. Walking through Zero Gravity as the boat pitches down a steep wave is akin to dropping suddenly in an aeroplane or jumping in an elevator as it reaches the ground floor.

The mess is the share-house kitchen of the *Steve*: this is where crewmembers relax, eat meals and gossip over cups of tea and coffee. It's divided into two rooms: one section is a cafeteria-style dining room, while the other is ringed with well-loved couches and armchairs that are filled only for crew meetings and lunchtime viewings of the *Daily Show with Jon Stewart* and the *Colbert Report* – both downloaded, much to Watson's satisfaction, via a satellite dish donated by the Prince of Monaco.

One whole wall of the mess is a bookshelf whose contents evoke a Brooklyn youth hostel: as well as Huxley, Hemingway and Fitzgerald, dog-eared favourites include *American Hardcore: A Tribal History* and a well-thumbed copy of *The Vegan Guide to New York City 2010*.

Just as I quickly acquaint myself with the *Steve*, so too am I soon familiar with its crew. There are forty-three on board, including me – thirty men, thirteen women – from fourteen nations. With ten nationals, Australia is the best represented country, followed by the United States (nine), the United Kingdom (six) and Canada (four). The bulk of the crew falls into five main departments: the deckhands, who maintain the ship and operate the small boats; the quartermasters, who keep watch; the galley; the engine room; and the media team. An in-house camera crew filming the top-rating US reality TV show *Whale Wars*, this last department is effectively Sea Shepherd's propaganda arm.

Once names and faces start to stick, I can't help but play amateur anthropologist. Unlike on dry land, the engineers seem to be the popular gang here, led by Brian, a handsome American who smiles about as often as Gerard Henderson. His second-in-command is Pablo, a lanky Melbourne hipster with a Victorian-era strongman's moustache, while the third engineer is 'Little John' because he's two metres tall and from Nottingham. 'Squid', a slight, sixty-something Liverpudlian with a friendly face full of creases, rounds out the quartet.

The deck is the *Steve*'s biggest department and is led by Chad, a high-school-jock type with long hair, elfin ears and the collective ink of a bikie gang. With their tattoos, body piercings and foul language, the deckies fit my preconceptions of both sailors and eco-saboteurs.

The crew's average age is thirty-two, with Bruce – or 'Uncle Bruce', as his avuncular nature soon leads him to be called – the oldest, at sixty-four. Many have recently left university or are of university age and, being predominantly white and middle-class, remind me of sufferers of the quarter-life crisis – as if a summer spent saving whales will be more fulfilling than one cleaning shit out of cages at an African elephant orphanage or one teaching English in China. And this is no pleasure cruise either. Crewmembers are unpaid and work seven days a week in often challenging conditions (try tying a sailor's knot in a blizzard). No alcohol is consumed other than on special occasions (Christmas, New Year's Eve, some birthdays) and anyone caught smoking is dropped off at the next port of call. Outgoing emails are screened by the ship's overworked IT guy, Tux, with all references to location, strategy and even local weather and wildlife censored for fear of leaking intelligence to the whaling fleet. Showering is discouraged to save fresh water.

Nor is this *The Love Boat*. Amongst the myriad whaling-related newspaper clippings and letters from well-wishers pinned to the mess noticeboard, one laminated page takes prominence: 'Sea Shepherd Policy: Ship and Field Personal Relationships'. The first few rules relate to work ethic and avoiding inter-crew fisticuffs, but then comes the juicy stuff: 'Officers (and field/project leaders) are prohibited from fraternising or becoming romantically involved with one another or with any other crewmember, volunteer or contractor.'

In the event that nature takes its course, there is an escape clause: anyone in a relationship that violates this personal relationship policy, or in a platonic friendship that may progress to violating it, must immediately disclose the situation to their manager. Asking Watson for permission to conduct a summer romance would surely be as awkward as any father–son sex-education session – not that I will even have the option ('No crewmember or volunteer may fraternise or become romantically involved with any media representative covering Sea Shepherd').

Do all these rules make Sea Shepherd sound like the army? Watson lists his chief strategic influence as Sun Tzu, the ancient Chinese military strategist and author of *The Art of War*. At all times while on campaign, Watson's crewmembers are required to wear the black Sea Shepherd uniform, and many choose to sew Royal

Navy patches onto their sweaters. The language of war is everywhere too: vintage US World War II propaganda posters adorn the galley and companionways (*Somebody blabbed! Button your lip! Don't talk about ship movements! Don't talk about war production!*), while previous campaign titles read like military operations (Operation No Compromise; Operation Leviathan). Already encouraged by the good-versus-bad dichotomy propagated by the media, Neptune's Navy considers itself to be on a crusade.

But like all good sailors – even naval officers – the crew of the *Steve* also enjoys having fun. Katy Perry singalongs are surprisingly common, as are dress-up parties: I arrive a week after Watson's birthday party, where the crew surprised him by coming in *Rocky Horror Picture Show* fancy dress. Practical jokes and bizarre wagers are commonplace, with Will, one of the cameramen for *Whale Wars*, having been challenged to eat from a dog bowl for the entire campaign.

'We don't take ourselves too seriously,' explains 'Grug', the mastermind behind the dog bowl challenge. 'It's a really fun atmosphere; you'll love it. We're all weirdos who stick out in some way back home, but here we all get along.'

Grug, a 24-year-old physiotherapist from Melbourne, is the first friend I make on the *Steve*. His nickname comes from his supposed likeness to the benevolent Burrawang cycad from a series of Australian children's books, but with his round face, mushroom mop of straw hair and beaming smile, I reckon he looks more like a cartoon depiction of the sun. My favourite childhood pet – a farm tabby whose voracious appetite for native wildlife would have contravened both Sea Shepherd's conservationist philosophy and its strict adherence to veganism – was also named Grug, so I'm immediately drawn to his whale-hugging namesake. We strike up a quick friendship based on a shared love of Australian Rules football, our joint New Year's resolution being to kick the footy I've brought on an Antarctic iceberg. It doesn't come true, but kick-to-kick on the aft deck does become a near-daily ritual.

Grug tells me he joined Sea Shepherd because 'it's Sea Shepherd and Sea Shepherd's fucking cool', but his motivation runs deeper than the louche world of high-seas piracy. 'I was eating a salami sandwich a few years ago, and I was halfway through it when it struck me: why did an animal have to die for me to eat lunch? I became a vegan that day and have slowly grown more interested in animal rights and conservation issues.'

Over 500 people applied to crew on Sea Shepherd campaigns in 2012. Chief recruiter Peter Hammarstedt tells me crewmembers are selected to represent a cross-section of society, and include Vietnam vets, single mothers, students and PE teachers. Some are chosen for particular skills (welders, carpenters, navigators or doctors), but most bring nothing more than a demonstrated passion for the cause. 'In some ways,' says Grug, 'I think the only thing we all have in common is the desire to save whales. Everyone on this boat thinks it's shocking what the whalers are doing down there.'

*

When a snowy-haired kid with freckles and Mickey Mouse gum-boots pulled a carving knife from his pocket, passed it to his dad and casually watched him butcher a pilot whale, I think it was the only time I've had culture shock. That was *shocking*.

The Faroe Islands rise from the North Atlantic like giant upturned billiard tables, their jagged felt-green mountains punctuated by thundering waterfalls, stone shepherds' huts and the occasional hamlet of colourful cottages with roofs often topped with turf. This spectacular archipelago, a semi-autonomous Danish possession perched between Iceland, Scotland and Norway, is celebrated for plump sheep, cute puffins and a national football side that punches well above its weight. But the 50,000 Faroe Islanders are also widely condemned for the *grindadráp*, a semi-regular summertime pilot-whale hunt that has come to define their national identity.

The first record of the grindadráp is from 1298: a pod of whales (*grind*) is spotted, the alarm is raised with a bellow and every man within earshot drops what he is doing, arms himself and rushes to the water's edge. Within minutes the sea runs red with blood and entire communities are provisioned with meat.

On my second-last day in the Faroes, on assignment for a newspaper's travel section, I am woken by a knock on my door and the same call that has galvanised Faroese men into action for centuries: 'Grind!' My hosts have heard of the grindadráp on the local radio; minutes later we are on the road to the town of Vestmanna, an hour's drive away on the island of Streymoy.

'It is perhaps the most communal event we have,' a Faroese friend tells me of the grindadráp. So communal, in fact, that although the pod of fifty-nine long-finned pilot whales was first spotted off the coast of Vestmanna early that morning, news of the hunt was deliberately not broadcast until long after the animals had been killed, to prevent the town from being overrun with volunteers.

We arrive in Vestmanna hours after the slaughter, but the sea still has a pink tinge. The whales have been arranged in rows on the town's wharf; neat offal escape hatches have been carved out of each carcass, while blood is still being washed away with a hose. Noisy seagulls linger. The stench is distinctly unpleasant.

With four whaling foremen supervising, men are butchering each carcass while their children hang about: first the blubber is flensed (peeled back) with the aid of axes, then the meat is filleted with purpose-made knives, their sheaths ornately decorated with carved whale motifs. With rare exceptions, whaling in the Faroes is a non-commercial activity, and in typically Scandinavian-socialist style, a strong emphasis is placed on ensuring that as many people as possible gain a share of the prize. 'Everyone who participated will get a share,' one hunter tells me, arms folded, while behind him locals load cuts of meat and blubber into car boots and wheelbarrows. 'If there is any left over it will go to the rest of the town, and then to the neighbouring town, starting with the nursing home.'

I am profoundly shocked as I wander among the carcasses, but it takes me a few minutes to realise why. It isn't the sight of the whales, nor the rich, wet smell of death. It's the children all around me: they're bored. A brother and sister are sitting on one carcass as if they're waiting for the school bus; a nearby girl seems oblivious to the carnage as she slowly rides her bicycle straight through it, her pink helmet matching the intestines spilling out of the whales' stomachs. Other kids sit with chins resting on hands. After Mickey Mouse Gumboots gives his dad the knife as if it were a TV remote, our eyes meet. His is the universal expression of the spoilt brat: *I would rather be playing Xbox.*

I must have been the same age as that boy – perhaps seven or eight – when I saw my first whale, a humpback rounding Cape Byron. My family was en route to visit my hippy uncle in Nimbin, and our frequent highway stops to look for migrating humpbacks were, I suspect, a convenient way for my parents to stop back-seat fights between my three sisters and me. That first glimpse wasn't much – a lump and a spout – yet I was filled with awe, because I'd been raised to treat the very *idea* of this creature as awesome: rare, intelligent, peaceful. But those Faroese kids didn't seem to be filled with any awe. And that, I think, is what so disturbed me.

For many in the Western world, whales are considered 'flagship species', defined by the British biologist Vernon Heywood as 'popular, charismatic species that serve as symbols and rallying points to stimulate conservation awareness and action'. A South African zoologist and anti-poaching advocate I know prefers the term 'ambassador species', with whales and elephants – large mammals whose supposedly unique qualities deem them worthy by many of special treatment – at the top of the animal kingdom's diplomatic corps.

The Book of Genesis tells us the first model off God's production line was the whale; in the Old Testament, Jonah is saved from drowning by a whale sent by God to swallow him. By 1977, when conceptions of existence had moved beyond our own planet, a whale-song recording was sent into outer space aboard the *Voyager* unmanned space probes as one of the representations of life on Earth for any aliens who happened to be passing by.

If you'd asked me when I was in primary school why whales are special, I would have told you that they are the world's biggest mammals, among the rarest, the smartest, that they dive the deepest and sing the best – and I would have been blurring the characteristics of blue whales, bowheads, bottlenose dolphins, sperm whales and humpbacks, respectively. The environmental anthropologist Arne Kalland called this 'the creation of a Superwhale', in which distinctions between whale species are often not made by those of us who live in non-whaling nations, creating a mythical creature whose virtues and conservation status do not correspond with any one species.

The tourist industry of watching these swimming superlatives, whether they be dolphins, orcas, humpbacks, minkes, southern rights or the roughly forty other cetacean species found in our waters, contributes $300 million to the Australian economy annually, while whales and dolphins – irrespective of their species or abundance – are the only marine animals to be afforded their own sanctuary under Australian law.

With distance, I can review the grindadráp with the aid of reason rather than the emotion that comes from my cultural upbringing. It would make sense to me to oppose the grindadráp if it were unsustainable, but it is not: the Faroese have kept annual records of their whale drives since 1709 and, amazingly, the catch has held steady over that time.

Although the method of killing is undeniably confronting to the unaccustomed – the whales are herded by motorboat to shallow water, where waiting men kill them with knives and hooks – it was designed by veterinarians to minimise cruelty, replacing an earlier technique involving spears and gaffs. The meat I eat is procured in a similar way; it's just that the killing occurs behind closed doors.

I would also feel comfortable to denounce it if it were now, as some allege, more about bloodlust than food-gathering, but those wheelbarrows and car boots were filling pretty quick – in spite of the fact that pilot-whale meat has been shown to contain high levels of mercury. While the Faroe Islands, an affluent society heavily subsidised by the Danish purse, is no longer the remote, impoverished outpost it once was, why should the Faroese swap what is locally available for the diet of their contemporaries in Western Europe – countries whose industrial waste helped poison pilot-whale meat in the first place? Implicit in this argument is that it is more moral for the Faroese to burn fossil fuels importing Australian beef than to harvest the whales on their doorstop because cetaceans are somehow more special than cows. Who determines the currency of morality?

I cannot condemn the grindadráp by treating it as illegal, either, because long-finned pilot whales, not much bigger than dolphins, are considered small cetaceans rather than great whales, and thus there is no consensus on whether they fall under the umbrella of the IWC's 1986 moratorium on commercial whaling (and, anyway, the grindadráp is a not-for-profit activity). Sea Shepherd has repeatedly claimed that the grindadráp places Denmark in contravention of the 1982 Bern Convention on the Conservation of European Wildlife and Natural Habitats, under which long-finned pilot whales are a protected species throughout the European Union. But the Faroe Islands have a high degree of autonomy within the Kingdom of Denmark, are not part of the European Union and are thus not accountable to its laws.

What's left? Intelligence? Which intelligence? Pilot whales have sophisticated sonar capabilities, but probably don't have the problem-solving skills of pigs or the tool knowledge of crows. If, as a benchmark, we take the presence of spindle neurons – brain cells that facilitate complex thought-processing and empathising – pilot whales, unlike several cetaceans, don't have them. If we go on self-awareness, plenty of mammals eaten by most Australians – as well as octopuses – are also thought to possess sufficient brain function to be conscious of their existence. Surely, then, my initial view that the Faroese shouldn't polish off pilot whales because they are 'majestic giants of the deep' is a cultural projection? It hadn't even crossed my mind that perhaps the only thing the Faroese consider majestic about whales is their taste when cooked in pepper sauce.

In time my initial shock gives way to understanding: of course those kids were bored – I was bored too when I was dragged to

Woolies with my mum, or, perhaps more applicably, when my dad, a farmer, made me help out at the cattle yards.

Travel-writing assignments to the Arctic and my love of cold, remote places expose me to another side of this debate: those who want to save the whales – for supper. In Greenland my Inuit friends Kjeld, Naja and Aqqalu nearly break my jaw the day they feed me a strip of *mattaq*, the rock-hard raw skin of the narwhal. Júlí, a ghostly-white Icelandic fisherman I know who holds vegetables and vegetarians in equal contempt, mesmerises me with tales of his father's involvement in Iceland's own 'scientific' whaling program. In the early 2000s, Paul Watson even sent Júlí's dad a threatening letter demanding that he stop hunting whales. When I ask how his dad reacted, Júlí breaks into a wry smile. 'He framed it.'

*

I don't, of course, tell anyone on the *Steve* about my whale-eating friends. While I don't share Júlí's zeal for killing whales (in Iceland he offered to take me shooting dolphins with a shotgun for fun), nor do I still view whales as ambassador species deserving of special treatment. Setting aside the legality of Japan's Antarctic whaling program and the veracity of its claims to 'scientific' research, I am not sure anymore why I should be opposed to the sustainable hunting of whales, whether it be in the Faroe Islands or elsewhere.

But I accept that this is an inherently anthropocentric point of view, which for Sea Shepherd misses the point of its campaigns in Antarctica. Neptune's Navy sees the whale wars as a question of philosophy: whether whales are resources to be exploited or sentient beings to be respected. And besides, it took only five days for the hostages of a 1973 Swedish bank robbery to start empathising with their captors – Stockholm syndrome, a local criminologist called it.

I'm spending three whole months at sea with Sea Shepherd's crew,
and nowhere to go but south.

HOMINIDS

It's New Year's Day when I'm accused of murder. To be honest, I'm surprised it took so long: during my time with Sea Shepherd I've made no secret of my omnivorism back on shore. I was still brushing flakes of sausage-roll pastry from my face when I boarded the *Bardot*, the remnants of a dockside last supper that also included a ham and cheese sandwich and a carton of flavoured milk.

But the identity of my accuser does surprise me. During the few times I'd spoken to Squid, I'd typecast him a sad, gentle man. 'Me wife died last year,' he explained to me soon after we met, 'which was really shit. I was a bit lost what to do next, to be honest, and then I heard about Sea Shepherd. I'm just so lucky I was accepted here; it's set me back on track.'

On 28 December the Japanese whaling fleet left port in Innoshima and Shimonoseki and commenced its journey south; it will be late January before it reaches the whaling grounds of the Southern Ocean, meaning we will be drifting off New Zealand's South Island for another week. On the first day of 2013 I'm in the mess library with Squid, hoping to identify a bird we've just seen outside. Squid leafs through his wildlife book to a page on Australia and tells me how proud he is to have successfully lobbied for an end to the sale of kangaroo meat in UK supermarkets; I tell him I eat kangaroo meat all the time back home because it's cheap, delicious and better for the Australian environment than heavy-hoofed sheep or cattle.

'You *what*?'

Clearly, I'm in for it.

'You should be ashamed of yourself! It's a beautiful creature: it cares for its young, it's quiet, and it doesn't hurt anyone.'

I tell Squid I agree with all those points, but I grew up on a farm and feel no moral qualms with ending one life to feed another.

Squid grows beetroot-faced; the veins in his neck have inflated. He now reminds me of a Quentin Blake illustration from a Roald Dahl book – all beady eyes and haystack hair. He brings his face close to mine. I get the impression that, were my nose not made of meat, he would bite it off. 'Yeah, I'm fookin' sanctimonious,' he hisses, reading my mind. 'And I Don't. Give. A. Fook! If you haven't opened your eyes to this and changed your murderin' ways by the time you get off this ship … God help you, boy!'

By now I am expecting a punch, and I frantically change tack in an effort to calm Squid down. What is it about whales that captures his imagination?

'Because they're better than humans, that's why. They don't harm anythin' else; they just peacefully go about their business. They have grand societies and make beautiful music. When they breach out of the water, it's like they're making love to the air. And what've we done? Us fookin' ratbags have done nothin' for the planet except fook it up because we're so greedy. Humans are nothin' but greedy fookin' parasites, fookin' up the planet until it's completely fooked!'

Does Squid remember the first time he saw a whale?

He scratches an itch on his neck; the colour is starting to leave his face. 'I've been in the engine room the last few times they've been spotted, so I haven't seen one yet, unfortunately. I've never seen a whale in me life.'

*

'On planet Earth,' wrote Douglas Adams in *The Hitchhiker's Guide to the Galaxy*, 'man has always assumed that he was more intelligent than dolphins because he had achieved so much – the wheel, New York, wars and so on – whilst all the dolphins had ever done was muck about in the water having a good time. But conversely, the dolphins had always believed that they were far more intelligent than man – for precisely the same reason.' I'm not so sure Neptune's Navy would get the joke.

When I ask Eleanor, a 21-year-old quartermaster from Jersey, why whales are special, she says they are important to the ecosystem but also that they 'are as intelligent as us, so deserve our protection'. One afternoon soon after boarding the *Steve*, I find myself beside Gav, watching a pod of dusky dolphins surfing the ship's bow. 'They're just so much more advanced than us,' he marvels.

Animals, the French anthropologist Claude Lévi-Strauss famously argued, are important to humans not so much because they provide nutritional nourishment but because they are 'good to think' with – they are the 'other' that defines our very humanity. For the sociologist Ted Benton, 'all thinking about animals is covert thinking about humans'. Indeed, the history of the animal rights movement is closely linked with that of human rights, from the nineteenth-century abolitionist and founder of the RSPCA, William Wilberforce, to the ethicist Peter Singer, who argued in his seminal 1975 book, *Animal Liberation*, that the liberation of animals is the final step in a civilising process that began with the emancipation of slaves.

Perhaps more than other animals, whales and dolphins are 'good to think' because they are seen to possess qualities that are easily compared to our own: like us, they have sex for fun; like us, they babysit for their friends; like us, they are intelligent – never mind that this gross generalisation of around ninety cetacean species buys in to the myth of the Superwhale. It's little wonder that in his 1988 study of North American attitudes towards animals, the social ecologist Stephen Kellert found that the second-most important factor in determining people's desire to save endangered species (the first being aesthetic appeal) was a perceived evolutionary link between humans and the animals in question. In the *Steve's* copy of Watson's book *Ocean Warrior*, someone has written in the margin in a wobbly cursive that hints at heavy swell: 'No one should be able to hunt whales under a fishing licence/company title – it's a highly evolved, social mammal.'

Arne Kalland went so far as to suggest that whales have become a social critique of modern society, encapsulating all that was once good about humanity but which had been lost in the industrial age: kindness, playfulness, enjoying life in the slow lane. In this way, the whale is an elegy for a halcyon era, one in which humans supposedly spent their time mucking about rather than fookin' up the planet.

*

The history of Antarctic whaling is a parable of humanity's capacity to destroy its surroundings. When, in December 1774, Captain Cook sailed the *Resolution* towards the Antarctic Circle for the third summer in a row, the Southern Ocean contained, according to Cook's second lieutenant Charles Clerke, 'a greater abundance of whales and seals [rolling] about these straits than I supposed were to be met with in any part of the world; a fair account of them would appear incredible – the whales are blowing at every point of the compass and frequently taint the whole atmosphere about us with the most disagreeable effluvia that can be conceived.'

Within 150 years the only disagreeable effluvia being emitted in Antarctica came from blubber being processed into oil within beachside try-works.

Subsistence whaling has been conducted by indigenous peoples in various parts of the world for thousands of years, but commercial whaling – what the British author Callum Roberts calls 'the first global industry' – first emerged in the Basque country. A document from AD 670 is the earliest known receipt of the trade, recording a sale in northern France by two Basques from Labourd of 'forty pots' of whale oil.

The Basques – rough-hewn mountain folk with hubcap berets and doorstop noses – spotted migrating whales from purpose-built watchtowers and launched rowboats into the Bay of Biscay to harpoon the beasts by hand. Whales were considered gifts from God, providentially blessed with abundant reserves of meat, oil and – in the case of sperm whales from the eighteenth century – ivory, ambergris and a mysterious wax known as spermaceti, obtained from the animals' oblong heads and incorrectly thought to be its semen. It would be used in cosmetics for the next 250 years.

Even with such rudimentary techniques, the Basques managed to severely deplete the Bay of Biscay's right whales by the 1530s, forcing the whalers to cross the Atlantic, where, off the coast of Labrador (now part of Canada), they were soon competing with Dutch, British, French, German and, by the end of the seventeenth century, Yankee fleets.

When the Labrador ground was exhausted, the whalers moved

on to the waters off Svalbard and, in turn, Greenland, Hudson Bay, Hawaii, the Antipodes and Japan. It was a process that would be repeated over and again: whaling grounds were emptied then discarded like a shucked oyster or a slagheap. In fact, sperm whales, that most valued of cetaceans, were said to move across the world's oceans in 'veins', as if they were a mineral deposit or well of petroleum.

Whale oil quite literally lubricated the cogs of the Industrial Revolution, as well as lighting streets and heating homes. Fleets of whalers – ragtag itinerants in search of wealth and adventure – operated throughout the world, amassing great fortunes for their employers on both sides of the Atlantic and becoming de facto colonialists in remote corners of the globe. Maori were crewing on whaling vessels long before the annexation of New Zealand, and the communities on Bass Strait's islands survived the genocide of Tasmania's Aboriginal people partly because of their long history of contact with sealers and whalers.

In the nineteenth century, however, candles were increasingly made from beef tallow instead of the more expensive spermaceti; from the 1840s, kerosene, derived from coal, began usurping whale oil as a fuel for lamps and heaters. The commercialisation of petroleum in the 1850s sounded the death knell for the whale-oil industry: in one day, an oil well could fill as many barrels as a whale ship on a three-year voyage. But by then whales had become a kind of deep-water Aldi: a cheap source of everything you needed (meat, paint, soap, glue, brooms) and everything you didn't need but wanted anyway (collar stiffeners, paper creasers, parasol handles, corset stays, jagging wheels for pastry decorating).

The world's whaling grounds were systematically picked clean until only one remained. Antarctica had long been protected not only by its remoteness and icy conditions, but also by the species found there: blue, fin, sei, minke and humpback whales are rorquals, which feed mainly on krill, and are fast-swimming enough to evade most rowboats and hand-thrown harpoons.

Antarctic whales lost their natural advantage in the 1860s, when the Norwegian Svend Foyn invented the modern whaling process, in which a gun mounted on the bow of a steamship fired a grenade-tipped harpoon that exploded on impact. From the 1890s Foyn's compatriots were applying his techniques in the Antarctic, and by 1910 Norwegian entrepreneurs had taken their expertise to much of the world, including Japan.

By the mid twentieth century whales were being killed less for industrial oil than for fertiliser, pet and stock feed, and to put on the tables of Japan, Norway, Iceland and (even if they didn't particularly like it) the Soviet Union. But the combination of high-powered industrial fleets able to withstand Antarctic conditions, 'factory ships' equipped to process their catch at sea and a competitive quota system, which resulted in a killing orgy colloquially known as the 'Whaling Olympics', made this the most devastating period for whales yet.

It was a lesson in the tragedy of the commons: unchecked killing of a resource that belonged to no one and, consequently, everyone. In 1946 fifteen whaling nations signed the International Convention for the Regulation of Whaling (ICRW), a treaty aiming to conserve global whale stocks for future exploitation and to regulate the industry through the creation of a governing body, the IWC. Both aims failed miserably.

In 1960 global whaling – the majority of it conducted in Antarctica – peaked, with nearly 70,000 animals reportedly killed; tens of thousands more deaths went unreported during this period, with the Japanese and, especially, Soviet fleets the main offenders.

Three years later, humpback whales were deemed too scarce to be hunted in the Southern Hemisphere, with blue whales protected two years after that. Quotas were tightened, and by the mid 1970s only Japan and the Soviet Union were still sending fleets to the Antarctic; it's an inconvenient truth that commercial whaling had become economically unviable for most countries long before it was halted.

With several large species on the verge of extinction in 1982 – around 2 million whales had now been killed in Antarctica – a moratorium on commercial whaling was passed by the IWC, with exemptions for aboriginal subsistence whaling and whaling for so-called scientific research – with the by-product allowed to be sold for human consumption. The moratorium came into force in 1986, designed to be lifted once whale stocks had sufficiently recovered. It's still in place today.

*

Paul Watson subscribes to biocentrism, an offshoot of the deep ecology movement pioneered in the 1970s by Arne Næss, a Norwegian philosopher and mountaineer, who argued that no species is worth more than another, and that all life on Earth is inherently valuable. Where the two ideologies differ is on whether humans are capable of peaceful coexistence with nature.

'Think of it like this,' Watson tells me on the squally January day when we finally start motoring south. 'The Earth is a spaceship, travelling through space right now at 500 kilometres a second. Like any spaceship, it has a life-support system. That life-support system is the biosphere. And the biosphere is run by the crew. Humans are just passengers: we're just basically having a good time entertaining ourselves. But the crew that runs Spaceship Earth – the plumbing and everything that goes with it – are the bacteria, the fish, the insects, the plants, the trees, things like that. The crew provides the air we breathe, it regulates the temperature, it provides the food we eat and it takes care of our waste.

'These species are the working crew, but rather than appreciating them, we're killing them. And you can only kill so many crewmembers on a spaceship before the whole thing starts to break down.'

Watson says the work Sea Shepherd does in Antarctica is, first and foremost, to protect biodiversity: 'If you lose one species, you diminish everything else. There simply isn't enough life in the oceans to continue to feed the ever-expanding population of humanity.'

When I point out that in 2012 the IWC's Scientific Committee estimated the population of Antarctic minke whales to be at least 515,000, Watson says we don't know how many there are, because they are considered 'data deficient' by the International Union for Conservation of Nature. He's right, but even the IUCN, a UN affiliate with a globally recognised inventory of species numbers, admits the population is 'clearly in the hundreds of thousands'.

'There could be a million of 'em and it wouldn't matter,' says Watson, 'because they are protected within the Southern Ocean Sanctuary.' In fact, they're protected from commercial, not scientific, whaling; Watson has a habit of ignoring such troublesome technicalities.

I ask whether there might be a time when he accepted the killing of whales for food if it was done sustainabl—

Watson interrupts my question. 'First of all, I don't believe in the word *sustainability* – that was a catchphrase coined by [former Norwegian prime minister and chair of the UN's World Commission on Environment and Development] Gro Harlem Brundtland in 1992 at the Rio Conference. It just means business as usual under another name. It's crap!'

I sense that I have just glimpsed the real Paul Watson. When he is selling his message to the media, Watson presents a donor-friendly view of Sea Shepherd – a high-seas police force upholding international conservation laws where governments do not. But there's also a misanthropic thread to his thinking that rarely emerges when he's rattling the tin on Sunset Boulevard.

As a young activist, Watson was influenced by the work of Henry Beston, an early twentieth-century nature writer, who wrote: 'the animal shall not be measured by man. In a world older and more complete than ours they move finished and complete, gifted with extensions of the senses we have lost or never attained.' But Watson seems to go further: he once labelled cancer a 'cure' for the Earth's problems and has said he believes the life of an earthworm is more valuable than that of a human. In 1999, when Washington State's Makah Tribe resumed whaling for the first time in seventy years, Watson held a protest against the hunt under a banner that read: 'Save a whale, harpoon a Makah'. On 11 March 2011, immediately following the Tohoku Earthquake, Watson posted a poem online about Neptune's 'fearful wrath' that 'smote' the 'Land of the Rising Sun'. Four months later, when Anders Behring Breivik killed sixty-nine people on the Norwegian island of Utøya, Watson posted on Facebook that the gunman was 'probably inspired by the butchers of the Faeroes'.

'Sea Shepherd isn't like other environmental groups who say they act for their children or grandchildren,' Watson tells me. 'It always bothers me when people say, "Oh my, if we don't protect this species then we might not find a cure for cancer," or "There might be all kinds of medicinal reasons for what we might discover in rainforests" … It's always about *us*, but you know, other species have a right to exist on their own – they don't owe us anything!'

Watson sees the Judeo-Christian worldview of plants and animals – as God-given gifts to exploit – as arrogant and offensive, and believes that the moment the first hunter-gather decided to become a farmer, humans commenced the downward spiral that has led to the world's current environmental problems. 'The forbidden fruit was agriculture,' he tells me, providing a context for his frequent religious rants in the mess.

In the Watson universe, human beings are called 'hominids' to put them on a level footing with animals. But whales and dolphins are 'people' and killing them is 'murder'. A Wild West–style poster in the *Steve* has a photo of the Japanese factory ship *Nisshin Maru* with the caption 'Wanted for Murder'; in November 2012 Sea Shepherd offered a US$20,000 reward for anyone with information leading to the conviction of a 'dolphin serial killer' wanted for 'murdering' dolphins that washed up along America's Gulf Coast with stab wounds and missing jaws.

Watson's not the only person on the *Steve* to use this kind of rhetoric. Throughout the campaign I hear Antarctic whaling casually referred to as a 'holocaust'. Vera, a middle-aged Hungarian cook with a penchant for bumbags, tells me whales and dolphins are not her favourite animals but 'brothers and sisters'. Every year on 6 August, the day when Japan commemorates the bombing of Hiroshima, she holds a solo protest against Japanese whaling outside Tokyo's embassy in Budapest. When I politely tell Vera that perhaps she should choose another day to voice her opposition, she scoffs: 'Why? For the whales it is their Hiroshima!'

Watson insists such language is biocentric, not misanthropic, and that above all Sea Shepherd opposes Southern Ocean whaling because it is illegal, not because whales are better than humans. Despite this, hating humans does seem the flipside to worshipping whales for some sailors in Neptune's Navy.

*

At 6am on 11 January we cross the Antarctic Convergence, the confluence of the cold waters of the Subantarctic and the colder waters of the Antarctic. Within an hour the temperature has dropped from 12 to 8 degrees and we are enveloped in a thick curtain of fog. By 4pm the temperature is 3 degrees; by 6pm snow is settling on the forward deck.

The next day we see our first iceberg, shaped like a clenched fist and the size of a sedan. Within hours they are everywhere. Like clouds, each one's resemblance depends on the beholder: an anvil, a sphinx, the (pre-Liz) jowls of Shane Warne.

By mid January the *Bob Barker, Sam Simon* and *Brigitte Bardot* are pitching through the marbled waters of the Southern Ocean beside us; we are a four-pronged flotilla heading south to the Ross Sea, a favourite haunt of Japan's whaling fleet in previous years and again suspected to be its likely first stop this whaling season.

The days grow progressively colder, forcing me to wear my puffy down jacket inside and, eventually, to bed. The hours of light, too, increase with each day: the sun doesn't set below the Antarctic Circle between late December and early February, hovering on the horizon to port for five hours late each night, bathing the Southern Ocean in streaks of pink before shooting skywards again by 1am.

But the most prominent feature of our increasingly southerly latitude are the whales. Most rorquals migrate to Antarctica each southern summer to feast on the most krill-rich waters on earth; athletes may now flog krill-oil capsules, but these whales have long fattened up on the miniature shrimp before giving birth to calves in winter off the coasts of Australia, New Zealand, South Africa, Hawaii and South America. I lose count of the whales we see: humpbacks theatrically flapping; inquisitive minkes and shy sei whales, the latter rarely showing more than an exhalation and dorsal fin.

There is undoubtedly something powerful in these moments, and when a minke calf passes under the *Steve* I find it hard to remain objective until it has safely resurfaced on the other side, but I'm still more fascinated by those watching them. In sleet, snow and shine, at 4am or 4pm, the crewmembers of the *Steve* never fail to be enthused by the sight of the beasts: high fives, hoots and hollers abound at the merest sight of a fluke or fin.

'I am a great believer,' wrote the American journalist Ted Conover, 'in the value of a writer witnessing something firsthand, of putting himself in others' shoes, be they huaraches or ski boots. Of writing from other than a sitting position, you might say.'

If I pulled on some leather huaraches, I'm sure Squid would throw me overboard, but luckily I packed some gumboots. After one month on the *Steve* I have been warmly received by most of the crew and have made a few friends. But I still feel like an outsider. To really penetrate Sea Shepherd, I feel I must join it. I trade my pen for a mop and ask to be put to work.

The toilet (or head, as they are known on ships) closest to my cabin belches like a geyser, regularly jetting water onto the seat, the floor and anyone unfortunate enough to be in the bathroom at the time. This is 'Old Faithful', the closest thing the *Steve* has to a bidet. Cleaning it is my first job. When I'm finished, I'm directed to help Grug build a shelf in his cabin. I find him fiddling with a cordless drill; a few minutes later, while holding the shelf in place, I ask him if he's a misanthropist.

'I wouldn't say that I'm a misanthropist, but the thing I have a problem with is speciesism: that one species thinks they can do whatever they like to other species. I mean, we're just fucking up the planet and what do we have to show for it?'

'Okay,' I say rather lamely, 'I agree that humans have wrought incredible damage on their environment, but what about the collective cultural and artistic tradition of 150,000 years – surely that counts for something?'

Grug shrugs. 'But it's still done nothing for the planet.'

I ask Grug if he thinks whales deserve special treatment because they are smart.

'So does that make it okay to kill a retarded baby or a dumb puppy?' he rebukes. 'I don't think whales are any better than other animals; I'm here to promote biodiversity and to promote animal rights. When I hear this talk of whales being far more superior than humans,' he continues, 'frankly, it makes me wonder if some of the people on this boat were bullied a bit too much at school.'

*

Life as a deckhand quickly assumes a routine, with mornings spent doing chores (sweeping and mopping companionways, cleaning heads and the mess, washing up) and afternoons dedicated to general upkeep (making shelves, doing odd jobs, repairing bunks, painting over and grinding away rust).

One drizzly morning I'm on the aft deck emptying a garbage bag full of used toilet paper overboard (the *Steve*'s 1970s plumbing can't stomach flushed paper), when a gust of wind catches the lip of the bag and blows a dozen pieces of shitty paper back on deck, causing me to slip about as if I'm playing Twister, frantically trying to catch them with my gloves.

While I'm on my haunches, I notice three exhalations from a distant pod of whales, the resulting mist producing a mini rainbow. Such a display of natural beauty reminds me of Watson's 1975 epiphany with the sperm whale, when he realised where his allegiance lay. But had he actually changed teams much earlier?

Watson was born in Toronto in 1950 and raised in the maritime province of New Brunswick, the eldest of six children (a seventh was stillborn when Watson was thirteen, a birth that also killed his mother). His parents endured a fraught relationship; by all accounts, Watson's childhood was tough. In *Seal Wars*, another memoir published in 2002, Watson wrote that he was beaten at home and bullied at school, and sought refuge in nature: 'I knew I was different, and accepted it. I was a loner, except for my five younger siblings, who all shared my sensitive nature and understood my passion for animals.'

In the summer of 1959 Watson spent much of his time playing in the woods with his 'best friend', Bucky. Bucky was a beaver. When Bucky was killed by a fur trapper, Watson started destroying every animal trap he could find; later, he wrote, he shot a boy in the bum with a BB gun to prevent him from shooting a bird. 'By his account,' wrote Raffi Khatchadourian in a 2007 *New Yorker* profile, 'he was an eco-warrior before puberty.'

Soon after boarding the *Steve*, I'd been told I was forbidden from asking Watson about his private life. But it isn't hard to pick up the story.

Hillary Watson, a 22-year-old environmental scientist from London, Ontario, tells me she lost her father to cancer last August, and that she decided to join Operation Zero Tolerance in part to bond with the uncle she has never known. Diminutive and covered in freckles, Hillary is softly spoken and a great listener, bearing no resemblance to Watson.

'They had an abusive father,' Hillary explains one morning during smoko, 'but I think Uncle Paul had it worse than my dad because he was the oldest. They [the Watson siblings] all left home pretty early, but my dad had a sister who was much older to look after him. Uncle Paul didn't have anyone. Dad told me a story once, that Paul – about fifteen at the time – got onto the roof of his school and wouldn't come down. When he eventually did, my grandfather beat him with a piece of wood.'

Watson ran away from home soon after that incident, though not before punching his dad, which he has said was a 'very therapeutic moment'. Uncle Paul, Hillary says, spent time jumping freight trains and living on the streets in Vancouver before finding his way into environmental activism via brief stints at university and in the merchant marine.

I ask Hillary if she thinks her uncle's upbringing led him away from humans and towards animals.

If she is offended by my question, she doesn't show it. 'I think so. He's never been very close to our family. It hit him hard when my dad died; I think he regrets now that they weren't closer. I think he's a bit lonely, and perhaps a little bitter at humans because of what happened in his childhood. He's always been very clear that nothing comes before Sea Shepherd for him. We all recognise and respect that; the fact that, for my Uncle Paul, whales and dolphins will always be number one.'

LABELS

Brian wears his heart on his sleeve.

I'd noticed it at mealtimes in the mess, a statement running down his right forearm in bold, black ink: 'Vegan'. I'd been bemused, at first, by his decision to have a tattoo of what seemed a most prosaic characteristic – it'd be like me having 'Lived at home nearly as long as John Howard' running across my chest in Old English typeface. But getting my mum to do my washing well into my twenties isn't how I choose to define myself.

'It's the most important thing in my life,' says Brian, twenty-six. I've been told he got the tattoo last year to celebrate ten years as a vegan. 'Some people have beliefs that they just absolutely know, in their heart, it's what they believe in the most. For me, that's veganism.'

Brian isn't alone. Kelly, Paul Watson's personal assistant, has the Animal Liberation Front logo – a paw and a clenched fist – tattooed on her back, while Eliza, one of the campaign's two official photographers, is often seen (ignoring the crew uniform) in a T-shirt that says, 'Vegans don't eat anything that has a family.' A doll-eyed cow and calf peer out from behind the caption, berating anyone who even considers becoming a home-wrecker.

'It's like a fucking religion!' complains Chase, a *Whale Wars* cameraman hired for his skills, not his diet, one night in the safety of the office I share with Giacomo. 'Everyone's trying to convert me,

54

telling me how guilty I should feel for eating meat back on land!' They will fail spectacularly in that endeavour: Chase has smuggled a cache of Spam on board and throughout the campaign regularly locks himself in the toilet to get his fix. I never do work out what he does with the empty tins.

Chase's appraisal isn't as far-fetched as it may seem. Pablo tells me that veganism is 'a great journey', while Tamara, a fashionably glum tattoo artist from Perth, explains that she recently 'found' it. Within days of Chase's complaint, it seems the evangelists are on my case too: I return to my desk to find the plastic wrapping of an unopened three-pack of Moleskine notebooks defaced with a texta tirade: '1 moleskine = 3 dead baby moles = exploitation = murder.'

*

Sea Shepherd is not officially an animal rights organisation. When Watson steered the *Sea Shepherd* out of the Port of Boston in 1979 to hunt for the *Sierra*, he did so with the aim of conserving a group of species whose numbers had been greatly depleted over 500 years. He tells me the campaign is vegan solely for conservation purposes: 'We first promoted this as a vegan vessel because of the understanding that we're eating the oceans alive. We've already removed 90 per cent of the large fish. That's why I think not eating fish is more important than not eating meat. Veganism has nothing to do with animal rights as far as I'm concerned.' I've heard rumours his personal bar fridge is stocked full of non-vegan snacks.

Watson's narrow rhetoric of marine conservation notwithstanding, the vast majority of the *Steve*'s crew are animal rights activists: Gav spends his days on land raiding 'puppy farms' in Australia, while Squid is a veteran picketer of fox hunts in the United Kingdom (known as 'hunt sabbing'). Upholding international law and conserving whale stocks are secondary to the bigger picture of opposing what Gav says is 'a system that places a hierarchy on life'. If you disagree, the crew of the *Steve* will stop just short of making you walk the plank.

An example of their fervour is the time a vegetarian crew-member was wrongly accused of committing a cardinal sin – going to Macca's – while the boat was docked in Barcelona. 'I'd actually gone to a vegetarian restaurant next door to McDonald's, but there was still a witch-hunt when I came back to the boat,' he explains.

I picture the scene: La Rambla is packed with flabby tourists flicking loose change into buskers' caps, while down at the dock, the accused stands before a phalanx of black capuches, forced to empty his pockets for an offending receipt, or maybe show his palms for signs of French-fry grease.

'I tend to keep my eating habits to myself now,' he says. 'You're the only one who knows that as soon as I get off this boat, I'm going to eat a cheese sandwich and a block of milk chocolate!'

'The sad thing is, it doesn't reflect Paul's vision for Sea Shepherd,' says Elissa, a 25-year-old ecologist from the Gold Coast, and one of only a handful of crewmembers aboard who tell me they are principally here to 'uphold the sanctuary'.

We're speaking on the bridge. It's dark outside and our faces glow green in the light of the radar; the blips of icebergs upon its monitor resemble germs under a microscope.

'For Paul,' she continues, 'as long as you oppose whaling, and as long as you believe in the sanctity of marine life, then you are welcome to join the organisation. I mean, Sea Shepherd is not PETA [People for the Ethical Treatment of Animals]; we're *not* an animal rights organisation and we're *not* about bullying people into believing in animal rights.'

I tell Elissa about Squid's accusations against me; she casts a furtive glance for spies lurking in the shadows and lowers her voice: 'I call them the Vegan Gestapo.' She smiles; our conversation has gone underground. 'Just because you are a vegan, it doesn't mean that you are absolved of any wrongdoing,' she tells me later in the privacy of my cabin. 'Corn and soy are the two worst products for the environment – we should be eating meat rather than corn or soy!'

Even in the dark on the bridge, I can tell that Beck, the first mate and officer on watch, is grinning silently beside us. 'Don't worry,' Elissa reassures me. 'He's one of us.'

'I piss some people off here, because back home I eat meat,' Beck, a forty-something hippy from Hawaii, elaborates without my asking, 'but I'm not real big on the moral high ground thing.' Beck is wearing a synthetic Russian-style winter hat with a Jolly Roger buckle, which glints in the light of the monitor. His eyes leave mine and return to the germs on the radar. 'As far as I'm concerned, I'm here to save whales – not have someone else's ideology rammed down my throat.'

Elissa is on board because she feels that Antarctica – 'the last pure and pristine place in the world' – should be absolved from human exploitation. Beck is on board because he used to be a humpback researcher; 'knowing how smart these animals are', he can't condone their killing. But just about everyone else is on board because they think it is morally wrong to exploit any animals for any purpose.

'It's about being compassionate towards sentient beings,' explains Squid, using a phrase I will come to consider to be as trite as 'working families', when I pluck up the courage to talk to him again. 'Either you're a compassionate person or you're not. If you know about the 'orrible killin' that goes on and you are compassionate, you will go vegan. It's as simple as that.'

But is it that simple?

'Vegans and marathon runners,' a friend once chaffed when I was boasting about my high turnover of running shoes, 'you never meet one without knowing it.' And it's true. Just as no reference to whaling from the Japanese government appears without the word 'scientific' in front of it, it seems like every second noun on board the *Steve* is prefixed by 'vegan'. From the 'cruelty-free vegan dinner' advertised on the mess whiteboard each evening to Tod's planned homecoming drinks ('There'll be vegan snacks and a vegan dinner') and all the tatts and tees, the V-word is ubiquitous.

It raises the question: is it more important to be vegan or for others to know it?

The victim of the Barcelona inquisition is unequivocal. 'It's about distancing yourself from the herd, isn't it? Showing that you're not just an average tosser who doesn't give a shit.'

*

The Moleskine texta tirade is a joke. My nostrils sniff out a good muckraking when I realise I am being judged for publicly supporting the cardboard industry. I perversely destroy the prank's evidence in order to open a new notebook and record it. The prankster reveals himself faster than I can write 'overly earnest deadshit granola heads'. Grug leans in the doorway, giggling at my gullibility and a little concerned at how readily I took the bait.

'We're not that fucking bad,' he protests, shaking his scruffy head. '*Jee-*zus!'

I'm impressed. He must have overheard me talking with Chase about the missionaries, or perhaps lending enthusiastic support to Giacomo's own culinary frustrations ('I'm Italian – I must eat mozzarella on my pizza!').

Later on, during another bout of high-latitude, pre-season footy training, I ask Grug whether his cause defines his being. We're getting cocky today, doing those kicks that dribble along the ground and then shoot up unexpectedly; they remind me of fireworks nights from my childhood when the Catherine wheel would escape from its fence post because Dad hadn't set it up right, cartwheeling across the paddock, sparks and father trailing in its wake.

'It's an interesting one, isn't it?' Grug's obviously thought about this before. 'I used to work with these two gay guys. For one, being gay was everything: it wasn't just his sexuality, it was his personality; it dictated his friendship group, his weekends – you name it. For the other guy it wasn't a big deal at all; it was just like me being straight.'

'So which one are you?' I ask.

'I'm just Grug – I don't need a fucking label to tell the world who I am.'

I point at the tattoo on his wrist: 'Strong but Few'. Is it something to do with being vegan?

'Nah, Sammy, it's just a lyric from a punk song. I thought it was a cool message; something good to stand for.'

Standing for something. Giving a shit. It's a powerful statement to make for a member of a generation often dismissed as entitled and apathetic. Tommy, a clean-cut deckhand from Vancouver, tells me that after he realised he wouldn't make it as a professional baseballer he wanted to be *something*, and animal rights activist was that something. Grug, Chad, Pablo and a lip-ringed Welshman named Chris – all members of the much-maligned Generation Y – tell me they disagreed with the idea of following a career and instead want to 'make a difference'.

Is there anything wrong with this? Of course not. And I'm not suggesting these people aren't genuinely compassionate towards animals; when two petrels fly into the side of the *Steve* late in the campaign, I'm amazed at how the crew tenderly nurses them back to health and successfully releases them. But for some on board, I suspect that what matters isn't so much who they are, but who they aren't.

GUNBOAT DIPLOMACY

P ercy strikes me as the kind of guy who would karate-chop a piece of four-by-two – or maybe even attempt to bend a spoon with willpower alone. 'I choose to take direct action on behalf of the whales and dolphins,' he tells me earnestly. 'I'm quite willing to risk my life to save the world, in that sense.'

Skinheaded and bespectacled, Percy is thirty-seven, British-Indian and intense. A yoga teacher from London, he holds a steely gaze at all times, speaks in military clichés and largely keeps to himself, spending his spare time on the communal PC watching Vietnam War movies (*Apocalypse Now*, *Full Metal Jacket*, *Apocalypse Now* again) and on the aft deck doing tai chi in bare feet and Thai fisherman pants. He looks a bit like Gandhi, but a pacifist he ain't.

It's mid January and the *Steve* is preparing for attack. It's hoped the whaling fleet will soon be found and preparations are being made accordingly: constructing prop foulers, filling paint bombs and tinkering with the engines of the small boats. On an overcast morning in gentle swell, I help Grug and Percy erect a series of steel spikes around the gunwales. Welded onto frames that are in turn fastened to the hull with nuts and bolts, the spikes are ostensibly to protect the *Steve* in the unlikely event that the whalers try to board it, but Grug tells me they're 'really just to make us look tough'.

The first one locks into place surprisingly easily, and Grug pats

Percy on the back. 'It's getting serious, Perce!' he says with a smile.

'Let's hope the spikes work,' replies Percy, 'because if the fuckers still manage to board us, I *will* be using violence against them.'

Grug gives me an embarrassed glance; I sense he regrets I heard that. 'That's not how aggressive nonviolence works, mate,' he says. 'We don't harm them if they don't harm us.'

'But if they board us,' Percy protests, 'we are entitled to use violence against them. After all, they'll be coming aboard shooting!'

'You seriously believe that?' I ask.

'Absolutely – look at the *Ady Gil* [a Sea Shepherd vessel totalled in 2010, with both sides blaming the other]. There's no doubt they want to kill us, but they would try and do it in sneaky ways: claiming they were trying to shoot a whale if they shot one of us or pretending they didn't see a small boat they've run over.'

I tell Percy that despite the mutual animosity between the whalers and the anti-whalers, from what I've read there is a certain boundary that either side has yet to cross, and that surely neither party wants to see casualties. In 2007, when two Sea Shepherd activists were lost at sea, a brief truce was called and the *Nisshin Maru* helped in their rescue; three days later, when the *Robert Hunter* collided with the spotter ship *Kaiko Maru*, the whalers issued a distress signal and Watson offered his assistance. (It was politely declined.)

'And besides,' I add, 'I don't think your government or mine would condone such a dramatic escalation in hostilities.'

'I hope you're right,' Percy tells me, 'but to be honest, I don't think any government gives a fuck – that's why we have to take matters into our own hands in the first place.'

*

The closest thing to a bible aboard the God-loathing *Steve* is severely dog-eared and brown with stains (soy milk? seitan?). It's *The Monkey Wrench Gang*, and if you want to read it, you'd better join the queue.

In Edward Abbey's famous novel, four environmentalists disillusioned by the political process try to protect the last wild places of the American southwest in the only way they think works: sabotage. They blow up bridges, uproot surveyors' stakes and seize up the engines of bulldozers, backhoes and bobcats with a cocktail of sand, sugar and Karo syrup (perhaps *that's* what those stains are).

When it was published in 1975, *The Monkey Wrench Gang* was dismissed as a provocative but ultimately harmless tale of loveable pranksters, a work of 'symbolic aggression'. Nearly forty years on, the book is still quoted at rallies for organisations ranging from Earth First! to the Animal Liberation Front, and is considered nothing less than the blueprint for the form of activism – direct action, which condones property damage but not physical violence – that Sea Shepherd has made its own.

Back when he concluded that neither Greenpeace's peaceful 'banner waving' nor the IWC's attempts to tighten whaling quotas were saving whales, Paul Watson decided a new approach was needed. It's the very reason Abbey's protagonists – an exiled Jew, an outcast Mormon, a libertarian surgeon and a haunted Vietnam vet – gave for taking up wrenches against the system: they felt they had no other option.

Desperate in its reasoning, conservative in its goals and profoundly simple in its execution, direct action has a certain romantic charm. Like the Luddites smashing new-fangled cotton mills in Britain of the Industrial Revolution, or the Brazilian *índios* who still take on miners and ranchers with bows and arrows, it's about resisting change head-on. Raging against the machine. Halting the progress of Progress.

The parallels between Abbey's Monkey Wrench Gang and Sea Shepherd are so obvious that the book could be about Neptune's Navy. Like the Monkey Wrenchers, Sea Shepherd does not use firearms, does not consider the destruction of property as violence and purportedly will not act where there is a risk posed to human life. The Monkey Wrenchers' archenemy is the Glen Canyon Dam, while for Sea Shepherd that role is played by the *Nisshin Maru,* the 8000-tonne, 130-metre factory ship of the Japanese whaling fleet, which for them is a symbol of greed, environmental destruction and pointless killing on an industrial scale.

Indeed, whether it's true or another example of Sea Shepherd's self-mythologising, rumour has it that Abbey based one of his characters on Watson, though I'm not sure which one. When I finally read the book under the flickering bedside lamp in my cabin, I suspect it's the ex–Green Beret George Hayduke: 'Though still a lover of chipmunks, robins and girls, he had also learned like others to acquire a taste for methodical, comprehensive and precisely gauged destruction. Coupled in his case with a passion for equity (statistically rare), and the conservative instinct to keep things not as they are but as they should be (even rarer); to keep it like it was.'

There is, however, one major difference between Neptune's Navy and the Monkey Wrench Gang: Hayduke and his cabal openly flout the law, while Sea Shepherd claims to uphold it.

*

Watson is brilliant at manipulating the law to his own ends. A favourite – and historically successful – tactic is the 'Brer Rabbit

Ploy': after acting in a way that may be unlawful but is also publicly popular, he actively dares the authorities to convict him at their political peril. Watson dons his seafaring finery for the occasion – a merchant master mariner's uniform, complete with gold braid – even though he doesn't actually hold a sea captain's licence (his title is self-proclaimed). The Brer Rabbit Ploy has proved successful on several occasions because, according to Watson, authorities grow reluctant to prosecute if they fear he will use the spotlight to highlight their own inaction about or complicity in the issue at hand.

There was the time in 1982 when he chartered an aeroplane and dropped sixteen paint-filled light bulbs on what he claims was a Soviet trawler operating as a spy ship off the Pacific Northwest coast, in protest at that nation's whaling industry. Watson was charged with four violations of Canada's Aeronautics Act and gleefully appeared in court, knowing it represented an opportunity to publicise his cause without fear of prosecution: the crew of the Soviet trawler could not be subpoenaed, leaving Watson as the Crown's only witness in the case against himself. The flabbergasted judge had no choice but to dismiss the case.

Then there was the aftermath of the Reykjavík scuttlings four years later. Icelandic prime minister Steingrímur Hermannsson, unused to his small nation being the focus of international attention, called an emergency cabinet meeting and angrily told local journalists, 'The saboteurs are regarded by the Icelandic government as terrorists,' and that 'all efforts' would be made to bring them to justice. Watson had been in Canada at the time of the incident, but once his two agents had safely left Iceland, he publicly claimed responsibility for the sabotage. Pleasantly surprised by the amount of media coverage the incident had generated – coverage that pointed out that Iceland was killing whales after the moratorium on commercial whaling had come into force (they said it was for science too) – he voluntarily returned to Iceland to call their bluff.

'I flew to Reykjavík in January of 1988 to present myself to the Icelanders,' he reminisces to me. 'I said: "You guys have been making a lot of accusations that we're criminals for what we did but I don't see any charges, so what are your charges?" They didn't charge me. They told me to leave the country!' Watson is convinced the Icelanders backed down for fear of increasing the attention the incident had already brought to their whaling industry.

In recent years Sea Shepherd has even begun claiming a legal mandate to ram, harass and prop-foul vessels. Call Watson an eco-terrorist and he will say he is in fact an eco-policeman, a high-seas watchdog enforcing international conventions which nations sign up to but fail to uphold. His instrument of choice is the UN World Charter for Nature, a resolution passed by the General Assembly in 1982, which enables non-state actors to 'safeguard and conserve nature in areas beyond national jurisdiction to the extent they are able'. Watson considers this to be Sea Shepherd's licence for vigilantism, and his key weapon in garnering public support for his actions: it's his proof that Sea Shepherd has not just moral but legal justification for its actions. Most crewmembers of the *Steve* would at some stage of the campaign spout the World Charter for Nature as an unambiguous justification for their actions. But ideological twenty-somethings tend not to be experts in international law.

The charter is non-binding, and has no enforcement provisions. Moreover, the UN Convention on the Law of the Sea, also passed in 1982, asserts that sovereign states alone have the authority to police the world's oceans. Watson sees no contradiction here but international lawyers do: when I email Don Rothwell, head of school at the Australian National University's College of Law and a close observer of the whale wars, for his view on Watson's mandate to play Captain Nemo, he dismisses it as 'completely nonsense' with 'no basis in international law'. In any case, adds Rothwell's colleague Don Anton, while the charter recognises that each person shall strive to ensure that the objectives and requirements of the present charter are met, such striving is, of course, limited to lawful avenues of action.

Watson claims he has no choice but to act because the whalers are operating in a jurisprudential vacuum, and that if the Australian government was doing its job, he wouldn't come to Antarctica at all. Here he has a point: despite repeated protests by successive Australian governments for Japan to halt its program in the Southern Ocean and threats to send a Customs vessel to monitor it (on which they made good in 2008), such calls had no effect.

Instead, the Rudd government announced in 2010 that it would try to stop the whalers not at sea but in court: an application was filed to commence proceedings against Japan at the International Court of Justice (ICJ), the judicial organ of the United Nations, located at The Hague. Japan, Australia argued in its submission, was conducting commercial, not scientific, whaling in Antarctica, thus breaching the moratorium, the Southern Ocean Sanctuary, and its obligations as a party to the ICRW.

For this season, prior to the ICJ's ruling on this case, whether the whalers are poachers or scientists – and whether Sea Shepherd's crewmembers are terrorists or vigilantes – is largely irrelevant: the remote theatre in which they operate leaves states either unwilling or unable to intervene. The Southern Ocean may as well be the Wild West, Paul Watson its de facto sheriff.

The whalers have an injunction on their side this season, issued by a US court and ordering Sea Shepherd, under Watson's command, to stay at least 500 yards (about 450 metres) from the whaling fleet. In a move calculated to render the injunction irrelevant, Watson stood down as captain a few weeks ago and transferred onshore control of the campaign to Sea Shepherd's Australian chapter, under the direction of former Greens leader Bob Brown. Watson told me at the time that Sea Shepherd had 'no intention' of flouting the injunction. But late one evening soon afterwards, his replacement, former first mate Sid Chakravarty, tells me quietly that he 'has a feeling that [on] this campaign there will be one big fuck-off boat action'.

It sounds like fun, this direct-action caper. But does it work?

*

The sky was starless that night, Tommy remembers: dark like the cinema. 'It was really hard to see what we were doing,' he recalls, 'but we couldn't use our own lights because we didn't want to alert the Japanese to what we were up to.'

The night was 7 January 2012; the location was sixteen nautical miles off the West Australian coast. Tommy, who was then just twenty-two years old, is telling me about his role in the biggest of Sea Shepherd's eleven 'actions' from the last Southern Ocean campaign: the boarding of the Japanese surveillance boat, the *Shonan Maru 2*.

It wasn't the first time the *Shonan* had been boarded by anti-whaling activists: in 2010 former Sea Shepherd crewmember Pete Bethune – some say armed with a knife between his teeth – climbed aboard the refitted harpoon ship and subsequently spent five months in a Japanese prison for his troubles.

Two years later, it wasn't a Sea Shepherd activist doing the boarding but three members of the Fremantle-based direct-action group Forest Rescue. The Forest Rescue boys decided to board the *Shonan* to distract the crew and allow the *Steve*, moored off Rottnest Island

and being followed by the Japanese ship since the previous December, to shake its tail – a plan approved by Watson. It was Tommy's job to ferry them to the *Shonan*.

A former mixed-martial-arts competitor, Tommy, though short, is fit, strong and the *Steve's* undisputed man of action – small-boat navigator, paint-bomb hurler and prop-fouling line unfurler. He's a good kid, hardworking, helpful and cheerful, if a little too high on life, as only Canadians can be.

Tommy tells me he always tries to calm himself down before going on an action ('You can't be angry when you approach the target – that makes us look unprofessional and can pose a danger to yourself and your crew'), but that night he couldn't help but be nervous; boarding was clearly a much riskier action than simply hurling a paint bomb.

Around midnight, the two small boats on the *Steve* at the time – the *Bindi* and the *Delta* – were lowered into the Indian Ocean loaded with the Forest Rescue activists, their liaisons from Sea Shepherd and a camera crew from *Whale Wars*. Moments later the *Bindi* was forced to return to the *Steve* after experiencing engine troubles. Like a farcical scene from a Wes Anderson film, the activists all piled into the *Delta* and headed onwards to the *Shonan*.

The *Steve* started its engines and headed south; knowing the *Shonan* would follow it, the *Delta* sat with engines off, posing as a fishing boat until the Japanese vessel was within striking range. Shortly after, the *Delta* stormed alongside the *Shonan*, the Forest Rescue trio crouched and ready to board.

'There were alarms going off and crewmembers rushing all over the deck,' remembers Tommy excitedly. 'I lifted the guys on and a huge block of ice was hurled at one of them. He moved out of the way just in time!'

The *Shonan* was bordered by barbed wire, but the Forest Rescuers scrambled underneath like rabbits into a veggie patch; Tommy had done his job, and Chad, behind the wheel of the *Delta*, turned for the *Steve*.

'I just remember screaming with joy and hugging Chad,' says Tommy. 'Without doubt, it's the best feeling I've ever experienced in my life.'

When they returned to the *Steve*, Watson was on the bridge wing with a grin on his face. He had reason to smile. Not only did the action break the tail (albeit only after the *Shonan* continued to follow the *Steve* south with its new guests aboard for five days), it put whaling spectacularly in the spotlight when the Australian Customs vessel *Ocean Protector* was diverted to pick up the trio. The then federal attorney-general, Nicola Roxon, criticised the irresponsibility of the activists, saying she was 'not holding her breath' that they would pay back the cost of their rescue.

The media exploded, predictably polarised between those applauding the supposed Aussie tradition of civil disobedience and those lambasting the costs incurred by the taxpayer, although, as *Good Weekend*'s Fenella Souter later pointed out, the estimated $155,000 price tag was a bargain compared to the $6 million to $7 million – also never repaid – the government spent in 1997 saving the lone British sailor Tony Bullimore.

Tommy says he understood the significance of what he had done when he went online the next day. At sea, too, the move seemed to have worked: when the *Shonan* stopped tailing the *Steve* to transfer the Forest Rescuers to the *Ocean Protector*, the harpoon ship *Yushin Maru 2* was temporarily forced to stop whaling until the *Shonan* returned, which Tommy cites – along with the ten other small-boat actions that season – as the principal reason that Japan's 2011–12 catch was just 266 minkes and one fin whale, woefully short of its quota of 850 minkes, fifty fins and fifty humpbacks.

Indeed, with the exception of 2005–06 – the first season during which Sea Shepherd found the Japanese whalers – every time Neptune's Navy arrives on the scene, Japan's neutrally named Institute of Cetacean Research (ICR) fails to meet its quota. And for Japan, the problem appears to be getting worse. In the four seasons between 2008 and 2012 – harassed by an increasingly large flotilla with more sophisticated resources – the whalers have caught 681, 508, 173 and 267 whales respectively.

The ICR has repeatedly blamed Sea Shepherd for these numbers, and Watson gleefully agrees. 'Whales don't die on our watch,' he boasts to me. On a season-to-season basis, at least, Sea Shepherd appears to be saving whales. By its very nature, however, direct action isn't without risk: in the space of a ten-minute conversation, Tommy tells me about nearly falling out of a boat in front of a harpooner, and having nuts, bolts and flashbang grenades thrown at him – not to mention the risk posed to the whalers themselves by Tommy and his chums tearing around their vessels, disabling their propellers and hurling paint bombs onto their decks.

To date, there have been no lasting significant injuries on either side: in 2007, a whaler claims to have been temporarily blinded by a canister of butyric acid; when the *Ady Gil* collided with the *Shonan Maru 2*, a Kiwi cameraman broke a few ribs; and Brian was bruised last year when a piece of metal hit his face. But given the nature, passion and remoteness of the confrontations, the question must be asked: how long will it be before someone gets killed?

As Monash University's Gerry Nagtzaam and Pete Lentini have argued, herein lies Sea Shepherd's conundrum: direct action may not aim to harm humans, but inherent in its methods is the risk of doing so inadvertently. All it would take is a small boat's engine to cut at the wrong time, or an action to be taken over by activists intent on harming humans to further their cause. Hijacked by pirates, as it were.

*

Days pass with the crew remaining in a state of heightened anticipation. I mop, sweep, read *The Monkey Wrench Gang* and write up my notes – all while keeping one eye on the empty grey sea. It's so cold now that mist rises from Old Faithful every time I take a piss, but we are told to stop using the oil heaters in our cabins to save fuel and thus prolong the campaign. At least I have my woollen thermals and eiderdown jacket to keep me warm – two products eschewed by the *Steve*'s core group of militant vegans.

One day I help Grug varnish the shelf we built. It's wild outside and the boat is listing giddily, so we have to carefully time our visits to the paint locker above for supplies to avoid being soaked by the waves sloshing across the deck. The sea seems thicker today – we are ploughing though it rather it than sailing on it – and rain falls in diagonal sheets. The only wildlife I can see is a defiant sooty albatross being buffeted above our starboard quarter.

This is the kind of weather in which I'd expected to be slouched over a bucket in my cabin, swimming in my own bile. But I'm not – I'm loving it. In the hold, I'm overcome with childish delight each time books fly off shelves, mugs lose their handles and the Jenga tower of dirty washing up loudly clatters within its enclosure; outside, too, it's great fun rushing between the paint locker and Grug's cabin – and even more fun when we mistime our run and end up ankle-deep in saltwater.

While we're in the paint locker seeking shelter from one such deluge, I ask Grug about Percy's outburst. 'He's a bloody psycho,' says Grug, shaking his head. 'When we were docked in Williamstown he wanted the *Steve* to be under twenty-four-hour guard!'

Grug believes Sea Shepherd's strict adherence to nonviolence is crucial to maintaining the group's credibility and the community perception that Neptune's Navy is a direct-action group, not an eco-terrorist cell. 'Sea Shepherd can't afford to have crewmembers who are willing to cause harm to others. That's why Pete Bethune got in such trouble – he knew what he was doing boarding the *Shonan* with a knife. And for Percy to say those things in front of you, of all people – I bet it's going straight in that bloody book of yours!'

Three days after Percy's outburst, Olav, the translator, pins a Japanese newspaper article on the mess noticeboard. It includes photos of a group of people, all dressed in giant cartoon-character suits, waving to the camera beside a boat with a new lick of paint. It is, Olav explains to me later, the launch party for a new Japanese security vessel that may or may not be currently looking for us. Beside it Olav has written: 'From the official site of the Japanese Coast Guard. We should be afraid.'

Percy descends the stairs and catches me reading the article. 'You still want to go to that country?' he asks. I've told him I intend to visit Japan in order to better understand the whaling debate.

'Yeah, it's certainly a unique place,' I say, trying to work out what animals the costumes are meant to be.

'Bunch of motherfuckers,' Percy declares. 'I want to smash them.' This time he has an audience.

That afternoon Captain Sid calls a crew meeting. 'We've put these anti-boarding spikes up,' he announces in his sing-song Indian accent. 'Obviously, the intention is to stop anybody from trying to board the vessel. Now, in the Southern Ocean campaign it's a remote possibility. But in the eventuality that somebody does board us or is attempting to board us, all attempts will be taken by the ship to stop the boarding, using the water cannons or manoeuvring the ship, or pitching the *Delta* on the access side so that nobody can come on.

'But in spite of all of that, if somebody comes on board, they are *not* to be met with violence. You are *not* to go and punch people and stop them from coming on board. You are supposed to stand back if they've come on board and let them come to the bridge, and I'll deal with them. There's no need to start throwing people overboard or start punching them or disabling them from coming on board. It will be an extremely serious situation if that happens, but resorting to violence is absolutely not on. Are there any questions?'

Percy has a question. 'In the unlikely event that they board, if they use violence, can we—'

'What sort of violence do you think they'll use?' Sid interrupts.

'Weapons or physical acts.'

'They won't. And if it comes to that, let me make the call – you, as a deckhand, shouldn't approach them or try to use violence against them.'

Beck has heard enough. He raises his hand. 'We're a nonviolent group,' he implores. 'We're direct action! So, interacting with equipment is one thing, but causing injuries to people is another.'

The room falls silent; again the chug of the engine takes over. As surreptitiously as I can, I move my eyes across the carpet – itself covered with stains – to find Percy towards the back of the room. He sits silent, arms folded and cross-legged, a scowl on his face and his head hung low, peering into space like a condemned man in the dock.

SOUND BITES

Weeks pass with no sign of the whalers. On 24 January we round Scott Island, a miserable black outcrop covered on its windward side by a snowdrift, and so desolate that I can't see any vegetation, let alone birdlife. 'Fook me,' says Squid from over my shoulder, 'imagine being shipwrecked on that fookin' thing – I'd find a nice *sharp* rock to jump onto!' Days later we are deep in the Ross Sea, just thirty nautical miles from the Antarctic ice shelf, which shimmers like a saltpan.

The ICR 'samples' whales from a swathe of ocean, divided into two sectors of six areas, ranging from the coast of Queen Maud Land, the Antarctic territory far below Mozambique, to the eastern basin of the Ross Sea, on the same longitude as French Polynesia. This season it purports to operate in the Eastern Sector, between 130 degrees east and 145 west, and below a latitude of 62 degrees south. It's a huge body of water, and Neptune's Navy has split into two groups to maximise coverage. On a morning when snow is settling on the aft deck, Uncle Bruce reveals that, while the *Bob* and *Bardot* are in another part of the Ross Sea, we have been paired with the *Sam* but are keeping apart a distance of at least seventy miles, so that if any of the Japanese fleet's six vessels finds one of us, the other will be outside the whalers' radar range.

The idea is to form a giant net and trawl the Southern Ocean for the *Nisshin Maru*; if the factory ship is found, and Sea Shepherd can block its slipway (the ramp below the stern for hauling carcasses aboard), it will be extremely difficult for its three harpoon vessels – the three *Yushin Marus* – to offload their catches and for its Panamanian-flagged refuelling vessel, the *Sun Laurel*, to give the *Nisshin* a drink. Conversely, should one of the three speedy harpooners or the security vessel *Shonan Maru 2* find a Sea Shepherd vessel first, they could help shield the *Nisshin* from the activists by advising the mothership via radio contact. The problem for the whalers is that this season they have four vessels to evade – and a quota to reach.

'It's become a game of poker,' says Uncle Bruce, chuffed with the analogy. I can't help but think that Battleship would more apt.

The *Steve*'s radar really only starts to pick up vessels within a radius of eighteen miles, but there are clues where the whalers will be found. Uncle Bruce explains that the *Steve*'s command believes the Japanese fleet, having moved south so late in the season, will head straight for the whaling grounds, so Tod is using NASA satellite imagery to map the Southern Ocean's chlorophyll hotspots. Chlorophyll, the green pigment found in algae, is eaten by plankton, which is eaten by krill, which is in turn consumed in vast quantities by the great whales of the Antarctic. By pointing the compass at waters that are both rich in chlorophyll and calm enough for whales to feed, it is hoped at least one member of the whaling fleet will soon be found.

Until that happens, I continue to immerse myself in the everyday tasks of crew life. I move to the bridge, waking at 4am for a week to shadow Beck, Eleanor and Elissa. Though these mornings are punctuated by the occasional whale sighting, I find the tasks of the quartermaster – plotting coordinates, logging banalities and watching for obstacles – extremely tedious; to pass the time I resort to reading the bridge's copy of *Italian Waters Pilot* (fully revised eighth edition), becoming strangely familiar with the challenges posed to yachties docking at the ports of Palermo and Pisa, Bari and Brindisi.

More engaging is my week in the galley. Feeding forty-three crew three meals a day for upwards of four months is no mean feat. The head chef is Amber, a six-time Antarctic veteran whose end-of-empire accent hints at expensive schooling in the lee of Table Mountain. 'We've been told to ration until the fifteenth of March, but that doesn't mean we should start cooking shitty meals from today,' she says, throwing me a tea towel. 'The campaign might last until the fifteenth of March, but it might be over in a few days. We might be underwater in a few days!'

Amber's galley – a narrow, loud space cluttered with cauldrons and a mantelpiece from which herbs hang like stockings – is stocked by a cool room filled with produce acquired in New Zealand, and a dry store brimming with suitably ideological food donations from Australia – vegan chocolate, organic peanut butter, ethically farmed quinoa and fair-trade chia seeds.

The trio of cooks, Amber, Tamara and Vera, work tremendously hard, and nothing less is expected of me: I spend a week cleaving pumpkins, dicing onions, scrubbing the floor and peeling potatoes. Their squabbles over what music we listen to remind me of the radio wars that occur every day on worksites across Australia ('Triple J makes kids slit their wrists', a Christian rock–loving plumber told me during my short-lived career as a concreter's labourer), as do the nature of their arguments (sharks vs dolphins instead of Holden vs Ford; almond milk vs rice milk instead of Carlton vs Collingwood).

My back soon grows sore from standing, and I become tired of chasing mushroom escapees under the workbenches. But being a galley slave has unexpected benefits. With crew constantly popping their heads in to see what's for dinner and the room presenting a convenient shortcut between the mess and the lower cabins, when news breaks on the *Steve* it immediately reaches the galley. On the evening of 28 January, I'm about to knock off when Grug appears. One hundred and twenty miles from our current position, the *Bardot* has found the *Yushin Maru 3* in the ice; two days later, the *Steve*'s helicopter pilot finds the *Yushin Maru* drifting with its engines off, thirty miles to our east. By nightfall it is tailing us.

The next morning I'm emptying a bin of cabbage peel over the side of the ship when I see the *Yushin Maru*: handsomely painted in gunboat grey, it is slimmer than I expected, riding high in the water about five miles behind us. A tingle runs down my spine; the campaign suddenly feels very real.

The conversation during that afternoon's bout of kick-to-kick is dominated by the newest addition to the seascape. As Grug nurses the ball, he passes on Sid's news that the *Sam* is now the only free vessel of the fleet: the *Bardot* is embroiled in a strange face-off with the *Yushin Maru 3*, both vessels sitting in the ice with their engines off; the *Bob* is now being followed by the *Shonan Maru 2* and is heading northwest to Macquarie Island in a bid to lose its tail – because the island forms part of Tasmania, should the whalers go near it, they would be breaching the ban on whaling vessels entering Australia's Exclusive Economic Zone (EEZ). If the ploy works, the *Steve* may do the same.

This means the *Yushin Maru 2* is conceivably the only vessel currently whaling. It also means that, sometime in the past few days, the injunction was likely breached, probably as the *Bardot* approached the *Yushin Maru 3*.

'D'ya reckon kicking the footy onto the deck of the *Yushin* would constitute a breach of the injunction?' jokes Grug.

'They're getting so close we should give them some love!' offers Arthur, a mohawked deckhand from Wellington, blowing a kiss in the *Yushin*'s direction.

Percy, busy working on his yogic energy flow in the corner of the aft deck, is predictably less jocular. 'What's the point of spreading love to people who want to kill us?' he asks. 'I say we prop-foul them immediately!' Whether such a move would break our tail is uncertain. But it would make great TV.

*

The caricature is unflattering but unmistakable. Paul Watson, drawn with puckered eyes, a whisky nose and no neck, shuffles across the screen, his exposed gut wobbling like a lager lout's on an Ibiza dance floor.

'That's definitely a Japanese boat,' the cartoon Watson splutters to a bridge full of animated activists, his eyes pressed to a pair of binoculars. 'Pull up next to them,' he orders. 'The fight is on!'

Moments later, the *Steve* is parallel with the '*Herro Maru 3*', a catcher boat (harpoon vessel) brimming with angry, spear-wielding whalers dressed in kimonos.

Watson outlines the plan of action to his charges. 'How about I pretend to be shot? Then we can tell the media the Japanese shot me, and start an international crisis!'

'Wait,' a new crewmember protests, 'we don't want to just lie about stuff.'

Watson looks confused. 'Why not?'

You know you've entered pop culture when *South Park* takes the piss out of you. After having their way with Kanye West, neo-atheism and the Book of Mormon, in 2009 *South Park* creators Matt Stone and Trey Parker trained their crosshairs onto Neptune's Navy.

The timing was pointed. As late as 2007 Sea Shepherd had a relatively low profile outside of activism circles. That summer, the US cable TV network Animal Planet sent a camera crew to live on the *Steve*. The result was *Whale Wars*, an Emmy-nominated reality TV show that shot Sea Shepherd to stardom in living rooms across the world, and in the space of five years increased the group's annual income from US$2 million to US$12 million.

'Before the show, Sea Shepherd had one rusty vessel and struggled to find crew,' explains Beck, a man whose game-day eloquence and GI Joe jaw have made him a regular fixture of the program. 'Now we have four new boats and reject thousands of applicants. Is our personal experience cheapened by [the *Whale Wars* crew's] presence?' he asks rhetorically. 'Perhaps. But if it's ultimately saving whales then I'm all for it.'

Combining stunning scenery, all-American sound bites and action shots from hand-held GoPros lashed by sea spray, *Whale Wars* is how many people were introduced to the Antarctic whaling controversy – and to Paul Watson's love of histrionics.

In series one, two crewmembers board the *Yushin Maru 2* and are dramatically 'held hostage' by the whalers for two days; after the campaign, the *Steve*'s then first mate, Peter Brown, admitted to his hometown newspaper, the *Cape Cod Times*, that it only became a hostage situation because the *Steve* deliberately left the duo behind, describing the ploy as 'giant street theatre'. In the series finale, Watson – who is wearing a bulletproof vest, despite not usually doing so – claims to have been shot by the Japanese whalers, an allegation verified only by a piece of crumpled metal that resembles one of Uncle Bruce's fillings. Over a million Americans tuned in that night.

In *South Park*'s spoof, *Whale Whores*, Stan, attracted by the ideology of saving whales with hardcore activists, joins the crew of the *Steve* only to find himself surrounded by lying Watson syco-phants, whose real adversaries aren't the Japanese whaling fleet but the Alaskan crab-fishing reality TV show *Deadliest Catch*. It's a war for ratings, not whales.

I'd seen *Whale Whores* years earlier but the offer to watch it aboard the *Steve*, with the makers of the very program it lampoons, proves irresistible. We start watching it in the *Steve*'s media room with Squid, who leaves in disgust after a few minutes, and Paolo, a usually taciturn Italian deckhand, who laughs more than any of us.

Then the door is unexpectedly flung open. 'What are you guys watching?' asks Watson.

Erin, the *Steve*'s *Whale Wars* field producer, turns tail-light red. On the laptop beside her, Stan has just assumed the helm of the *Steve*; behind him, a statesman-like portrait of Watson, who has earlier been harpooned in the head, has been defaced by the word 'TURD' daubed in red paint.

For one surreal moment, the two Paul Watsons lock eyes: they seem to be sizing each other up like two dogs at the park.

The real-life Watson is unfazed. 'Oh, that crap again,' he says, before disappearing down the companionway. He later tells me he sent a letter to Stone and Parker congratulating them on the epi-sode, but they never replied. Parker told a TV interviewer, 'Matt and I are just as against whaling as anybody, but dude, we're way more against people going out and basically saying, "My cause is so just that I can say people shot me when they didn't!"'

In our interviews to date, I'd felt silly even contemplating asking Watson about the shooting. But when I finally do, he is strangely nonchalant.

'Oh, yeah, I was shot,' he says. 'What year was that again? Oh, yeah, 2008.'

I press him to tell the story.

'What happened is we were out on deck and [the crew of the *Nisshin Maru*] were throwing flashbang or concussion grenades at us and I felt something prick in my chest. I looked inside and I found out that I had been shot.'

Watson claims the prick he felt was the pin of a badge he was wearing on his sweater, which was pushed into his chest when the bullet struck. It's Bible-over-your-heart stuff, and I'm not convinced. How did he not so much as stagger from the impact of the bullet?

'People say, "You know, it's not really real," because they expect me to have been thrown against the thing [across the deck]. But that's not the way ballistics works – the impact of a bullet can never exceed the kickback of the weapon that shoots it, and so therefore if it doesn't knock the person who's firing the bullet off [balance], it's not going to knock anybody back.' That's how it happens in real life, he shrugs.

But why was so little made of it in the media?

Just then, the ship rolls and a racket comes from the cabin adjacent to Watson's office. The fridge door has swung open; I cast a furtive glance to see if I can spot some of the captain's alleged non-vegan treats – perhaps he has one of Chase's Spam tins?

'The interesting thing about it,' says Watson, his assistant shutting the fridge before I can check its contents, 'is the Japanese government immediately informed the Australian embassy [in Tokyo] that they had fired shots. That was reported in Reuters, and about two hours later it was pulled out of the reports and the shots were changed to "warning balls" – whatever the hell "warning balls" are.'

On the afternoon of 7 March 2008, a media release was issued from the office of Australia's then foreign minister, Stephen Smith, stating that Japan had advised that a 'crewmember on board the Japanese whaling vessel fired warning shots'. Soon after, an update clarified that 'three "warning balls" – also known as "flashbangs" – had been fired'. Flashbang grenades are distraction devices commonly used in military training that emit a small explosion – and the sound of a gunshot.

The ICR categorically denied the shooting. 'No one shot at Paul Watson,' the institute's then director-general, Minoru Morimoto, said in a statement at the time. 'His claim that we shot at him and he has the bullet that was stopped by his bulletproof vest is more fiction for articles for the Australian media.'

Some of the *Steve*'s crew agree with Morimoto. 'I don't believe it for a second,' Grug says of the shooting. Arthur's appraisal is sardonic: 'Of course he just *happened* to be wearing a bulletproof vest at the time.' Beck grins when I ask him his view. 'The shooting? No, we don't talk about that!' But none of these men was on board at the time.

For Watson, it seems the purity of his cause justifies his means. This is a man who, in his book *Earthforce! An Earth Warrior's Guide to Strategy*, wrote: 'If you don't know an answer, a fact, a statistic, then ... make it up on the spot.'

'Paul Watson has been lying for thirty years,' a senior member of the *Steve* tells me late one night, while we're feasting on Vegemite toast. 'Lying is part of his DNA.'

'Does that bother you?' I ask.

'Well, sure,' the activist says, 'but he's pretty damn good at his job. At the moment, this organisation – though not perfect – is the most successful at saving whales. If another one forms that's better at saving whales, then I'll join it. But right now that organisation doesn't exist.'

Of most importance for Watson is exposure, and he's brilliant at getting it. Not counting Watson himself, no less than thirteen of the *Steve*'s forty-three crew are on board essentially to conduct PR, whether as photographers, media liaison officers, live internet-stream coordinators or *Whale Wars* camera operators, technicians or producers. And that's just on one of four boats, all of which are supported by a full-scale operations centre in Melbourne.

This is why I have no difficulty believing Watson when he tells me how grateful he was to Stone and Parker for featuring him on their show – even if it was as an adipose sociopath. 'From my point of view, they had just elevated me to the level of Tom Cruise and all the other people they make fun of,' he tells me delightedly. 'It gave us an awful lot of exposure.'

*

As January gives way to February, the *Bob* successfully loses the *Shonan* by approaching Macquarie Island, with then federal environment minister Tony Burke stating that vessels associated with Japan's Antarctic whaling program 'are not welcome in Australia's Exclusive Economic Zone or Territorial Sea'. The *Steve* starts heading north – away from the ice and back towards heavy seas – to do the same trick.

This is when I realise I've hit the wall. For Watson, the sea is a passage to freedom; I'm beginning to feel like I'm on a prison hulk. I'm profoundly homesick, missing my friends, family and the luxuries of land: running as fast as I can, smelling blossoms, or turning a corner to see something new – a stranger, a dog, a dead-end.

Instead, in these milder waters there is nothing to look at but the ever-present *Yushin Maru*. No icebergs. No whales. No birds. No islands. Just the same bubbling sea and the same foreboding sky.

We may as well be floating through space; there is very little to suggest we are on a planet of 7 billion hominids.

I'm not the only one losing it. A packet of chips is taken from Squid's cabin, provoking hysteria from its owner; a mobile phone disappears and is never found; bickering starts to creep into sea life. There is an overwhelming sense of monotony; we are waiting for something – anything – to happen.

In this atmosphere I struggle to find the motivation to take notes, instead sleeping like a koala and watching more TV than I have in my entire life. So, too, do I start losing self-respect, blurring the hitherto separate public and private spheres of the *Steve* by showing up to the mess in boxer shorts and attending crew meetings in ugg boots or, if I can't even be bothered putting them on, bare feet. My life has descended to watching period dramas in my undies with eco-terrorists.

And then, an unexpected reprieve. After abandoning the plan to head to Macquarie Island and instead turning southwards once more to look for the *Nisshin*, in early February we start seeing icebergs again: one looks like a teapot with a busted spout; another resembles a gingerbread cottage with icicles hanging off its eaves; both are backed by a sky streaked with pink. While I'm on the aft deck admiring the bergs with Grug and Gav, three humpbacks appear, diving and slapping their pectoral flippers as they feed around the *Steve*.

The whales, the teapot, the ethereal red glow: even my lump-of-coal heart is moved by the sight, and I rush to the bridge to tell Giacomo to take some photos. On the way up I nearly bowl over the comms officer Tux, so I tell him about the whales.

'So you've become one of us!' he says, before cheekily quoting one of the many derisive emails about his organisation that I've sent home – and that he's screened. 'You've become a cultish whale hugger!'

*

The next day a second vessel appears on our radar: the *Yushin Maru 3*, fresh from tailing the *Bardot*, which is on its way back to Hobart for engine repairs, is trying to replace the *Yushin* on our hammer. As the *Yushin* is low on fuel – evident from how high it is riding in the water – when it leaves us we chase it, using both engines at our near top speed of fourteen knots, in the hope it may lead us to the *Sun Laurel* or perhaps even the *Nisshin Maru*. This is the Southern Ocean: if you run out of fuel, you can't walk to the nearest service station with a jerry can.

The *Yushin*, outrunning us at seventeen knots, is eventually lost, but we keep heading west in the hope of bleeding it dry. On 7 February we turn northwest to meet the *Sam*, which that morning spots the slow-moving *Sun Laurel* 1250 miles south of Albany, in effect severing the whalers' refuelling supply, as the *Sam* can interfere with any attempt by the *Sun Laurel* to tie up to the *Nisshin Maru*. Sid tells us that by his calculations the *Sam* and the *Sun Laurel* are 600 miles west of us; we are due to intercept them in two days.

One sunny day we approach a tabletop iceberg the size of a suburban shopping mall. Waves are licking at the bottom of its sheer cliffs; its surface has the sugary sheen of a meringue. Two-thirds of every iceberg sits below the water: what we can see is but the tooth that emerges from a gum.

'Imagine kicking the footy on that!' says Grug.

Watson has another idea. 'This'll fuck with 'em,' he says, gesturing to the *Yushin 3* as he takes the helm of the *Steve*, spinning it hard to starboard with all the care of a gambler playing roulette. We turn sharply; the necks of those admiring the berg are jarred. Within minutes the *Yushin 3* has slipped from sight. For twenty minutes we circumnavigate the iceberg before sharply returning to our original course, Watson chuckling to himself as the *Yushin 3* comes back into view, having chased us around the (ice)block.

Confusion sets in over the next week: we go north but then west, speed up then slow down. Sid is tight-lipped when I ask him what's going on; rumour has it we are no longer chasing the *Sun* but are stalling the *Yushin 3* to give the *Bob*, 200 miles away in the ice, some space. I'm still in bed at 1.50pm on 15 February when I learn the purpose of this move:

'Attention all crew, attention all crew: at 13.42 the *Bob Barker* got on the slipway of the *Nisshin Maru*! I repeat: the *Bob* is on the *Nisshin*'s slipway!'

MOMENTS OF TRUTH

Captain Siddharth Chakravarty stands at the helm of the *Steve* wearing a black hoodie and the look of a man about to piss his pants. His teeth are bared; his nose is pinched. 'Somebody hand me a bottle to pee into!' he barks at a startled quartermaster. For two hours Sid hasn't moved, one hand on the *Steve*'s steering lever, the other clutching a thermos of coffee. A loudspeaker suddenly blares to starboard. That bottle will have to wait.

'Warning, warning. This is the Fisheries Agency, the government of Japan. Stop your violent, obstructive actions immediately! Keep away from the research vessel! The government of Japan *strongly* urges you to stop your activities threatening the safety at sea!'

'Which one's the research vessel?' somebody quips.

It's shortly after noon on 20 February 2013 in the Australian Antarctic Territory's ironically named Cooperation Sea, where nine vessels are about to face off in the biggest ever confrontation between the two fleets. Two nights earlier, Sid had made official the worst-kept secret aboard: Sea Shepherd would be using its vessels to physically block any attempts by the *Sun Laurel* to refuel the *Nisshin Maru*. This is D-day: with the nearest friendly port in Indonesia, if the *Nisshin* cannot refuel from its tanker it will likely be going home; for Neptune's Navy, stretched to its own fuel limits, if it cannot end the whalers' season within the next week, it too will be heading for port.

Amid hearty applause and the allocation of 'action roles', testosterone had run high. 'Finally!' Tommy told me afterwards in the mess. '*Finally!* We should *totally* watch something *epic* before we go to bed!'

Percy, too, could not contain his excitement. 'This is what I've been waiting for!' he declared with uncharacteristic happiness. 'I will be operating our water cannon, which is actually quite a dangerous job, you know – I'll likely have stun grenades and pieces of metal and bolts thrown at me.'

Percy was ready for war. 'Ideally I'd like to be wearing a bullet-proof vest and have a riot shield,' he told me, 'but despite my requests to buy some, we don't have any, so I'll just be wearing my helmet and goggles.'

*

The *Nisshin Maru* is a slaughterhouse at sea. The great survivor of the industrial age of whaling, it is an evolutionary anachronism: the saltwater crocodile, the Wollemi pine, the National Party of its class. In the 1960s Antarctica was full of these behemoths, factory ships loaded up by their catcher boats like Tonka trucks in the sandpit, their contents processed, packed and frozen on below-deck production lines. With this new technology, the whale hunt, once a zero-sum game summarised by Melville as 'a dead whale or a stove boat', was now not a contest but a cakewalk: whaling had become mechanised, depersonalised, sanitised even.

'We came across a factory ship,' wrote Luis Sepúlveda in *The World at the End of the World*, 'more than 100 metres long, with

several decks, stopped but with its engines running at top speed ...
With a hose two metres in diameter it was sucking up the sea, removing everything, creating a current we could feel under our keel and
leaving in its wake something that was no longer sea but a sort of
soup, dirty and dead. The hose sucked up everything without regard
for threatened or protected species; I was left breathless by the horror
of it all, seeing several baby dolphins inhaled and disappear. But
worse was the realisation that through an overflow pipe fixed to the
stern, offcuts of this butchery were being spat back into the ocean.'

Sepúlveda is a novelist, but his nautical hoover is surely based
on the *Nisshin*: the Chilean crewed on Greenpeace vessels in the
years leading up to Japan's first post-moratorium season of research
whaling. Even by then, most of the world's factory whalers had
been retired or sold for scrap; today there is only one.

Sepúlveda paints the image of a killing machine concerned only
with efficiency: whaling as a function, a chore – like picking up a
child's toys from the floor or mowing the lawn. And this, I think, is
partly what upsets so many of us: like the 'super trawler' denied
access to Australian fisheries in 2012 after immense public pressure, the naked pragmatism of the *Nisshin Maru* is a far cry from
aboriginal subsistence whaling, which – small-scale, personal and
rooted in tradition – presents a more ambiguous target.

And now, there she blows. Even bigger in real life than I had
expected, the *Nisshin* is 130 metres long and twenty metres high,
8000 tonnes of reinforced steel with a hull painted in bad-guy black-
and-red stripes. Its deck is cluttered with nets, masts and propaganda signs: 'Animal Planet Promotes Ecoterrorism; Legal Whaling
Under the ICRW; ICRwhale.org'. Three water cannons jet from its
main deck like crop sprinklers; the word 'Research' runs boldly
across its midship.

For its part, the *Sun Laurel* is distinctly less imposing, a clapped-out rust bucket of peeling cream-and-tangerine paint, sailing under a tatty Panamanian flag. Its woefully underdressed Filipino crew mills about on deck in op-shop parkas, tracksuit pants and, in the case of one poor bloke, thongs. Cigarettes hang from everyone's lips in a comic violation of the 'No smoking, safety first' message running across the tanker's superstructure.

Supporting the *Nisshin* in its bid to refuel is its full suite of harpoon vessels, each blasting water cannons. The *Shonan Maru 2* has just appeared. Sea Shepherd's plan is to use its three ships to surround the *Sun Laurel* – essentially, to double-park it.

*

At twenty-nine, Captain Sid is Sea Shepherd's rising star. Born in Bhopal eighteen months before the industrial disaster for which the city is now infamous, he served seven years in the merchant marine doing 'stuff you wouldn't expect of an environmentalist' – transporting palm oil from Borneo to Rotterdam, floating lumber down the Amazon, shipping petroleum from Texas to China, before the chilling fact of carrying a consignment of an odourless and lethal cargo similar to methyl isocyanate – the chemical that killed more than 3000 people in Bhopal in 1984 – channelled him towards activism. He's navigated oil tankers through the bustling Singapore Strait and crewed on ships skirting (actual) pirates off the coast of Somalia. But he's never been tested like today.

The bridge Sid commands is full of people: Beck helping on controls, Uncle Bruce on internal comms, Tux on external comms, quartermasters on radars, *Whale Wars* on the job. The mood is generally calm, although Sid seems more irritable than usual. The cobalt ocean is still and has the consistency of a margarita. It's a sunny day and the soft light refracting off the *Steve*'s windscreen creates the false impression of warmth; the temperature outside is minus 0.9 degrees Celsius.

Since 10am, Sid has positioned the *Steve* 100 metres behind the *Sun Laurel*. The *Sam* is trailing a long rope ahead of the *Sun* to try to disable its propeller. The *Bob*, the *Nisshin* and the three *Yushins* are exchanging positions behind us.

The radio crackles to life with broken English: 'All crew, you stan-by.' Ciggies are hastily stamped out and fenders lowered over the *Sun*'s port side. Drift ice – soupy white and cowpat-flat – is forming on the water's surface, preventing Sea Shepherd's small boats from reaching the fenders to cut them.

I pull on my balaclava and step onto the bridge wing. It's loud outside: I can hear the rumbles of nine vessels' engines and the hiss of ten water cannons; somewhere behind me the *Shonan*'s obnoxious radio loop runs. On our lower deck, I can see balaclava-clad figures in orange jumpsuits shifting ropes and operating the cannon; the one standing with his hands clasped at his waist, like a cop at a picket line, is instantly recognisable as Percy, who will be reprimanded for swearing at the whalers today.

On the *Yushin* I can see four grim-faced crewmembers on the lower deck and two in the crow's nest, one of whom is filming me on a camcorder. It's strange to finally see the whalers: with their legionnaires' hard hats and novelty-sized utility belts, they remind me of nerds at a *Star Wars* convention.

The *Nisshin* has overshot its mark and makes a 360-degree turn. By the time it is ready to approach again, the *Steve* and the *Bob* are tightly blocking access to the *Sun Laurel*. The *Nisshin Maru*'s captain, Tomoyuki Ogawa, radios the *Bob*, asking it to move; Hammarstedt's reply is unequivocal: 'You are conducting an illegal whaling operation and illegal refuelling operation within the Antarctic Treaty Zone. If you do not move, the moral and legal responsibility will be yours!'

Ogawa asks again; again, Hammarstedt denies his request.

We soon receive our own strangely polite ultimatum: '*Steve Irwin*, this is *Nisshin Maru*. How are you? I advise you to stop your obstructive actions immediately. Please move away.'

Suddenly the bridge is full of refugees from the upper deck. They are blocking my view out the back windows, but their faces – afraid, excited, awestruck – illustrate the looming presence of the *Nisshin*. I bend my knees and grip the bench, ready for the crunch.

*

I look at Chase, a camera on his shoulder and a bemused look on his face: *Was that it?* The impact – a dull thud on the heli-deck – later becomes legendary among the *Steve*'s crew as 'the ramming', but in Giacomo's words, 'Let's face it, it was more of a nudging.'

On the *Bob*, Hammarstedt, under fire from the water cannons of the fast-approaching *Nisshin*, continues to warn the whalers: '*Nisshin Maru*, this is the *Bob Barker*. I will not move for you; you'll have to sink me. Back off!'

He radios through that his engine room is taking on water: this is serious. For ten minutes I watch the maritime equivalent of a pile-up, the *Nisshin* sandwiching the *Bob* between itself and the *Sun*. I count the flashes of Japanese 'warning balls' – one, two, three, four – and try to mentally untangle each vessel from the mass of paint and metal.

Hammarstedt verifies that the water in the engine room has come from a cannon through a chimney, not a breach of its hull. The *Sam*'s captain contacts Tux to float the idea of asking the *Sun*

Laurel if it would be prepared to refuel the *Nisshin* north of the six-tieth parallel – outside the Southern Ocean's boundaries and thus legal under the terms of the Antarctic Treaty.

Tux turns to Sid: 'Diplomacy?'

Sid cracks his knuckles and stares ahead. 'No time for thinking about that right now.'

The *Nisshin* pulls alongside the *Steve*, pounding our windows with water. One of the windows is slightly ajar, and Tod cops the ricochet, his long black hair plastered to his neck. The *Nisshin* falls behind the *Steve*, and, to everyone's surprise, soon slams into the *Sun Laurel*, cracking the *Sun*'s port lifeboat and crumpling the davit used to launch its starboard lifeboat. Sid is incredulous: 'Why the fuck are they ramming the *Sun Laurel*?'

A messenger tells Sid that crewmembers on the *Sun* have thrown a message in a bottle onto the deck of the *Bob*. Paul Watson – disguised in a ridiculous (fake) fur Russian hat and bandito's black kerchief – has appeared on the bridge, and he too hears the *Sun* crew's claim that they weren't told they were coming to Antarctica and are now being forced to refuel the whalers.

Sid suggests announcing the message over the radio. Watson, who since January has supposedly been just a 'special observer', overrules: 'No, don't do that.'

On the radio Hammarstedt claims the *Nisshin* is now ramming the *Bob*, but my view is obscured. Later, a Sea Shepherd press release will announce that the encounter destroyed one of the *Bob*'s radars 'and all of her masts'. Afterwards, I see the broken radar and four crumpled navigation masts, but the two main masts are fine.

The two-hour skirmish comes to an end when the Japanese vessels break away and head north. Sid embraces Beck, sighs and hurries down from the bridge to relieve himself.

*

The refuelling has been thwarted for another day, but for Sea Shepherd the real war has just begun: Kelly has already issued a press release about the *Bob*'s damage and Watson is locked away in his office writing another, in between fielding calls from journalists. Sea Shepherd focuses on its suspicion that the *Sun* is illegally carrying heavy fuel too far south; it also points out that whaling vessels have entered the Australian Antarctic Territory and are thus, it claims, in breach of the ban on such boats in Australia's EEZ.

As well as the damage to the *Bob*, structural damage to the *Steve*'s heli-deck is alleged. I step outside and notice that some of those spikes I helped erect have been violently twisted, and the balcony is indeed badly broken and fenced off with tape.

Much is also made of the mysterious messages thrown to the *Bob* by crewmembers of the *Sun Laurel*. They make their way to the *Steve*'s bridge and I carefully unfold them on Tux's desk. The first is written in loopy black biro by a non-native English speaker:

> To Research Ship
> Please: 'May day' 'Help'
> ALL CREW DIDNOD KNOW   TO   THIS
> ANTARCTIC TRIP. SO ALL CREW DON'T
> LIKE TO SUPPLY THIS FISHING VESSELS
> WE CANNOT USE TELEPHONE SO WE CANNOT
> SPEAK 'IMO'. PLEASE YOU AS SOON AS
> POSSIBLE CATCH ACTION.
> Thank U.

The IMO is the International Maritime Organization, the United Nations' regulatory body for world shipping. The letters, scrawled on pages ripped from exercise books, paint a sad tale of exploitation and explain why the deckhands are so underdressed: they didn't know they were coming here. Filipino sailors are the Kiwi kitchenhands of the sea: cheap, hard-working labourers, whose wages provide a lifeline for thousands of families back home.

I'm angry these people have been brought here against their will, but I'm also angry they are about to become victims of shameless opportunism from Sea Shepherd. Last night, Sea Shepherd publicly dobbed them in for smoking on an oil tanker. But now Watson has become a champion of the proletariat as well as of the great whales. He claims that the *Sun Laurel*'s crew 'found common cause' with Sea Shepherd's crew after the *Nisshin Maru* rammed it, and even 'surreptitiously gave them thumbs up and applause' for their efforts to block the refuelling.

But the euphoria is short-lived. At 6.30pm on Sunday 24 February, all hands are called on deck. One of the *Yushins* has been spotted by the *Bob Barker*, a few miles from us, successfully transferring a harpooned minke whale to the *Nisshin Maru*; it happens during an episode of the bacchanalian period drama *The Tudors*, when many of the *Steve*'s crew are eating dinner on their laps in the mess. Do the whalers know this is when we are at our most vulnerable? 'C'mon,' says Olav, reluctantly pressing pause, 'not now – King Henry is about to get laid!'

But he is the only one who sees humour in the situation. On the bridge, Beck is shattered that a whale could be caught under his nose; Eleanor and Elissa are tearing up.

The chopper is sent up to retrieve photos, returning with shots of workers on the deck of the *Nisshin* sharpening a set of curved knives that look like scimitars. Tommy stands in the mess afterwards, dismayed as to how this could happen. Hands on head, he exhales like a horse. 'Cheeky, cheeky fuckers,' he says.

The next day, further north, the nine vessels again congregate for the attempted refuelling of the *Nisshin Maru*. Once again, Hammarstedt uses the *Bob* to block it; once again, he is sandwiched by the *Nisshin* into the *Sun Laurel*. But this time the *Steve* is afforded a clear view. It is sickening: at one stage the *Bob* lists violently, and the risk of it capsizing in below-freezing water seems a real possibility.

Thankfully, that doesn't happen, the *Nisshin* pulling back and again abandoning its refuelling attempts. Sea Shepherd rightly tells the media that the *Bob*'s crew was in grave danger, but leaves out how the skirmish started: the *Bob* had unexpectedly turned and run into the factory ship. It reminded me of a blue heeler nipping at the hooves of a cow: if we were rammed on 20 February, the *Nisshin* was rammed today. Once again, Chase and I share a look of bemusement: *Did that just happen?*

Later, in the privacy of my office, Bruce confesses that 'it looked bad because it was bad'. The rules of the open sea, Bruce explains, dictate that the vessel being overtaken must maintain course and speed. 'In the second incident [the sickening sandwich] the *Bob* had nowhere to go, but in the first incident [the blue heeler nip, in which the *Nisshin* was overtaking], it clearly didn't have to turn into the *Nisshin Maru*!'

*

I'm still up at 1.45am, and I head to the bridge to retrieve a forgotten notebook. On the way, in the adjacent communications room I encounter Gav, Kelly and Sid, all hunched over a computer, intently editing footage taken from yesterday's encounter. I walk a little way past them, then drop to retie my shoelaces and eavesdrop.

'The ICR released two clips from this angle that make it look like the *Bob* is at fault,' says Kelly.

'Hold it back a bit,' says Sid (of, presumably, the footage). 'That's perfect.'

Four days later a crew meeting is held in the mess, where an interview conducted between 7.30's Leigh Sales and Bob Brown on 26 February is shown on the TV. Sales is characteristically going for the throat, accusing Sea Shepherd of putting the *Bob* in a position where it couldn't help but be rammed, and of reckless vigilantism in general. Footage is shown of the previous day's contact from both sides: a Sea Shepherd clip of the *Bob* being pummelled, and a clip from the stern of the *Nisshin Maru* of the *Bob* turning into it. I stifle a laugh. Both clips are correct, of course – it's just that each has been selectively cut from the same sequence to further each side's respective cause. Put together, they show the full picture.

*

The whalers are eventually left to refuel in peace, with Neptune's Navy's own low tanks forcing it to head for ports in Australia and New Zealand in early March. By this point, the fast onset of the Antarctic autumn, with its shorter days and icier seas, will soon put an end to the whaling season anyway. On Tuesday 19 March 2013, in international waters off Tasmania's King Island, the *Bardot* appears to the *Steve*'s starboard side and collects Paul Watson, cruising him back into hiding. It will be another eight months before he resurfaces.

As we all squeeze onto the starboard deck and wave to the fast-fading *Bardot*, Tod tells me something so emetic I nearly reach for my seasickness tablets. 'For me, Paul Watson is a real-life Davy Jones,' he gushes. 'He may be unable to return to land but at least we know he'll be out there, somewhere, looking over the oceans.' Two weeks later, the ICR announces its fleet has taken 103 minke whales, zero humpbacks and zero fins from a revised quota of 935 minkes, fifty humpbacks and fifty fins. Outside of the two world wars, it is the lowest seasonal catch in the history of Antarctic whaling.

WHALE HUNTERS

CULTURE

Contrary to what you may have imagined, whale doesn't taste like fish at all. And no, it doesn't taste like chicken but rather faintly bovine – a bit like the ox tongues, tough and rich and blue like cold lips, my grandpa would eat for lunch.

I was nineteen when I first ate whale. 'You must try it,' the beaming blonde waitress had insisted. 'No visit to Norway is complete without it.'

This was long before my trip to the Faroe Islands; I ordered a serve of whale through a combination of curiosity and teenage ratbaggery. I remember feeling vaguely ashamed when it arrived, as if I was about to break a taboo. To my mother's dismay, I carefully cut off a slice, raised it to my mouth and – as if theatrically flirting with cannibalism – let the meat rest between my teeth for a moment before I began to chew.

In Norway and Iceland, minke whale is most commonly barbequed as steak and smothered in gravy; in the Faroe Islands, pilot whale is traditionally wind-dried and eaten as jerky to fortify fishermen and shepherds, in between globs of the moist tobacco powder called *snus*, which is stuffed inside the upper lip.

But it is Japan – famously homogeneous and fiercely parochial – that has the most diverse culinary tradition in the whaling world.

Whales have been eaten in Japan for perhaps 10,000 years;

middens from the prehistoric Jomon Period suggest that the Ainu of contemporary Hokkaido, like pre–European contact Indigenous Australians, took full advantage of whales that had beached themselves. In the ensuing centuries, some coastal communities started scavenging and later hunting whales, a practice encouraged by a seventh-century imperial edict forbidding the eating of most four-legged animals, which wasn't overturned until the Meiji Restoration in 1868.

Whaling towns arose in various parts of the archipelago, resulting in differing regional tastes today. In Arikawa, on western Kyushu, right whales were traditionally the most highly valued; once they were hunted to virtual extinction in Japanese waters, the salted blubber of Antarctic fin whales (themselves now endangered) took precedence. In Ayukawa, on northern Honshu, if you order whale you'll likely get a bloody red block of minke sashimi; in Taiji, below Osaka, dolphin is favoured; while in the town of Wadaura, on the Boso Peninsula adjacent to Tokyo Bay, Baird's beaked whale is preferred – a meat considered offensive elsewhere because of its strong smell.

Shintaro Sato isn't so fussy. 'I like whale heart, whale brain, whale sushi and whale sashimi – many whale dishes, but all whale makes me strong!' he tells me, beating his chest like King Kong for emphasis. Sato is the owner of Taruichi, Japan's most famous whale-meat restaurant.

Wandering among Shinjuku's fashionistas and neon, I begin to think I wrote down the address incorrectly; Tokyo's ultramodern commercial centre seems an unlikely site for a purportedly ancient tradition. But then I stumble upon an educational poster by a stairwell with the title 'Cetaceans of the World'. In Australia, it would be hanging on a classroom wall; at Taruichi, it's the menu.

Amid the blue fug of cigarette smoke inside, any lingering doubts about what's for dinner are dispelled by the decor: traditional Japanese watercolours depict whaling scenes, while above the doorway hangs a novel take on the members' entrance: a dried whale penis the size, shape and colour of a faded traffic witch's hat.

I visit on an unseasonably cool weeknight and at 6pm, early for dinner by Japanese standards. Despite these factors – and despite recent Greenpeace claims that only 5 per cent of Japanese people regularly eat whale meat – Taruichi is buzzing: every table bar two is packed with a crowd of older after-work diners tucking into whale and drinking sake from traditional wooden box-shaped cups called *masu*.

At the next table a shitfaced businessman with a glistening forehead notices my Japanese-made camera and proudly proclaims that he works for the company that made it. When I compliment him on my camera's performance he takes personal credit. 'Thank you very much!' he says, doing a classic Elvis impression for reasons that aren't clear to me.

Shintaro Sato is equally friendly as he approaches my table to see why he has a *gaijin* in his midst, chuckling when he learns of my provenance and admitting he doesn't get much business from Australians. When I ask him, through my interpreter Ryoko, what he thinks of Canberra's desire to see Japanese vessels stop whaling in the Southern Ocean, he adjusts his Karate Kid sweatband. 'It's a question of respect,' he says earnestly. 'We don't tell Australians what they should do. We respect the whales and don't hunt them for no reason – we hunt them for science and use what's left over to keep the culinary tradition alive.'

'And Sea Shepherd?'

'They are terrorists, like Osama bin Laden!'

There are no less than thirty minke whale dishes on Taruichi's menu to help 'keep the culinary tradition alive', including boiled whale blubber with jellied broth, deep-fried whale dressed with spicy cod roe, deep-fried whale brains in dashi broth, whale bacon, whale cutlets and – should you feel so inclined – whale tongue, whale penis and whale testicles.

Taruichi, Sato tells me, was started in 1968 by his father, Takashi ('he's 100 per cent made of whale meat!'), and was initially dedicated to the high-quality sake made in the city of Shiogama, Miyagi Prefecture – a prefecture that once had a thriving minke whale fishery. Just as you might pair roast chicken with a good bottle of chardonnay, Shiogama sake is traditionally matched with minke whale.

When I ask Sato whether the whale he serves is from the North Pacific or the Southern Ocean, he says he mainly sources minke meat from Japanese waters, but Antarctic specimens occasionally end up in his kitchen. 'But, of course, it is only after research has been conducted,' he is quick to add. 'Scientific research.'

My own scientific research determines that minke sashimi, marbled like a wagyu steak, becomes as black as tar when dipped in soy sauce, and that mashed ginger and pickled okra give whale sushi a fierce kick. Less palatable are the testicles, which come thinly sliced and topped with diced shallots and a decorative daisy. They remind me of cookie dough, in both taste and appearance. As for the sliver of whale penis I order, my cumbersome chopstick skills land it on the floor before I have a chance to taste it; it's retrieved and discarded by a waitress before I can pick it up. I'm off the hook.

With the help of Ryoko, I ask some of the diners around me why they are here. 'Whale is not my favourite meat,' says one woman in her sixties, 'but I think it's important to maintain this tradition. I grew up eating it at school, so it has a certain nostalgia.'

'Everyone is entitled to their opinion,' adds her male companion when I ask him about the whale wars. 'What's important is that the relationship between [Australia and Japan] isn't harmed.'

'Whale meat suits my taste,' says the Elvis-impersonating camera company employee. 'Australians eat lamb; we eat whale.' He then switches to English for his catchphrase: 'Thank you very much!'

'See you next time you want to eat the whale!' Sato ventures in English as I leave.

'I'll bring some Australian friends!' I joke in response.

*

From his office on the eighth floor of Rakuno Gakuen University, Professor Jun Morikawa points out the hazy silhouette of the city of Sapporo below us and, beyond it, foothills cloaked in spruce and fir that give way to lead-grey mountains flecked with snow. Spring has arrived on the island of Hokkaido: as I walk through the grounds of the agricultural university, I pass two students in shower caps and gumboots leading a dairy cow to pasture; fat bumblebees land on lupins around me and Shrek-green leaves rustle above. The brisk air, the soft light, the tell-tale clumps of grass recently weighed down by snow: it reminds me of Reykjavík.

'This view always reminds me of the Adelaide Hills,' says the professor of international relations, nose pressed to the glass. I raise an eyebrow; Morikawa-sensei starts giggling.

In conformist Japan, Morikawa is something of a maverick. Within minutes of meeting me, he's boasting of the guerrilla garden he's started on campus: 'These people – these *bureaucrats* – always need documentation when you do anything! So I completely ignored them and soon they were asking me for the pumpkins I am growing. Just like that' – he clicks his fingers – 'I changed the culture.'

Then there are the maps that adorn the walls, tables and ceiling of his office – they're upside down. 'I like looking at the world differently,' he explains as he shows me his favourite, the Japanese archipelago centred on Hokkaido, the sparsely populated frontier-island shaped like a kite with streamers flailing from its tail.

But it is Morikawa's distinctly nonconformist stance on whaling that is the reason I've come to see him.

'There are no objective conditions to support the government's whaling policy,' he tells me bluntly. 'Market forces should be allowed to determine whaling policy – and market forces say that Australian beef – Angus beef! – tastes much better [than whale].'

We're sitting on a couch eating strawberries and drinking kiwifruit tea. The office around us is classic mad professor: hundreds of esoteric books spilling from shelves (*Japan and Africa*; *Namibian Independence*), reams of paper piled in leaning towers, essays long-ago submitted and never returned, and all those topsy-turvy maps. Slight and neat, a pocket watch in his palm and mischief in his eyes, Morikawa wears bone chinos and a matching vest. His English is heavy with Japanese vowels and interspersed with ocker idioms and outback anecdotes, souvenirs from a research fellowship at the University of Adelaide in the early 1990s.

'The Japanese government would have us believe we all eat the whale meat – like you Australians and your Vegemite,' Morikawa tells me, smiling. 'They have created the myth that a national whale-eating tradition exists from Okinawa [in the sub-tropical south of the archipelago] to Hokkaido [at its chilly northernmost]. But it doesn't.'

When the moratorium on commercial whaling came into force in 1986, Norway's objection to it was on economic grounds alone: whaling was an industry and the ban would result in unemployment and depopulation. But Japan, which accepted the zero-kill policy and thus is bound by it, has frequently used cultural arguments in its calls for the moratorium to be overturned. In the 1990s, Japanese delegations to the IWC presented several papers that argued the moratorium has 'contributed to declining community solidarity and the loss of a rich cultural tradition as many customs, such as the giving of whale meat, can no longer be fulfilled'.

There's no doubt that in the Japanese communities which have practised whaling, it has historically held far greater importance than as a mere food-gathering exercise. Buddhist rituals, festivals, dance and art serve to reinforce a mutual relationship of dependency between humans and whales. Temples and memorials are dedicated to the souls of whales, with one national historical monument (Kogan-ji, in Yamaguchi Prefecture) even containing a tomb for foetuses found inside killed whales.

In what is a deeply hierarchical society, eating whales has long been a source of social stratification too. In his 1832 book *Geiniku chomihho* ('The Way to Season Whale Meat'), scholar Tomokiyo Oyamada writes that of the more than seventy cuts of whale, the outside of the gum is tender and thus suitable for the nobility, whereas the trachea is 'given to servants in the countryside' and the duodenum is worthy only of the landless poor.

But whaling and whale-eating, Morikawa tells me, have a history of cultural importance only in a handful of Japanese communities – most notably the four towns of Taiji, Ayukawa, Abashiri and Wadaura. He points out that in far more Japanese coastal communities, whales have never been eaten, and in some they were even perceived as gods of good fortune whose presence was believed to bring happiness and a good catch of fish.

And yet for years the Japanese government, through its organs the ICR, the Fisheries Agency (which pays the bills) and the various pro-whaling groups it supports, has promoted whale-eating as a pan-prefecture celebration, releasing pamphlets like the recipe book *Protecting and Enjoying Whale Meat – Let's Cook!* and the *Motto Shiritai Kujira Bukku* ('Let's Learn More about Whales'), a 22-page booklet for schoolchildren in which whales are referred to as 'gifts from the sea', their consumption in Japan is described as a 'prehistoric tradition' and whale is vaunted as a 'healthy meat' full of protein, iron and omega-3 polyunsaturated fatty acids.

At first glance it seems merely like marketing: in its efforts to satisfy the requirement in the ICRW that whales caught for research be 'processed', since 1988 the government has offered for sale the by-product of its research whaling programs. That job is assigned to the Tokyo-based company Kyodo Senpaku, which also provides the whalers who man the *Nisshin* and its entourage.

In the decade prior, with the moratorium an increasing threat, the whaling-as-culture narrative appears to have been cultivated by the whaling industry to gain political and public support: following the 1972 UN Conference on the Human Environment in Stockholm, at which a clear anti-whaling consensus emerged, the Japan Whaling Association employed the public relations firm Kokusai PR to boost its domestic image. The result, as researchers Atsushi Ishii and Ayako Okubo have shown, is that the word *tampakushitsu* (protein) was suddenly replaced with *bunka* (culture) as the principal justification for whaling, both in the *Asahi Shimbun* newspaper and in Japan's parliament, the Diet.

The strategy worked: Jun Morikawa tells me that Japan's cunning Cold War–era prime minister, Yasuhiro Nakasone, a close friend of Ronald Reagan, was initially happy to let whaling die to placate US sensibilities (his government accepted the moratorium), but eventually bowed to domestic calls to support it (his government started research whaling).

But there is now something distinctly nationalistic – Orwellian, almost – about the government's promotion of whale as cuisine, which has included school visits from members of the ICR during which children are strongly encouraged to eat whale meat and given samples and propaganda to take home. It reminds me of the way John Howard so effectively invoked the Gallipoli landing to justify Australia's presence in Iraq and Afghanistan; Antarctic whaling, less than ninety years old, has been linked with much older practices of coastal whaling to give it a grander narrative.

By elevating the consumption of whale meat to the status of national symbol, the Japanese government has politicised whaling to the point that it is no longer a matter of taste. Munching on minkes has become a point of cultural demarcation, a source of pride, a symbol of sovereignty. Ambassador species.

'But despite these efforts,' Professor Morikawa tells me confidently, 'whale meat is less popular now than ever before. While you are in Japan, Sam-san, I urge you to do one thing: ask young people wherever you go if they eat the whale, and especially ask young mothers if they are buying the whale and serving it to their children. Governments don't decide traditions; people do.'

*

There was once a time when whales were eaten on a national scale in Japan. When, on 2 September 1945, the Japanese Empire's last foreign minister, Mamoru Shigemitsu, bent his back, signed on the dotted line and formally ended World War II, he did so on behalf of a devastated nation. Japan's misadventure in empire building had left it bankrupt, occupied and in ruins. The most pressing concern for the Allied occupation's commander, General Douglas MacArthur, was feeding a starving population. On 19 May 1946, more than 250,000 people gathered outside Tokyo's Imperial Palace in what would become known as the 'Food May Day' protests. It was in response to this that the Allied powers granted permission for Japan to resume and expand the Antarctic whaling industry it had started – after much opposition from Western countries – in the 1930s. The first fleet sailed south on 4 November that year.

According to figures from the Ministry of Agriculture, Forestry and Fisheries, in 1947 Japan consumed 130,000 tonnes of meat – 69,000 tonnes of which were whale. Antarctic whales helped Japan get back on its feet. In 1954 the School Lunch Act mandated a free lunch for every school student in the archipelago; for the first time in Japan's history, whale was indeed being eaten from Okinawa to Hokkaido. By 1958, Japan's whale catch had become the biggest in the world, and when it peaked in 1962, over 200,000 tonnes of whale meat was circulating on the Japanese market.

'But these were abnormal conditions,' clarifies Morikawa. 'All of Japan was eating whale because it had no choice – I had to eat it!' Now in his late sixties, he remembers: 'I didn't care what it was – it was meat! Unlike Australia, [where you can] just get meat, in Japan pork and chicken was too expensive.'

But just as uni students stop eating $2 packets of instant noodles for dinner once they are no longer at university, Japan stopped eating emergency rations once it was no longer living in a state of emergency. As Japan's postwar recovery blossomed into a postwar boom, tastes started to change. From the 1970s, riding the wave of its all-conquering foreign legion of Toyotas and Hondas, Walkmans and Toshibas, Japan's burgeoning middle class started spending its newly acquired wealth on imported products that had once been luxuries afforded to a select few: chicken, pork and, most notably, beef.

The moratorium on commercial whaling did hammer Japan's whaling industry, but by 1986 whale meat was already considered an old person's habit.

When Japan's research program in the Antarctic, known as JARPA (and, since 2005, its successor, JARPA II), was launched in 1987, it was designed to be self-sufficient: whale-meat sales would offset the cost of the research. Although the program has enjoyed government subsidies since its inception, for the first decade the plan worked, with meat sales from the 330 to 440 whales caught each year largely covering operating costs. Since 1994, a much smaller number of minkes has also been caught in Japanese waters under Japan's research program in the North Pacific (JARPN, and, since 2000, its successor, JARPN II, which also takes limited numbers of sperm, sei and Bryde's whales), also initially sustained largely by the sale of whale meat.

According to Greenpeace Japan, between 1987–88 and 2006–07 the average annual subsidy for the Antarctic and North Pacific research programs combined was $6.23 million. In that period the subsidies stayed relatively stable, with a difference of only $2.1 million between those two seasons. But in 2007–08 the subsidy jumped to $10.3 million, hovering thereabouts for a few years before tripling to $30.9 million in 2011–12.

These increases coincided with decreasing sales of whale meat, and the increasing amount of whale meat in cold storage. In 1997–98 the combined catch for the two research whaling programs was 538 whales; that year the peak amount of whale meat in cold storage was 2600 tonnes. In January 2012 the *Tokyo Shimbun* reported that the stockpile of unsold whale meat was almost three times greater than it had been ten years earlier (over 5000 tonnes). A year later the stockpile was still growing, despite a disrupted North Pacific hunt in 2011 because of the tsunami – a disaster in which 300 tonnes of frozen stock was also lost. As of 2014, it has dipped back to 5000 tonnes, although, as Japanese investigative journalist Junko Sakuma tells me, this reflects JARPA II's recent low catches more than any increase in consumption.

Sea Shepherd cites the stockpile as proof that Japanese consumers are rejecting whale meat, a point echoed by the Western media. But it's more nuanced than that. Since 2010, endangered fin whales caught in Icelandic waters have been threatening the sales of Japan's whale meat. After begrudgingly accepting the moratorium under diplomatic pressure in 1982, Iceland left the IWC ten years later in protest at its continuation. Another ten years later, in 2002, Iceland was accepted back into the IWC in a controversial vote that allowed it to maintain a reservation on the moratorium and to resume commercial whaling from 2006; the company Hvalur H/F started exporting whale meat to Japan four years later, ending Kyodo Senpaku's two-decade-long monopoly on the market.

With lower overheads resulting in a cheaper product, Hvalur H/F has found a way of making money where Kyodo Senpaku cannot. But for how long? Everyone knows pensioners love a bargain, but Iceland's controversial catch appears to be a short-term spike on what has long been a flat-lining life-support system: as the generation weaned on whale begins to die, one with more cosmopolitan tastes is replacing it. Whale meat is increasingly a niche product with a fading market.

But still the Japanese government pours money into the ICR, with bipartisan support for the research programs, which, by Morikawa's estimates, employ no more than 200 people. On top of the existing subsidies – and the $28 million of the nation's earthquake and tsunami relief fund controversially given to the ICR because the affected region contains some whaling towns – in late 2012 it was announced the ICR was now to benefit from a no-interest loan program originally set up by the government to help fishery businesses modernise. This is why the *Nisshin Maru* was so late to sail south this year: the new loan was being used to give it a much-needed overhaul. Research whaling has effectively been nationalised.

On 26 February 2013 – six days after Percy was reprimanded for swearing at the whalers – Japan's fisheries minister, Yoshimasa Hayashi, stated that Japan would 'never stop whaling', and continued to frame the controversy as a culture war. 'In some countries they eat dogs, like Korea,' the Harvard-educated Hayashi said in fluent English. 'We don't eat those animals, but we don't stop them from doing that because we understand that's their culture. Whaling has long been part of traditional Japanese culture, so I just would like to say: "Please understand this is our culture."'

It makes sense that a generation which grew up under wartime austerity would be nostalgic about the first protein that filled their bellies, but Japanese society has changed beyond recognition since then. Why go to such effort to prop up a product the market now rejects? It'd be like Sydney lord mayor Clover Moore imploring Woollahra stockbrokers to start eating rat meat because it had served the winos who slept on their doorsteps during the Great Depression so well: *They used to eat it on a stick over a rubbish fire, but now, if you rub it in Maggie Beer verjuice then sear it on your Weber, it's simply divine.*

*

When does a habit become a tradition? And should it be forced on people who would otherwise let it fade? A friend from Victoria's High Country doubts her dad's claim that alpine grazing is scientifically sound – but concedes that, eighty years old, it's a way of life. My own dad, a free-market economist before he turned to farming, makes the brutal argument that any cultural pursuit that doesn't earn its keep should be left to the whims of the market (goodbye, Australian film industry).

I disagree: for years the French government has been subsidising its film, TV and music industries. The French call it *l'exception culturelle*: the notion that there is an intrinsic value in culture that sets it apart from other commercial products and makes it worthy of special treatment. Key to this is the belief that – Gérard Depardieu's occasional public urination on planes notwithstanding – culture can act as an ambassador for France in the wider world. But whaling is just the opposite: it has brought nothing but international condemnation on Japan. Surely, then, the most patriotic position would be to finally put this fish out of its misery rather than let it keep flapping about on the pier?

I return to Rakuno Gakuen University the next day to attend a guest lecture by Kotoe Sasamori, a local marine biologist and pioneer of Japan's nascent whale-watching industry. She's been invited to address Morikawa's second-year international relations class; the professor tells me he wants his students to learn that tourism is the world's biggest industry, so that when they inherit Japan they'd be wise to watch, not eat, its whales.

The lecture is in Japanese, a PowerPoint presentation full of purple bubbles and jagged yellow clouds that reminds me of a glossy supermarket catalogue. I sit at the front, where arriving students swipe their IDs, and those of their absent mates, against a reader on the wall – wagging, twenty-first-century style.

Afterwards, Sasamori, a petite woman with a neat fringe, tells me that no more than a handful of whale-watching ventures exist in Japan – and that the number is actually decreasing, something she blames on cowboy operators who just transport tourists to see the whales rather than educating them about the beasts. 'Between 1997 and 2000 was the peak,' she says. 'It is a very difficult industry; I am in a delicate position.'

I ask Sasamori why she likes whales and her answer is straight out of Squid's script: 'Orcas have a strong family bond and look after one another,' she tells me. 'We could learn from them in the way we treat each other.'

Sasamori came up against a suspicious whaling establishment: her venture takes schoolchildren to see orcas in Kushiro – the eastern Hokkaido city which is one of the home ports for JARPN II, with a 'research centre' for the program recently built there and hailed by its mayor as an answer to the blight of depopulation and unemployment. In 2003, when she first started researching the local orca population, the Japanese Coast Guard at one stage refused her permission to dock in Kushiro. 'I received the Sea Shepherd treatment,' she jokes.

Slowly, Sasamori, who does not position herself as being against whaling, convinced the Hokkaido local government that whale watching could also be a source of economic stimulation. It now sponsors the project; since 2008 she estimates she's taken 300 Kushiro primary-schoolers whale watching.

'I don't want to push my view but instead to present an alternative view, so that they can objectively make up their own mind. If I throw the ball very fast,' she analogises, 'people will try to dodge the ball. But if I throw it gently they might try to catch it. I am not Sea Shepherd: to be accepted by these people we must understand what they want and what we want – tolerance.'

Yesterday Morikawa had lauded Sasamori to me as a sign of things to come: whale eating to whale watching; changing the culture, just like he did with those pumpkins. But Japanese conceptions of nature extend much further than the veggie garden.

NATURE

The road to Chikatsuyu hugs the Kumano River, a trickle lost among sun-bleached boulders, exposed sandbars and the occasional shopping trolley stuck in the mud since a 2011 typhoon. Its steep banks are cloaked in oak, beech, pine and maple; in the dying days of summer their uppermost ridges are tinged with outbreaks of red and yellow.

At Hongu I stop to stretch my legs and climb the 158 stone steps to Kumano Hongu Taisha, a Shinto shrine to the three-legged crow deity Yatagarasu, who guided Japan's first emperor, Jimmu, through these forests and is now the mascot of the national soccer team. Massive cedars flank the thatched shrine; the pulse of unseen cicadas is staggered like an impact sprinkler. As with other postcard-worthy sites in this country, there's a gift shop in the car park where you can buy an icy pole. And, as with other postcard-worthy sites in this country, there's no bin to put the wrapper in.

Saving the planet isn't big in Japan. A 1991 Yale University study compared Japanese and American attitudes towards animals, wildlife, the concept of wilderness and awareness of conservation issues. While the American respondents displayed strong ethical and ecological perspectives (wilderness is for admiring, not eating for breakfast; it's worth paying a higher price for tuna caught in dolphin-friendly nets), their Japanese counterparts placed greater value on the satisfaction derived from controlling nature (not just keeping the wolves at bay but manipulating them to increase their aesthetic and emotional appeal).

In conducting the survey, the social ecologist Stephen Kellert wanted to address a seeming paradox: why the Japanese, a people widely broadcast as living in harmony with or having an appreciation of nature – think bonsai, haiku, Shinto, rock gardens, tea ceremonies, cherry blossom parties, ikebana and a vast national park system – have become some of the postwar world's worst environmental criminals, be it through unreported whale catches, illegal rainforest logging, high-seas driftnetting or the largely unchecked importation of endangered animal products.

Kellert concluded that what is perceived by outsiders as a Japanese 'appreciation' of nature exists in narrow, highly idealised forms that largely lack ethical or ecological depth; the appreciation isn't so much of nature but of the symbolic and artistic *experience* of nature. Nature is not merely defined by its relationship with humans but improved by it: for one of Kellert's respondents, nature isn't even natural until it has been 'touched by the hand of man'; another respondent described this as a 'love of semi-nature' in which the 'materials of semi-nature' are used to 'express human feelings'; for another, this reflected a desire to 'freeze and put walls around' nature. These views are consistent with what French Japanologist Allan Grapard calls the wider Japanese 'love of cultural transformations' – a world which, 'if left alone, simply decays'.

'Wilderness' – a state of nature supposedly unaltered by humans – is in this context not so much untouched as unkempt, raw instead of pristine. It's a pet to train, a bathing-averse toddler to tame. In another study by Japan's National Institute for Statistical Mathematics, 60 per cent of Japanese respondents said they preferred to spend time in 'nature influenced by man' instead of 'unspoiled nature such as the virgin forests and wilds'. Kellert cited a consumer survey from Japan's Environment Agency, which revealed that its citizens visit protected areas 'to admire beautiful … landscapes' (rather than to go spotlighting for rare gliders, as my mum likes to do, or gawk at the understory dynamics of an old-growth forest untouched by logging, as my dad likes to do). In other words, the desire to 'get back to nature' does exist – but from the safety of a tour bus, a garden path, the refuge of an umbrella or the viewfinder of a camera.

Furthermore, according to Kellert's respondents, such is the power of nature that – irrespective of their education level – they largely believed it was incapable of complete destruction by humans: 'If wild nature is beyond the human ability to control or grasp,' one said, 'if people are fundamentally inconsequential before an all-powerful nature, then one could hardly imagine people as being able to exert much harm or regulation over nature.' Another put it this way: 'People have to objectify nature, almost be arrogant toward it, to feel any particular ethical responsibility or capacity for meddling with it.'

The 1991 study was a long time ago, but in deeply conservative Japan, would the same results be found today? I think of my first trip to Japan. On Yakushima, an island of dripping rainforests off Kyushu's southern tip, I spent a day a few years ago researching a travel story about Jomon Sugi, a revered millennia-old cedar that lies deep in the mountainous interior. I hadn't planned on bush-walking when I packed my suitcase, so I wore jeans and sneakers; the Japanese hikers on the trail had brand-new boots, gators, backpacks, jackets and walking poles. They struck out in a careful caravan, barely leaving the trail to fill their drink bottles from the cool brooks in the forest. All around them were napalm-bright discs of fungi, flowering rhododendrons and matte-black butterflies, but the hikers' eyes didn't seem to leave the path.

When they reached Jomon Sugi – which was ringed by safety rails, its boughs supported by high-tensile wire like a giant bonsai – they all made V-signs for the cameras, banged the mud off their boots and made for the car park. I remember feeling frustrated: I was the only foreigner on the trail and it struck me that everyone else couldn't see the forest for the tree.

Kumi Kato gives a validating nod when I tell her about that experience over a beer in the town of Chikatsuyu. 'I went to Shiretoko [in Hokkaido] a few months ago,' she says. 'It's meant to be Japan's last wilderness and I felt like I was in a Kyoto garden or something – it was all organised!'

Kato is a social scientist with a unique perspective on Japanese conceptions of nature: for twenty-two years she lived in Australia, where she was a keen camper and vocal 'ecohumanitarian' activist – rare behaviour in her homeland, where she now teaches environmental studies at Wakayama University.

She's loath to indulge in national stereotyping but concedes there are significant cultural trends that can be applied to how Japanese and Australians view their surrounds.

The concept of wilderness as something untamed, which humans would want to enter to 'reconnect' with a primordial, pre-industrialised world, is largely foreign, she says. A journalist I later speak to tells me nearly all of Japan's national parks were established for cultural patrimony, not conservation – sites of a famous shrine (or tree), a great view or a mountain where an ascetic had achieved enlightenment, rather than sites to protect an endangered frog or a biodiversity hotspot.

Kato tells me the desire to conserve nature for nature's sake does exist, but it is usually restricted to younger people who have been exposed to Western concepts of nature's inherent worth. Once back in Japan, they're soon pulled into line. 'Activism is not anything too unusual in Australia, but in Japan, I think expressing individual ideas, individual ways of living, it's quite a challenge,' she says.

When I visit the office of Greenpeace Japan a few weeks later, I wander around the backstreets of Shinjuku for ten minutes hunched over Google Maps until I notice a lime-green Greenpeace sticker, the size of a chocolate bar, on a second-storey window. It is Tokyo's equivalent, I realise, of the bright flags of African migrants hanging from windows in grey Parisian suburbs: both admissions of defeat and markers of defiance. The world's second-biggest environmental NGO after the WWF, Greenpeace has a global membership of 2.9 million. In Japan it has 5000.

'It's not about who's got a deeper understanding of the human–nature relationship, but I think on an expression level, certainly in Japan people tend to express less,' says Kato. And when they do express themselves about environmental degradation, their concerns have tended to be about air, water and, lately, nuclear pollution; 'environmental problems' are framed through the prism of human health and wellbeing.

'People don't go off the path, conceptually,' she says. Nor literally. Kato tells me the story of a Buddhist nun she knows who lives on the other side of the mountain from Chikatsuyu. Her temple sits in a forest clearing where wild boar snuffle about the leaf litter and the mist sometimes doesn't clear until early afternoon. One morning the nun opened her curtains to discover a preternatural addition to the view: a lurid tent. 'That's probably unthinkable in Japan!' laughs Kato. The camper? An Australian backpacker.

*

The Japanese word for whale – *kujira* – translates as 'big fish' (in earlier days *isana* or *isa* was used, meaning 'brave fish'). Scientific discovery put paid to that assumption, but the insinuation remains: this is no Superwhale, just another animal to be hauled out of the sea. And yet it would be ethnocentric and overly simplistic to think whales have traditionally existed for Japan in crassly materialistic terms: fuel for the furnace or steaks for the barbie.

Traditional Japanese conceptions of whales are perhaps more closely aligned to those of the Inuit than of the Lutheran societies of Norway, Iceland and the Faroe Islands, where they are viewed as providential gifts which humans are entitled to harvest. In Shinto cosmology, humans, animals and even some inanimate objects are endowed with souls and involved in a partnership of reciprocity: prey 'give themselves up' for humans, and are thanked according to Buddhist custom. If in the Christian tradition the human–animal relationship is one of dominance and submission, its Japanese counterpart is one of equality.

Central to this notion of reciprocity is the Buddhist concept of *kuyo*. Literally 'offering and nurturing', kuyo is given in honour of Buddha, deities and the spirits of all beings. Offerings can be tangible (food, incense, flowers) or intangible (prayers): in Taiji, an old whaler told me that before he and his colleagues would sail south they would hold prayers for the whales, 'because whales provide meat for us'; Ayukawa's Kannon-ji temple contains glass cabinets full of wooden minke, sei and sperm whale carvings, shadow boxes to allay the souls of the dead.

Kuyo-to (kuyo monuments) are found throughout Japan and can be dedicated to the spirits of both humans, as with the Hiroshima Peace Memorial, built in 1955, and non-humans, as with the rat monument in Tokyo's Shoen-ji temple, built in 1903 after a two-year extermination program over health concerns. There are ninety-five kuyo-to for whales. In addition, other sites, like Taiji's Ebisu-jinja shrine, its entrance crossed by two right whale rib bones, are dedicated to all beings of the sea.

In this Shinto web of mutual exchange, little distinction is made between species according to perceived intelligence or sentience. On the drive out of Ayukawa, my interpreter Lily tells me the priest of Kannon-ji kept asking her why I was so interested in whales and not other animals; the old whaler in Taiji was equally perplexed: 'Japanese people have respect for every living thing,' he told me. 'Whales are just one of them.'

According to Kumi Kato, elevating the importance of one species over another is mostly a foreign concept in Japan; all beings, she says, animate and inanimate, have an inner spirit. But it makes sense that whaling communities would dedicate more spiritual energy to the animals from which they derive their living.

In Japan's whaling communities, natural disasters were traditionally perceived as punishment for failing to perform proper rituals or for breaking taboos. Off Ukushima Island, north of Nagasaki, seventy-two whalers drowned in 1715 after they attacked a blue whale which had a calf. A disaster in which 111 Taiji men drowned in 1878 occurred after they broke the same taboo, this time with a right whale and calf.

In the community of Kayoi, in western Japan, an elderly Buddhist nun even holds daily prayers for whales in the township's Kogan-ji temple – over 100 years after whaling ceased there. But in keeping with the sentiments of her colleague in Ayukawa, the nun also prays for dolphins, fish and any creatures that may have been killed during farming.

Kogan-ji contains a funeral register for whales killed between the eighteenth and twentieth centuries and, highly unusually, a granite tomb for foetuses found in mother whales killed by local whalers. On the tomb, beside the names of the donors, whaling captain and priest, a sutra is inscribed: 'Although your life as a whale was terminated with the mother's life, it was not our intention to take your life. We'd rather have freed you into the ocean, but you'd not be able to survive on your own in the harsh environment. Therefore we pray that you receive the virtue of impermanence like us human beings.'

Kogan-ji, like Taiji's Ebisu-jinja shrine, holds an annual whale memorial service (*eko*) each May, featured in 'A Memorial for the Whales' (circa 1930) by local poet Kaneko Misuzu:

A memorial for the whales
Held late in spring when flying
fish are caught
When the temple bell travels
across the bay's water
When fishermen dress in
their formal attire
and hurry to the temple
A lone whale child
listening to the temple bell
cries alone missing its mother
and father
How far into the ocean
does the temple bell resonate?

A monument for right whales, crowned by a whale statue, was erected in Hakodate, Hokkaido, in 1957 by an 83-year-old retired chief gunner of the Toyo Whaling Company. The inscription hints at a haunted soul, uneasy with how Japan's conservative spirituality sits with the realities of the industrial world it now inhabits: 'We engaged in whaling for twenty-six years from 1908 and we took some 2000 whales. Although among the groups of whales were mothers and calves, many of them were taken. The guilt of taking of the precious lives of these whales was truly regrettable. I have for some time preached the need to formally acknowledge this regretful act, and my desire to do it has grown stronger since the passing of my wife.

'I have lost three of my children and the anguish of the loss is unbearable. The mercilessness of this world is felt even stronger now in my old age. My wish is to commemorate the spirits of all living things and I therefore erect this monument to wish for the peaceful resting of all whale spirits taken by humans.'

The inscription goes on to say that the former gunner feels especially guilty because he was given a gold watch by his boss for his proficiency at killing whales. Whenever he checked the time he was reminded of the life he had taken.

Guilt, empathy, regret and undeniable compassion for sentient beings: these whaling community mores certainly contradict the prevailing Western depiction of Japan's merciless whale and dolphin murderers. But how compatible is this system – based on a spiritual assumption that nature balances itself out – with the contemporary realities of life in the world's third-biggest economy?

'It's a strange society to some extent because you have huge consumerism but huge respect to the old Japanese culture,' Greenpeace Japan's executive director, Junichi Sato, later tells me. 'When you see both, it doesn't really match: people still think their values are based on the Japanese culture but their actions are totally different from those values.'

Sato sees this disparity between the actual and the imagined to be especially applicable to whaling: 'The elderly people who support whaling, they think whaling is a part of the dealing with nature; they don't see whaling as an industrial thing – whaling is a cultural event [for them]. Their image of the whaling is really the small-scale, hand harpoon, more cultural events, when the reality is really large-scale industrial fishing vessels.'

That reality shocked Mark Votier, the first – and last – foreign journalist allowed to travel to Antarctica with Kyodo Senpaku. Votier, a British filmmaker, lived with the whalers for five months of the 1991–92 season and had free rein during that time: he filmed the freezers and processing facilities on board the *Nisshin Maru*, and life among the crew of the catcher boat *Toshi Maru 25*.

Less than half the whales Votier saw harpooned died a quick death, something he blamed on the scientists, who demanded the head of a killed whale be left intact so they could better study it. To do this, the harpooner was told to aim at the heart – something that required expert marksmanship and was rarely achieved. Whales that weren't killed instantly were speared with an electrified lance and juiced up with just 100 volts (by comparison, 2400 volts are administered to people killed by electric chair in Nebraska). The longest Votier saw a whale take to die was twenty-five minutes.

In a gutsy piece of journalism that both showed the on-water reality of research whaling and ended my hopes of getting the ICR to answer the phone, Votier's subsequent documentary – which aired around the world – slammed the failings of the electric-lance method and helped contribute to the eventual adoption of the rifle by the Japanese fleet to inflict a quicker death blow. The ICR remained unrepentant, however. After Votier's documentary the filmmaker visited the ICR, only to be berated. 'I am a scientist,' one

Dr Nagasaki told him. 'I am not concerned with humane killing.'

When Votier accompanied the whalers, it may have been possible to formulate an argument that whales' lives were being exchanged for human sustenance. Is it still accurate to speak of reciprocity in a program of negligible scientific worth conducted at a time when there is little demand for whale meat? Does Japan's Antarctic whaling accord with the give-and-take spirit of old Kayoi, or is it now just take-and-take?

*

For five bucks, three times daily, you can get a front-row seat to the paradox Stephen Kellert identified at Taiji's 'marinarium'. I arrive five minutes before the four o'clock show: the cashier, a heavily made up woman, flashes her purple eyelids; she wakes with a fright when I clear my throat.

Beyond the entrance and beside the Taiji Whale Museum, with its jars of whale parts in formaldehyde, twelve cetaceans – false killer whales, Risso's dolphins, short-finned pilot whales and bottlenose dolphins – cruise around a fifty-metre pool, their spouts of breath like the exhalations of snorkellers.

If manipulating nature for artistic appeal was a key theme of Kellert's findings, this place is a case in point: the pool is artificial but has been made to look natural, with rock blasted out of a hillside to exaggerate the beginnings of a canyon, although some of the boulders aren't quite lifelike enough to fool a critical gaze.

In an adjoining building made to look like the entrance to a cave, there's an indoor exhibition with artful photos of Antarctic whaling scenes: icebergs silhouetted at sundown; whales breaching; the ICR's fleet pitching through the southern swell. There's also a gallery of harpoon guns.

At four sharp, generic '90s dance music starts reverberating around the canyon from speakers discreetly hidden among its scrubby trees, and three trainers dressed in matching yellow anoraks and blue overalls appear to excited applause. They clasp buckets of dead fish and rest whistles in their mouths like officious soccer referees.

I take my seat beside the handful of Japanese tourists, camera phones at the ready. For half an hour three bottlenose dolphins and a Risso's dolphin, its skin speckled and grey like a well-worn bowling ball, respond to a series of elaborate hand signals: jumping two metres out of the water to touch a buoy held aloft; corkscrewing through the air; 'shaking hands' with a flipper (a crowd favourite).

The Japanese are unburdened by the notion of species ambassadorship, so watching dolphins or whales and eating them are both simply different forms of human gratification. Is the joy in the marinarium's bleachers any more hypocritical than my realisation, age eight, that 'Glowy', an orphaned poddy lamb I helped my dad nurse back to health, ended up on the dinner table? I still think lambs are cute, and I still eat them.

To exit the marinarium, you have to pass through the gift shop, where you can buy dolphin postcards, plush whale toys, whale fluke T-shirts and slabs of whale and dolphin meat from a fridge decorated with stickers of dolphins jumping through hoops. When Ric O'Barry, the famous dolphin handler from the 1960s TV series *Flipper*, visited this place, he derisively quipped that Taiji must be the only place in the world where you can have your whale and eat it too.

COCKROACHES

Masayuki Komatsu missed a spot shaving this morning, a black almond running down his right jawbone that is conspicuous on both its owner – with his finely parted hair, grey cashmere scarf and matching double-breasted overcoat – and in these surrounds, Tokyo's elite National Graduate Institute for Policy Studies, referred to as 'Asia's LSE'. Perhaps the spot is a glimpse at the boy inside the man; a peek at the knockabout country kid who, through a combination of balls and brilliance, leapfrogged the usual bureaucratic rungs to become the most bellicose postwar diplomat Japan has produced.

'For journalists used to the smooth diplomatic hum of the global conference circuit,' wrote the *Japan Times'* David McNeill in 2007, 'covering the poisonous annual meetings of the International Whaling Commission is akin to being slapped on the face with a slab of week-old minke bacon.' For the fourteen years that Komatsu was Japan's alternate commissioner to the IWC, it was usually him starting the food fight.

Komatsu's tenure as Japan's chief whaling negotiator was marked by a growing distance between the IWC's pro- and anti-whaling blocs. At the 1989 IWC meeting in San Diego, Komatsu framed the whaling controversy as a culture war between 'meat eaters' (Australia and the Anglos) and 'fish eaters' (Japan). He had previously accused America of coming to the aid of whales in the 1970s only to deflect public criticism of the Vietnam War, and he would later dismiss New Zealand as a feckless puppet of Greenpeace.

But his most infamous moment of high-level shit-stirring came in 2000, when he dubbed minke whales 'cockroaches of the sea'. Even in the nascent days of the internet the comment went viral, drawing outrage from whale huggers and official condemnation from Western prime ministers and presidents.

Komatsu slips off his coat, untangles his scarf and pours us two glasses of water from a carafe. I tell him that while researching this interview I found a meme on Google depicting a photo of two harpooned minkes being winched up the *Nisshin*'s slipway sandwiched by the following caption:

IM IN UR OSHAN
KILLIN UR ROACHES

He slaps a thigh and chortles; the old pest exterminator obviously hasn't grown tired of this one yet. The statement must have been known to cause offence, but I ask whether the extent of the backlash was anticipated.

'No, no, of course not!'

I'm sceptical of his sincerity, but accepting of his reasoning: minke whales, Komatsu tells me, are known in Norway as the 'mice of whales' on account of their abundance. They are named, so he says, after a hapless whaler called Meincke, who, every time he tried to nab a fin whale, ended up with a minke on the end of his harpoon.

Komatsu tells me he was thinking of Meincke when he made the comparison. He used the cockroach analogy, he claims, not because he thinks minkes should be squished with your shoe, but that – being widespread and common – they are ripe for exploitation. 'I wanted to pick up on [other] kinds of – in terms of number – abundant species,' he says. 'So I came to the minke whale – I mean cockroach.' Komatsu apologises for his English but I'm grateful for the gaffe. He's still getting his vermin mixed up after all these years.

*

Whaling makes such good copy because it encapsulates so many dichotomies: tradition versus modernity; nationalism versus globalism; local culture versus outside influence. But at its root is something more profound still: what is nature for? And what is our place within it?

Perhaps more than any other global forum, the International Whaling Commission has become a battleground for this dialectic. Multilateral attempts at regulating whaling date from the 1920s, but initial efforts largely failed until 1946, when fifteen countries signed (and later ratified) the ICRW; the IWC was set up three years later as the implementing body. Founded at a time when whales were seen as floating oil sumps, the IWC's remit was much like OPEC's today; its preamble is to 'provide for the proper conservation of whale stocks and thus make possible the orderly development of the whaling industry'.

Any amendments to the ICRW's whaling quotas, which can be achieved only with a three-quarters majority of member states, must provide for the conservation, development and optimal utilisation of whale resources, and must also be based on scientific findings. Such findings are provided by the ICRW Scientific Committee, made up of nominees of member governments as well as advisers from relevant international organisations and invited participants.

It was envisaged that the Scientific Committee would meet annually to make recommendations to the IWC on quotas, research and stocks based on analysis of biological and scientific data.

But the IWC has been dysfunctional from birth. Its first twenty years were characterised by a failure to set sustainable quotas – not so much a failure of the Scientific Committee as skulduggery by some nations, including claiming a take of one species yet taking another. This was a time when the whale-oil industry was still a powerful lobby with the ear of its nations' delegates.

Quotas at the time were measured in 'blue whale units' (BWUs), irrespective of species or stocks. The BWU was deduced from the amount of oil one blue whale produced, which was deemed equal to that from two fins, 2.5 humpbacks, six sei or thirty minkes. With whales reduced to the content of barrels, it made sense for whalers to prioritise blues and fins, both of which are now endangered. At this stage quotas were a system of first in, best lubed, encouraging whalers to behave like competing siblings at a garden Easter egg hunt – without the requisite parental divvying-up of the prize afterwards.

By the 1960s it was becoming apparent that the creation of the IWC had done little to stop the Antarctic ground being exhausted like other stocks before it. But the falling price of whale oil was making the whole escapade pointless to most IWC members. Japan (which was after meat) and the Soviets (not being beholden to the capitalist economy) still found whaling worthwhile, but most of the West no longer had an interest in keeping quotas high.

The waning influence of the British, Dutch and Australian whaling industries enabled the Scientific Committee to finally make its voice heard, with restrictions gradually introduced to reflect the conservation status of separate species. The Easter egg hunt was replaced by national quotas; humpbacks and blue whales were protected entirely. Whales were still seen as resources, but as renewable rather than extractable – more pine plantation than old growth.

In 1972 the BWU was replaced by species-specific quotas commensurate with their conservation status. Two years later the New Management Procedure (NMP) was introduced, whereby mathematical modelling charted stock sizes with a focus on comparing pre-exploitation and current populations. Species were divided into three categories according to abundance and governed by the principle that 'exploitation should not commence until an estimate of stock size has been obtained which is satisfactory in the view of the Scientific Committee'.

This was easier said than done: in remote Antarctica, how could stock sizes be gauged in order to determine their maximum sustainable yield? The NMP assumed nations told the truth about which whales they hunted. And most did, but not all. The USSR, in particular, took blue whales but reported its catch as a mixture of fin and sei whales. The scientists became more puzzled as their quota setting seemed ever less reliable, causing the NMP to be discredited – yet it was actually always working, it's just that the input data were false.

As the postwar movement of environmentalism gained mainstream credibility, a consensus began growing within the IWC that the safest way to ensure a sustainable population of whales would be a blanket period of zero-catch: a moratorium.

With a three-quarters majority needed to bring about a moratorium, the IWC – once a whalers' club – was inundated by countries solely wanting to halt whaling: membership increased from fourteen in 1972 to thirty-nine in 1982. And like the Jamaican bobsled team at the Winter Olympics, historical familiarity with the terrain wasn't a prerequisite for membership – nor was having a coastline. So Switzerland, Austria and even Luxembourg grew interested in whaling; the regulator became more cosmopolitan than the industry it regulated ever had been.

The moratorium on all 'killing for commercial purposes', passed in 1982 and enforced from 1986, was aimed at buying time until uncertainties over stock numbers had been clarified through the creation of a Revised Management Procedure (RMP).

In 1991, at its annual meeting in Reykjavík, the Scientific Committee recommended a mathematical model it had devised, effectively giving the green light to a sustainable resumption of commercial whaling. It estimated that with 761,000 Antarctic minkes – plus 87,000 in the North Atlantic and 25,000 in the North Pacific – an annual commercial quota of 2000 would not harm the population. Yet this didn't satisfy many who wanted the moratorium to continue. And so the Scientific Committee kept refining the model, without it ever being implemented.

For countries that had no consumptive use for them, saving whales had become, in the neat words of University of Sydney political scientist Charlotte Epstein, 'shorthand for saving the planet'. Sidney Holt, one of the architects of the moratorium, wrote on the eve of its implementation that 'saving whales is for millions of people the crucial test of their political ability to halt environmental destruction'. By saving whales – the humans of the deep – we were saving ourselves.

For the second time in its history the Scientific Committee thought it was being undermined, this time not by the pressure of big business but by a new force: environmentalism. In his letter of resignation as the committee's chairman after tweaked RMPs had again been rejected in 1992 and 1993, Cambridge University's

Professor Philip Hammond wrote: 'What is the point of having a Scientific Committee if its unanimous recommendations on matters of primary importance are treated with such contempt?' Ideology overruling science: sound familiar?

The IWC had split along philosophical lines: whether or not it was ethical to hunt whales. This was when Japan started playing hardball, and in Masayuki Komatsu they found the man for the fight. The son of a fisherman from the rural (and now tsunami-flattened) town of Rikuzentakata, he doesn't fit the Japanese cookie-cutter bureaucrat of elite Tokyo finishing schools. When we talk in his university's minimalist meeting room, Komatsu's famous combativeness asserts itself; throughout our interview he has the disconcerting habit of employing the pronoun 'you' for both me and my nation's whaling policy – as if I'm an official envoy dispatched by Canberra and not a writer who just happens to live there.

By the early '90s, Komatsu thought there could *actually* be as many minkes as cockroaches and it would make no difference to Australia: 'We felt that, even though we were playing baseball, you were trying to impose the rules of, you know, soccer game or cricket game,' he says. 'So I thought that perhaps it's in vain for us to keep this sincere response to the IWC.'

This was when the IWC descended into farce: Iceland left; Norway resumed commercial whaling. The mudslinging began in earnest, and Japan, rather than trying to have the moratorium overturned through diplomacy, was accused of trying to buy its desired outcome. Small developing states were wooed to the pro-whaling camp in return for not-so-discreet increases in aid – a landmine removal project in Laos, a cultural project in Mongolia. Japan has always vehemently denied this palm-greasing, but it doesn't try too hard to hide it: in June 2004 the then Japanese prime

minister, Junichiro Koizumi, expressed his gratitude to the Nicara-
guan president, Enrique Bolaños, for his newfound interest in commercial whaling; one month later Japan cancelled Nicaragua's
US$118.4-million debt. Nor is it restricted to bilateral aid: in 2010
undercover reporters from London's *Sunday Times* exposed widespread bribes from Japan of cash, prostitutes and flights to delegates of developing nations in return for their votes – by posing as
anti-whaling lobbyists offering counter-bribes for them to win back
their votes.

So while the 'antis', as Komatsu calls opponents of commercial
whaling, were the majority in 1986 (31–10), twenty years later they
had been supplanted (32–33). The IWC had entered its current
state: hopeless deadlock. Ostensibly, for a resumption of commercial whaling to take place, the commission has now decided on the
need for a Revised Management Scheme (RMS), incorporating
both scientific aspects of stock management (the Revised Management Procedure eventually agreed on in 1994) and non-scientific
aspects of management (on-board inspectors; DNA registers;
humane killing techniques). But the reality is the moratorium has
become a ban; Australia and its allies are opposed to any RMS,
irrespective of its nature.

Komatsu tells me he sees no end to the status quo but is frustrated by what he perceives a lack of 'fighting spirit' in the nebbish
Japanese delegations of today. If Japan loses the ICJ case at The
Hague, he thinks Japan should resume commercial whaling in its
own waters: 'Of course that would be controversial – you Australians might like to, again, fight the litigation, but chances of you
going to win may not be higher.'

Komatsu concedes the market for whale meat in Japan is 'dead
in the water' but thinks it could be refloated if there was a 'trigger'

to make it tempting to younger tastes: 'You know, Chicken McNugget or something like that. Whale meat could be served in similar fashion.' He claims that the '3000 tonnes' (which is actually closer to 5000) of whale meat in storage equals 1 per cent of the tuna currently in Japanese freezers, so it's not a sufficient stockpile to make prices competitive. It's an interesting point, but irrespective of your taste in meat, surely sending a whaling fleet to Antarctica will never be able to compete with the economies of scale of domestic chicken farming or even importing Australian beef.

Komatsu argues that it's not the whales themselves that are at stake but the cornucopia they represent: with the world's population rapidly expanding, he has no time for the argument that because Antarctica's marine resources were the world's last to be exploited, they should be locked up for good: 'It's an abundance there, a resource pool!'

This is what Jun Morikawa described to me as the 'domino theory' – the fear among some Japanese policymakers that if they give up whales, they will next have to give up other marine resources, most notably tuna. China's recent increased consumption of fish, land-poor Japan's tradition of looking to the sea to feed itself, and the government line – however apocryphal – that whales themselves are competition for fish all hint at an undercurrent of anxiety about resource security running through this debate.

Komatsu even thinks Australia has the same idea, with whale-loving a masquerade for future mineral, oil and fisheries exploitation. 'Antarctica is a place for exploitation, and you want exclude other countries from the profit! It's for selfish domestic reasons you want to exclude all other nations from Antarctica!'

My interviewee has transformed from friendly sparring partner to schooner-smashing icehead; is this, I wonder, what a minke-slap feels like? I'm reminded of another quote from that *Japan Times* article by David McNeill. It came from the IWC's 2006 annual meeting, held in the Caribbean state of St Kitts and Nevis, when, emboldened by the first pro-whaling majority since the moratorium and without giving any clear reason why, Japan declared its intention to kill fifty humpback whales a year in Antarctica for scientific research – a species it knew full well to be among the most popular of all mammals in the West.

'What is Japan *doing*?' the exasperated New Zealand conservation minister, Chris Carter, was heard to utter. 'It seems determined to anger the world.'

But what if that's the point?

SCIENCE

I'm on a commuter train and I'm on my best behaviour. I stuffed this up last time: a chance to interview a whistleblower gone begging. We had him lined up: found by Jun Morikawa, cautiously approached by my interpreter Ryoko and formally contacted by me. The plan was to phone him one minute before my train left Shinjuku for his suburban Keio-Nagayama station, which is 'precisely twenty minutes walk' from his house. We would then meet at the station, walk another five minutes to a local café and talk for half an hour. The man clearly liked structure; he used to make computer models for a living.

But then cross-cultural miscommunication intervened. A week before our scheduled meeting, Ryoko called, saying my man wanted more information about me. I sent him an outline of my questions. Two days later he contacted me directly: 'Email is a risky way of communication,' he wrote. 'If someone changes email address, the person can easily disappear from my contact range. Thus I have a policy that I do not interview [am not interviewed by] any person with whom I am acquainted only through email. It is unfortunate that you, and perhaps your publisher, meet such case [sic].' Whether that's the real reason he pulled out I will never know.

I let it thaw a few months and had my editor send him a fawning email. And now I have a second chance.

It's early autumn when I return to Tokyo; soft, flat light swaddles the afternoon commuters in a lazy stupor. Heads hang limp, mouths agape in half-sleep; grips on briefcases or mummy's hand slowly loosen; manga pornos, printed on *Green Guide* newspaper, slide unhindered across their owners' laps towards the floor. Everyone bobs in silent sync to the jolts and turns of the train.

I don't know much about the man I'm meeting today. 'From speaking to him on the phone,' Ryoko advised, 'he sounds like a pretty formal guy; a typical conservative old Japanese man. I think you better tuck in your shirt.' I have. I've also shaved. And consulted YouTube to tie my tie. I notice I'm even conscious of my posture as I sit on the train – back straight, knees together, palms clasped at the waist – as if through some kind of cosmic pre-emption I'm already reassuring him of my motives.

But my apprehension proves misplaced. Professor Toshio Kasuya greets me warmly when I alight at the tangle of mock Starbucks and twee boulangeries that is Keio-Nagayama station. He asks after my journey and apologises for being too busy running errands today to meet me in the city.

'I am flying to Bhutan tomorrow,' he explains as we cross the street. 'On vacations.'

'Flying to Bhutan! You know the international airport there is said to be the most difficult for pilots to land at? It's a steep descent through the Himalayas onto a tiny runway. That'll be very exciting.'

Japan's most venerable expert on small cetaceans has stopped walking. I bite my lip and curse my tactlessness; he looks up at me, ashen-faced. 'I know, Mr Vincent. My wife is *most* terrified.'

*

In the Western media, the 'science' of scientific whaling is almost always flippantly dismissed as 'so-called' or bracketed with a mocking pair of bunny ears (as I've sometimes done myself). Conversely, Japan's national public broadcaster, NHK, has a policy of always prefixing JARPA II and JARPN II with the words 'scientific research' – without the quote marks. Neither approach does much to further our understanding of what the ICR is actually up to.

They don't make it easy for those who try. My multiple emails and phone calls to the ICR and its approval-stamping Fisheries Agency go unacknowledged and unreturned. Because of this, I've had to go behind the ICR's back to find someone connected to the program.

The irony is that Japan's research program was sold to the world as an uncontroversial answer to the whaling controversy: science is rational where whalers and anti-whalers are emotional; science is neutral where activism and industry is partisan; science can navigate the gridlock of the IWC to reach the happy land of sustainable commercial whaling, free of the profligacy of the past. An ICR propaganda booklet, *Misinformation: The Protest against Japan's Whale Research,* picks up the story: 'In order to draw the best scientific advice, scientific whaling having as [its] purpose the collection of necessary information is the only way to go. Should this task be neglected, the best scientific advice would never be obtained.'

The problem is that scientists, like activists, don't exist in a vacuum. Science is pluralistic, hotly contested within its own community and subject to influence from money and power – especially when it becomes politicised.

This is the principal criticism of Japan's Antarctic whaling program: that it has been compromised to the point that it is science in name only. The crews (former commercial whalers), the ships (left over from commercial whaling), the waters (previously favoured by

Japan's commercial whaling fleet), the timing (immediately follow-ing the enforcement of the moratorium), the species (the principal quarry of the whale-meat industry), the method (lethal take), the fact that Japan hadn't previously shown an inclination for scientific whaling of this magnitude: they all suggest a continuation of Japan's commercial whaling industry, 'retro-fitted', in the Australian gov-ernment's words, under the artifice of the scientific exemption to the moratorium.

Japan's greatest asset in countering such criticism is that the scientific exemption from the moratorium and the Southern Ocean Sanctuary – found in Article VIII of the ICRW – is vague, simply requiring the government to grant a 'special permit' to kill, take and treat whales for 'the purposes of scientific research'. How 'special' must a special permit be? Special like Christmas or Special K? While governments must submit the results of such research, Japan has been pilloried for the paucity of peer-reviewed papers its research whaling has produced. And governments conducting such scientific research may take 'all practicable measures to obtain such data'. Is this carte blanche for Japan to set quotas as high as it likes?

It was Japan's interpretation of Article VIII that Australia asked the International Court of Justice to pass judgment on. Much of the world already had.

*

At seventy-six, Professor Kasuya has now retired from the IWC's Scientific Committee, although he attended meetings as late as 2013. No taller than the Himalayan rhododendrons he is subjecting his wife to aviational torture tomorrow to visit, he has a broad nose splintered with purple veins and wears a tatty flowerpot hat pulled down firmly over his face. His English is classical, formal and fired in staccato bursts.

We sit outside on a café's patio, squinting into the low sun over our coffee. Kasuya tells me a story that starts with a visit to his lab by the then vice-president of the Fisheries Agency one day in 1984. At the time Kasuya was working as a biologist at the National Research Institute of Far Seas Fisheries. He and his team were asked to design a program to gauge the ecology of Antarctic minke whales in response to the IWC's claims of 'uncertainty of scientific information' – they were to design, in other words, the management mechanism the IWC seemed incapable of designing itself. JARPA's aims were to determine mortality rates of Antarctic minke whales, their stock numbers and structure, the role the minkes played in the ecosystem and whether pollution was affecting them.

To do this, Kasuya and his team advised the collection and investigation of over 100 research items from the whales, including baleen plates, ovaries, testes, stomach contents, blubber thickness, parasites. I ask the professor if the development process was subject to political interference.

'What is "political interference"?'

'Influence from the Fisheries Agency or politicians perhaps; pressure. Were you and your colleagues allowed to independently create the research program to achieve its objectives?'

'I didn't feel pressure,' he says, 'except two or three cases. One was the proposal – the idea came from the Fisheries Agency, politically. Scientists didn't propose it. We were asked by the Fisheries Agency, and we were working under the Fisheries Agency, therefore we had no right to object to it. That is a kind of pressure, maybe?'

There was another kind of pressure. Members of the Fisheries Agency's whaling division accompanied the body's vice-president and told the scientists the program must meet two conditions: a long duration, and a sample size sufficient to cover the expenses of the program through the sale of whale meat. Lethal take was thus the only option – and it was one Kasuya was happy with: he believes lethal take is the only way to obtain such information.

JARPA, then, was a commercial operation from the start – albeit one in which data was scrupulously collected and measured. 'The scientists believe in what they are doing,' Mark Votier, the British filmmaker who accompanied the JARPA crew in 1992, told journalist Andrew Darby. 'It's not a sham in the sense that they nod and wink and say, "We don't really care about it." They are doing it because they are genuinely interested.'

But in Professor Kasuya's view, as a scientific venture JARPA was flawed from the outset because the program didn't kill *enough* whales. In 1987, in their final proposal, Kasuya and his team concluded that in order to meet the research objectives, a catch of at least 1500 minke whales was necessary. The Fisheries Agency deemed this number unacceptable to the anti-whaling camp, and instead brought to that year's IWC meeting, in Bournemouth, a plan to kill 825 minke whales and fifty sperm whales – itself later reduced to a final quota of around 330 minkes.

The sample size may not have been enough to achieve the program's purported objectives, but it was enough to increase the Fisheries Agency's whaling budget by $12.29 million between 1988 and 2003. It wasn't quite in the ballpark of King Leopold's Congolese kleptocracy but it was the same idea: private enterprise masquerading as the national interest. The profit margin was always slim: the *Japan Times* reports that in the first year of scientific whaling, sixty-four tonnes of meat went unsold from a catch of 1700 – a fraction of the 209,000 tonnes eaten in Japan in 1962. But it was a profitable balancing act while it lasted.

This is the primary reason that Tohoku University's Atsushi Ishii and Ayako Okubo of the Ocean Policy Research Foundation believe that Japan's IWC delegation – dominated by Fisheries Agency officials – has no intention of overturning the moratorium. If commercial whaling were resumed, they argue, any profit from meat sales would go to private enterprise, not the Fisheries Agency, so it would lose its power.

In his 1989 expat bible *The Enigma of Japanese Power*, Dutch writer Karel van Wolferen advises against assuming that 'Japan is a sovereign state like any other, a state with central organs of government which can both recognise what is good for the country and bear collective responsibility for national decision-making'. Rather, Japan has a nebulous political structure of overlapping, competing hierarchies without a clear leader. The Fisheries Agency is looking out for itself; it is, in Jun Morikawa's words, 'a horse with no rider'.

Ishii and Okubo assert that since 1991, the real goal of the Japanese IWC delegation, and through it the Fisheries Agency, has been to *undermine* efforts to overturn the moratorium, not facilitate it. 'I have no direct evidence,' Ishii tells me. 'For example, the Fisheries Agency officials saying' – he covers his mouth conspiratorially – '"Oh, we are not really trying," or an archived letter or so, but my analysis is based on a technique called counterfactual analysis, and that is a technique of political science. The basic idea is you set a hypothesis and you analyse the conditions if that hypothesis must be true. And then you analyse the conditions and [if] the conditions were not met, you can say the hypothesis is wrong.'

Ishii and Okubo proposed four conditions necessary to achieve a resumption of commercial whaling: creating an atmosphere at the IWC and in the Japanese body politic conducive to negotiation; placating critics of 'scientific' whaling through transparency and cooperation; negotiating with the 'antis'; and developing a fallback strategy for withdrawal from the IWC, should all else fail. They found that none of these has been met.

And such is the strength of the IWC's deadlock, Ishii and Okubo argue, that Japan's outspoken desire to lift the moratorium and its attempts at vote buying are actually ways of shoring up the impasse, not breaking it. Though he has publicly denied any corruption, Komatsu conceded to me it would be nearly impossible for Japan to get the three-quarters majority required to overturn the moratorium.

In 2009, even the outgoing IWC commissioner, Dr William Hogarth – an American whose government is opposed to commercial whaling – hinted that maintaining the moratorium was beneficial to the Fisheries Agency, telling the BBC: 'I'll probably get in trouble for making this statement, but I am probably convinced right now that there would be less whales killed if we didn't have the commercial moratorium … I'm not sure you'd need nearly so many whales if it were strictly for sustainable use.'

When I ask Professor Kasuya if he thinks research whaling is helping to meet the Fisheries Agency's stated objective of overturning the moratorium, he shakes his head. He then tells me something amazing. In the Scientific Committee's draft report into the success of JARPA in 2007 – a report to which he contributed – the program was unanimously deemed to have failed.

'But due to some unknown reasons,' he says, voice suddenly very low, news of the program's failure 'was deleted from the final published report'.

'So was it changed or was it deleted?'

'I don't know the reason. But I was a member of the review meeting; everybody agreed … that JARPA didn't achieve the initial objective.'

In its final 2007 report on JARPA, the Scientific Committee identified problems with age and mortality rate data, but, as Kasuya says, did not go so far as deeming it a failure. According to one of the Fisheries Agency's propaganda booklets, however, JARPA was 'highly appreciated by the IWC Scientific Committee'.

I wonder how this man, who was once a Japanese appointment to the Scientific Committee before participating in an independent capacity, is regarded by his compatriots in the pro-whaling camp. He tells me his work on small cetaceans at the IWC meant he was rarely put in a position to publicly condemn research whaling, but he's now scathing of what he sees as the Fisheries Agency's meddling in the work of actual scientists.

'The Japanese so-called scientists attending the IWC contain some politicians,' he fulminates. 'They always speak some unscientific logic. They always control the scientists toward their benefit. So Japanese scientists are not always free from their influence in the Scientific Committee meetings of the IWC.'

Kasuya ultimately rejects the prevailing view of Japan trying to overturn the moratorium for the same reason Ishii and Okubo do. 'No companies want to start whaling,' he says. 'The scientific whaling is just good for Kyodo Senpaku.'

Was good for Kyodo Senpaku. In 2008 the *Asahi Shimbun* reported that Japan's three biggest seafood companies – Maruha Nichiro Holdings, Nippon Suisan Kaisha and Kyokuyo – had transferred their stocks in Kyodo Senpaku to public entities free of charge, surely a sign they see no commercial future in whaling.

And if Kyodo Senpaku, the company being chartered by the Fisheries Agency to catch the whales, is seemingly the only current beneficiary of the program – they are being paid by the Fisheries Agency, after all – for how long? JARPA may have increased the agency's budget but JARPA II, with its inexplicably expanded quota to 850 minkes, fifty humpbacks and fifty fins – it's taken eighteen fins and no humpbacks since it started – is nothing but a financial sinkhole, each voyage south now losing in excess of $10 million.

'I doubt it will continue long,' says Kasuya. 'The survival of the operation is becoming difficult, due to the shrinking demand.'

So Paul Watson, Sea Shepherd and the Western press keep telling me. But if this were merely a matter of supply and demand, why would fisheries minister Yoshimasa Hayashi defiantly announce that Japan will 'never stop whaling' in the midst of the country's worst ever hunting season? The national subsidies, too, seem at odds with the prevailing view that the program is seen to possess a purely profitable value.

I feel like I'm back where I started; I'm no closer to understanding what this is *actually* about. This conflict is so minuscule in every respect – whales killed, money made, cultural importance, scientific worth – it surely cannot be a conventional case of the economy versus the environment.

In 1970, 39,000 whales worldwide were reported as being harpooned; in 2012, 1000 were. As Greenpeace Japan's executive director, Junichi Sato, wrote in the *New York Times* in 2013, whales are now under far greater threat from collateral damage than from harpoons: pollution, overfishing, climate change. 'Whaling is dying out,' wrote Sato, 'but the threats to whales remain real and urgent and apply to all of the ocean's creatures, not just to its biggest ones. To save the whales, we need to restore the health of our oceans.'

But 'save the krill' doesn't have quite the same ring to it, does it?

I find a 2010 editorial from the *Age* outlining its opposition to all whaling. *All* whaling. Can you imagine a respected Australian newspaper declaring its opposition to all logging or all mining? Saving whales is clearly no longer about saving whales. It's about Saving Whales. And as for 'pro-whaling', it reminds me of stances on abortion or guns: pro-life; pro-freedom. As if there's no nuance in the world.

But then I'm frequently being asked whether I'm 'pro-whaling' or 'anti-whaling'. Aren't I allowed to think that the efforts of Washington State's Makah Tribe to reclaim its cultural heritage by hunting gray whales, after being smashed by American expansionism for the previous 200 years, is a beautiful thing? Can't I recognise that Iceland returned to the IWC with a reservation on the whaling moratorium, but disagree with its subsequent decision to hunt endangered fin whales? Am I not able to celebrate the fact that the arrival of grog and missionaries didn't stop Alaska's Inupiat from hunting bowheads – and celebrate the fact that since commercial whaling ceased, bowheads, once threatened with extinction, are increasing steadily?

Can't I hold all those views and be baffled why Japan's Fisheries Agency maintains a program of negligible scientific esteem for a product its public doesn't want and a commercial opportunity its business community probably wouldn't take?

I don't seem to be allowed a nuanced view: it's one or the other, you're one of them or one of us. Whaling divides and unites: a demarcation, a fracture, a border between peoples. It's akin to the pattern on your kilt, the style of your handshake, the name of your tribe – and the colour of your ship. And it's been that way for nearly 200 years.

TRADITION

The whale wars didn't start in 1987. They started in 1820. That was when a multinational fleet of ships began appearing on Japan's horizon. Onlookers called them *kurofune* – 'black ships' – a reference to the last foreign vessels that had visited Japan, sixteenth-century Portuguese carracks whose hulls were waterproofed with tar. These ones weren't black in colour but the smoke they belched into the sky sure was. And, like the Portuguese before them, they had come to make money.

I'm travelling to the town of Taiji, in southern Honshu's Wakayama Prefecture, to find some contemporary whalers. Many Antarctic whalers have come from Taiji. But Taiji is also a fascinating example of a Japanese whaling community that went from pioneering a sustainable system of net-whaling in the seventeenth century to having 111 local men break the taboo of catching a mother whale and calf and subsequently drown in a typhoon in 1878 – after the black ships had done irreparable damage to the local baleen whale stocks.

A few decades after that, Taiji's whalers adopted modern whaling techniques – both in Antarctica and offshore, where they increased their pursuit of small cetaceans. This eventually led to the town's gaining international notoriety after the release of the 2009 documentary *The Cove*, which showed graphic footage of locals slaughtering dolphins. My hopes are slim of finding someone in Taiji who'll talk to me.

*

As we drive to Taiji, my guide, Simon Wearne, a former *Whale Wars* cinematographer who now lives in Japan and has spent much time building trust with the locals, points out citrus terraces climbing up the hillsides, deftly reinforced with stonewalls. Powerlines march across the landscape and tunnels plunge into it; the whole scene is dark green and glossy like the leaves of a camellia.

As with Japan more generally, the coastal communities of the Kii Peninsula have traditionally relied on the sea for survival. Surrounded by water on three sides and blessed by the nutrient-rich Kuroshio Current, Taiji is ideally placed.

By the late seventeenth century, Japan was starting to possess what Professor Mitsuhiro Takemura calls the 'uninterpretable something' that would later be the catalyst for the country's unparalleled transition from feudal hermit kingdom to industrial powerhouse.

The Tokugawa shogunate, effectively a military junta that came to power in 1603, instituted a period of isolationism that would last 250 years but also brought peace, unity and economic prosperity to an archipelago that had been wracked by civil war for the preceding 150. Roads were built to facilitate the circulation of commodities, banking and finance developed, a rigid division of labour was instituted to do the heavy lifting, and a sophisticated bureaucracy established to take care of the paperwork. Trades and crafts flourished, and the time was ripe for a whaling revolution.

'All it needed was an entrepreneur to bring together the technology and the natural providence at his disposal,' says Simon, scruffy and lanky and too excited to keep his eye on the road for longer than ten seconds at a time.

That entrepreneur was Wada Kakuemon, who, legend has it, sometime around 1675 was watching a spider trap a fly in its web and wondered if he could do the same with the whales that passed his town each winter.

Kakuemon contrived a method whereby sleek, fast dragon boats called *sekobune* were used to drive whales into 33-square-metre nets set between waiting boats. Enveloped like a Cornish pasty, the entangled whale would be attacked with harpoons and lances before having its life ended with a sword. Once killed, the whale was slung between two boats and rowed to land for processing.

From Taiji the system spread to Kochi, Chiba and Yamaguchi prefectures; at its height, Kakuemon's design was trapping whales in thirty villages throughout southern Japan.

The method was unremarkable but the scale and organisation of it was: more than 600 people were needed to catch and process one whale, with highly specialised skills and roles required. The preparation began in early autumn, with large amounts of hemp imported from afar and made into ropes by women from the host town and neighbouring communities. Next, the ropes were woven into nets by experts from a handful of villages that specialised in the trade. Coopers, smiths and boatbuilders were also brought to the site to maintain the vessels and replace harpoons and knives as needed.

Once the whale was hauled ashore, men in a waterside shed worked fast to prevent spoilage: flensing the blubber, rendering it into lamp oil in fire pots and butchering the meat into useable cuts from all parts of the whale. What couldn't be eaten was sent off to warehouses across Japan where it would be put to use in other ways:

baleen for fans, plates and parasols; crushed bones for fertiliser; pickled penises and vaginas for aphrodisiacs. The scale of the operation, the interconnectedness of the roles involved and the network that enabled it: in Edo Japan it's about as close to industrialisation you can get without Ned Ludd arriving with his minions to smash the joint up.

We arrive in Taiji after lunch, and I can see a tangible example of the myth-making Jun Morikawa was talking about: up on blocks by the town's entrance is the retired Antarctic harpooner *Kyo Maru 1*, painted red and robin's egg blue. Beached on this subtropical shore, the ice-reinforced ship sticks out like an Aussie in a whale-meat restaurant: a stand of feathery palm trees sways beside it, while a tatty fishing eagle sits on the vessel's empty harpoon gun.

Below the boat, the bronze, erect figure of a whaler, loin-clothed and muscles rippling, is about to throw a harpoon into some unseen leviathan. 'His harpoon's just been replaced,' Simon tells me as we drive past. 'It was looking a bit limp after a Dutch Sea Shepherd volunteer swung off it last year.' The Sea Shepherd volunteers who patrol Taiji each autumn – to protest the killing of dolphins for meat and their capture for live export to marine parks and aquariums – call themselves the Cove Guardians. They largely consider Simon a nuisance, he tells me, because he's doing a PhD in tourism with the ultimate aim of lifting the veil of shame that cloaks contemporary Taiji by celebrating the sustainability of its past.

Our first stop is the office of Hayato Sakurai, the curator of maritime history at the local archives who works with the Taiji Whale Museum, an institution dedicated to net whaling but bankrolled by the ICR in another neat example of its appropriation of tradition for political purposes. I have five copies of a translated request to meet some whalers. Following Simon's advice, I have also admitted to going on campaign with Sea Shepherd as an independent observer.

But was I independent? The once-black Sea Shepherd T-shirt I had to wear at sea is now so faded it's brown; hopefully nobody here was watching the live feed Tod had running throughout the campaign. And sure, I think Percy is a caricature and Paul Watson a megalomaniac with daddy issues, but I've also cooked dinner for them both and did my bit to keep the ship running so it could chase whalers. While I reckon my time with Sea Shepherd has probably made me tougher on the organisation than an outsider would be, I'm not sure how to convince the Japanese of this.

It's a stinker in Taiji: 33 degrees and 85 per cent humidity. Beads of sweat run down my nose and smudge the ink in my notebook while, without a word, Simon leaves me in the car park and marches inside the administrative building that houses Sakurai's office. I'm not sure if he wants me to follow him, but after five minutes in the heat I pop my head through Sakurai's open door. An irritable man, he speaks English with a twang and rebukes my tactlessness with his own.

'Well, I guess now that he's here I can spare five minutes,' he says to Simon loudly.

Sakurai glances at my letter before pushing it back at me. 'I'm glad people like you and Simon exist,' he says glibly, 'otherwise it would be impossible for us to tell our story. But why would Taiji people talk to you after all the trouble that Sea Shepherd has made for us?'

'That's why we're here,' Simon says. 'We were wondering if Sam could speak to the mayor, and perhaps he could recommend some whalers for Sam to speak with?'

'I can't do that! It would make my life difficult!'

'Okay,' reasons Simon, 'what about if we just go to the mayor's office ourselves—'

'What, so that I get a phone call from the mayor immediately after, asking what I'm doing bringing troublemakers into town? You guys just don't understand: you come from a country where you are free to speak your mind. *We* are *not*: we have pressure on us. If I help you, I will get into trouble. It isn't even up to the people you want to talk to whether they can talk to you – it's up to the politicians above them. You've got to understand that this is a very sensitive issue!'

Clearly.

'It took Simon two years to build trust in this community,' Sakurai continues, 'so what makes you think you can do it in a week? Taiji people are good people: they are just trying to make a living. They don't know about the whaling controversy in the out-side world – most of them don't even have the internet! The *radical extremists* come to our town and intimidate us; for the Taiji people you look like one of them – and you have spent time with them! How will they know you are not a radical extremist also?'

He has me there, but I persist nonetheless. I tell Sakurai I have come to Taiji not to *tell* the locals how to live their lives but to *ask* them how they live their lives; I say I understand I am unlikely to get anyone to speak to me, because of the climate of mistrust that exists between the whalers and anti-whalers, but that it would do little to facilitate Australian understanding of the Japanese position if they do not.

Sakurai theatrically exhales. 'I'll think about it. And that letter really should be sent to the mayor in the post – *not* delivered per-sonally.'

'Don't worry about Hayato,' Simon says as he beeps his Beamer unlocked. 'He's the meat in a whale sandwich.'

*

With Sakurai and the mayor not responding to my letters, I have plenty of time to read up on the nineteenth-century whale wars. By 1820 the Pacific had become the focus of commercial whaling. The New Zealand and Peru grounds were opened prior to the British–American War of 1812; afterwards, Western whalers moved on to Hawaii in 1819. The next year Captain Frederick Coffin of the British whaling ship *Syren* started working the Japan ground – not so much off Japan as on the way there – finding them rich in right, sperm and gray whales.

The British – and in their wake the American, French, Dutch, Danish, Russians, Norwegians and Australians – started plundering whales, severing their migration routes up and down the Pacific, but they were restricted by an inability to access Japanese ports to take on supplies. Japan was still closed for business, with foreign arrivals banned from entering its harbours on pain of death.

There were attempts to force the issue: in 1837 the American merchant ship *Morrison* naively hoped to conduct trade onshore after returning a group of local shipwrecked sailors; it was chased out of Edo Bay (now Tokyo Bay). An 1846 US trade envoy under the command of Commodore James Biddle proved similarly fruitless, the increasing number of black ships merely hardening the shogunate's mistrust of foreign investment – which already rivalled that of Barnaby Joyce – with coastal batteries built and Taiji's net whalers even deployed as sources of intelligence.

For the whaling barons of Massachusetts, the Texan oil tycoons of their day, this was unacceptable. While it is incorrect to assert that whaling alone forced the opening of Japan – desire to access markets in China and Japan was the principal factor – when in 1853 the US Navy's Commodore Matthew Perry led a squadron of four warships with sixty-one guns and 967 men into Edo Bay in pursuit of a trade treaty, he did so under pressure from his nation's whaling industry. As the secretary of the navy John P. Kennedy wrote two weeks after Perry left for Japan: 'The extension of the domain of the United States to the shores of the Pacific ... and the increased activity of our whaling ships in the vicinity of the northern coasts of Japan, are now pressing upon the consideration of this Government the absolute necessity of reviewing our relations to those eastern communities which lie contiguous to the path of our trade.'

Overpowered by this famous show of 'gunboat diplomacy', Japan's arm was twisted until eventually it begged for mercy.

Whaling activity in the Japan ground increased, but by then the damage had been done. Between 1839 and 1909, perhaps 37,000 right whales alone were killed by Western whalers in the North Pacific. Eighty per cent of the catch is thought to have occurred in the decade 1840–50. Several thousand more sperm and gray whales were also taken.

Australia, too, is not absolved of blame: on a windy summer morning I stand on a Hokkaido headland and peer out to the reef where the Hobart-based *Eamont* was wrecked while pursuing whales in 1850; nineteen years earlier the crew of the Sydney whale ship *Lady Rowena* had terrorised this coast on- and offshore, burning villages and taking a local hostage before releasing him with an ultimatum for the emperor to open Japan to trade. It is the first recorded meeting of Japanese and Australians.

Simon tells me Taiji's town records indicate that the whale population showed decline by the 1840s: by the time of the disaster in 1878, many young men had emigrated to the Californian goldfields, to the plantations of Hawaii or to Broome, where they worked as pearl divers. Of the 919 pearl divers buried in Broome's Japanese

Cemetery, many came from Taiji. The two towns have been twinned since 1981, though the partnership was suspended by Broome for three months in 2009, following the release of *The Cove*.

The collapse of the Japan ground by Western whalers is widely thought to have instigated the risk taken by the 111 men who drowned, because the scarcity of prey made them break a taboo they once never would have compromised. A new era of industrial fishing began, and with it Japan's Antarctic whaling venture. Steam ships replaced wooden boats and net whaling was abandoned for Svend Foyn's grenade-tipped harpoon – although in a precursor of things to come for everything from arms to automobiles, the technique was copied then improved, with two power heads added to the Norwegian's original design of three.

And as petroleum usurped whale oil, Japan found itself at the forefront of the industry. For Armstrong Atlantic State University's Meagan Chandler this is significant, because the very reason Japan kept whaling served to reinforce the notions of its backwardness that had predominated long before one of Perry's officers dubbed them a 'singular and half barbarous people'. 'While the United States became less economically reliant on commercial whaling,' Chandler writes, 'the Japanese consumption of whale meat and other by-products meant that Japanese industrial whaling was able to expand in the years when whaling was waning in the West. Thus, while the Western economies were no longer in need of whales, the Japanese economy and its people still supported whales as a natural resource; the West no longer understood the necessity and forced its "advancement" on the Japanese.'

There is a bitter irony here: the very nations who overexploited whale stocks are now lecturing the one that had developed a sustainable whale fishery on notions of progress.

Forced to open by the West in the nineteenth century, smashed into submission by the West in the twentieth and increasingly seen by the West as a pivot to checking China's rise in the twenty-first, could it be that whaling is a line in the sand for Japan: a symbol of postwar sovereignty that, once reclaimed, will not easily be surrendered?

*

I set myself a deadline of a week in Taiji to find a whaler who will talk to me. Maybe it's all in my mind, but everyone I pass in the street seems to regard me as a radical extremist, casting their eyes away or clutching their handbags a little closer as I approach.

I feel uncomfortable taking notes in public and find myself retreating to the town's many hilltop tsunami shelters to jot down my thoughts; one afternoon I go for a swim at *the* Cove, and after a few minutes notice a man watching from a nearby bridge. I wave; he takes a photo of me.

But after three lonely days, a breakthrough. Before returning to his home in Wakayama City, Simon had introduced me to Kita Yoji, a retired public servant in his late seventies whose grandfather was a harpooner and one of just eight whalers to survive the disaster of 1878. I asked Kita if he knew of any Antarctic whale hunters; he said his neighbour had been south four times and might be prepared to talk. When Kita calls me days later to confirm the meeting, he corrects himself: his neighbour hasn't been to Antarctica four times. He's been *forty* times.

Tameo Ryono is sitting up attentively at a table in Kita's living room when I arrive for our interview, dabbing his sweaty forehead with a folded white handkerchief. At seventy-six, he has ears reminiscent of Roald Dahl's BFG, horsey teeth and the sun-blotched skin of a gone-troppo cane farmer. I like him immediately when he asks me why I would want to interview him, an ordinary old man nearing the end of his life.

I want to interview him because his career bookends the peak and fall of commercial whaling. When in 1956 the nineteen-year-old Ryono joined the fleet of Maruha Nichiro Seafoods Pty Ltd – after first receiving permission from his dad to do so – the company competed against domestic and international wholesalers and had the run of the entire Southern Ocean; on his last voyage south, in 1994, Ryono was the navigator on a catcher boat conducting research whaling for the ICR in its restricted sample area. By then Japan was the sole Southern Ocean whaler, but it had company of a different kind: Greenpeace activists – 'a distraction from my job' – began appearing from 1989.

The early years, Ryono tells me, were tough. There was the time in the Ross Sea when his catcher boat was trapped in pack ice for two days as autumn came early to the Antarctic; back then, navigation was still done with a sextant and the only free time was spent gambling, trying to keep warm or, if the whalers were lucky, watching the green bands of the Aurora Australis pulse and writhe above. The presence of penguins, Ryono tells me, always made him feel safe.

'Those days in Antarctica were a kind of game,' he says, with Kita's son Yasunori interpreting. 'Many nations came to Antarctica and caught whales.'

In 1960 – two years before Japanese whaling peaked – 340 Taiji people were employed in its Antarctic fleet. 'It was a kind of dream,' Ryono says, 'for Taiji boys to go to the Antarctic sea.'

Two years later he was promoted to the role of navigator on a catcher boat, a position he would keep until retirement. He tells me he loved his job but other nations didn't share his view. He says he's disappointed and saddened by what he sees as Australia's current hypocritical stance on whaling – 'They were once hunting whales also' – and that he hopes Taiji boys continue to man Southern Ocean whalers, 'so the skills aren't lost and because we don't know how many whales are in Antarctica'.

I'm told that while no Taiji whalers went to Antarctica when I did, two local men manned the *Nisshin Maru* two summers ago. Frustratingly, they are currently whaling off Hokkaido.

What does Ryono think of Sea Shepherd?

At this question, he looks genuinely baffled. 'He says they are disjointed,' says Yasunori, who adds that Ryono has pride in his career and respects whales and all living creatures. 'Greenpeace was much more mild than Sea Shepherd, so if [Ryono's fleet] just keep straight they avoid [the activists].'

'What about you, Yasu? What do you think of them?'

'I think they are an eyesore,' my interpreter says. 'And I think they are doing it just for money.'

I know Ryono retired before they started campaigning but I ask him anyway: did he ever see Sea Shepherd?

'Only here,' quips Yasunori, before he's even interpreted my question.

*

Simon's Taiji connections afford me an 'informal chat' with Lieutenant Masaru Zukeran of the Wakayama Prefectural Police. Zukeran is off-duty and, although (at a guess) under forty, is dressed like a Tea Party enthusiast in his matching Nike polo shirt, cargo shorts and Navy SEAL baseball cap; he emphasises that he's meeting me in his capacity as an acquaintance of Simon's, not as the officer responsible for policing Taiji during the dolphin-hunting season, between September and April.

I'm performing a careful kabuki here: talking about Simon's efforts at trust-building while covertly trying to glean as much as I can about the way Sea Shepherd behaves in Taiji. While this book isn't about Taiji's dolphin hunters, such is the Japanese fusion of all forms of its whaling – one narrative, many theatres – and given that the same *gaijins* combat Taiji's hunters as the ICR's, it's fair to say the locals' view of Sea Shepherd is an accurate distillation of Japan's view of the organisation at large.

I ask Zukeran how he feels when dolphin-hunting season starts. 'It is much stressful work for me,' he says, 'because of the *dees-GUSTING* behaviour of some people with Sea Shepherd – and because the nationalists come from Osaka to try to stop Sea Shepherd. So I am trying to protect both sides!'

The nationalists he refers to are right-wing groups, apparently associated with the Yakuza. I ask Zukeran what the nationalists do to Sea Shepherd but he won't tell me; a few times now he's warned me that my questions are getting too investigative. I'm finding, though, that if I let him talk, he will.

Zukeran changes the subject and compares Sea Shepherd's approach with that of Edith Hanson, an American former TV personality and long-term Wakayama resident who has led several Amnesty International campaigns against capital punishment in Japan.

'The Japanese people do not always agree with her views,' explains Zukeran, 'but she is very polite and has the respect of the Japanese people. I think Sea Shepherd does not understand our culture. Their [Sea Shepherd's] view [that dolphins are sacred] is understandable,' he continues; 'this is a democratic nation. But the disruptive tactics and attacks on Taiji people are *dees*-GUSTING!'

What kind of disruptive tactics?

'I think this discussion is becoming very formal,' Zukeran warns, standing to take his leave. 'If you would like to know the exact cases of Sea Shepherd people breaking Japanese law, you should come to [nearby] Shingu police station and request a formal interview.'

I apologise and urge Zukeran to sit down. Then I stay silent. Two border collies lie outstretched like bear rugs on the gravel beside us; a nearby pot of azaleas has wilted in the midday sun. Finally, he can no longer resist elaborating.

'Some Sea Shepherd people are polite. They come to me and explain themselves. But some are *dees*-GUSTING: just shouting at local Taiji people and pushing and hitting them!'

He may not know it, but Masaru Zukeran is talking about direct action, of course. And for the first time it makes me think: what must the Sea Shepherd crew have looked like to the whalers down there, an urban camouflaged armada crewed by foreigners dressed in balaclavas and black hoodies? Just more *kurofune*, I suspect. More black ships engaging in gunboat diplomacy.

HARPOONED

Ayukawa was put on the map when it was wiped off it. A little-known hamlet of rusting hulks and geriatrics, its location on the southeastern tip of Honshu's Oshika Peninsula gave it the grim honour of being the closest community to the epicentre of the March 2011 Great East Japan Earthquake, the first landfall of the tsunami that followed and, for a time, the focus of world attention.

Eyewitness footage suggests a *Godzilla* movie scene: splintered houses floating in a ten-metre-deep grey soup, boats caught in the adjacent forest like flies in a spider's web, cars flipped on their backs like stranded beetles. More than a thousand bodies washed up in the steep coves of the Oshika Peninsula in the days following the tsunami. In Ayukawa, three out of every four houses were destroyed; seventy-eight of its 1400 residents were confirmed dead, while thirty-six remain unaccounted for.

I arrive long after the camera crews have departed and the town's survivors have relocated to temporary housing on a nearby hillside. What was once a town, though, is now a scene of devastation. At the port, the only building left standing is a bunker-like public toilet, while beside it a half-collapsed three-storey car park has a smashed boom gate and a twisted car still trapped on the ground floor. Assorted rubble – bricks, shoes, a pencil case – litters the ground.

But amid the debris it isn't hard to find signs of what was once this community's economic mainstay and what it hopes will help revive it. At the entrance to the town a mounted harpoon – prophetically, I'm later told – survived the tsunami, while on every manhole cover a cartoon humpback smiles at me from beneath a film of grime, goofily baring its baleen. A stylised sailor's cap hangs off the whale's head; a telescope is pressed to one eye.

Ayukawa, like the towns of Taiji, Wadaura and Abashiri, is engaged in what is known as 'small-type coastal whaling'. This activity – as well as the dolphin drives of Taiji and porpoise hand-harpoon hunts of Iwate Prefecture – is unregulated by the IWC because it has never decided whether the small cetaceans taken – Baird's beaked whales, short-finned pilot whales, Risso's dolphins and false killer whales – fall within its quotas mandate. Annual quotas are instead set by the Japanese government and hunts are conducted in domestic waters by a handful of companies.

Around 15,000 small cetaceans are killed in Japan every year, the vast majority Dall's porpoises. Japan has consistently lobbied the IWC – to no avail – for the four main whaling centres to also be allowed to kill minke whales – the second-smallest of the thirteen baleen whale species the IWC does regulate – under a cultural quota similar in nature to that allocated to aboriginal peoples in parts of North America, Russia, the Arctic and the Caribbean. The problem with this idea, according to Greenpeace Japan, is that there are two distinct stocks of minke whale found off Japan – one more abundant than the other – and it's impossible for whalers to know to which stock a minke belongs until they've killed it.

The up-on-blocks Antarctic harpooner *Toshimaru 16* also testifies to Ayukawa's earlier link with the Southern Ocean. Strangely enough, it was the only boat here the tsunami didn't budge.

*

Australians like to think of themselves as universally popular, readily and easily embraced abroad. The Frenchman is arrogant and the American ignorant, but the Aussie is a lovable larrikin who can blend in anywhere. The world's class clowns, we accept that we're sometimes dickheads (I've been to Bali too), but we're funny, kind-hearted and ultimately harmless – right?

I've come to Ayukawa to see the resumption of offshore whaling since the tsunami. As part of JARPN II, a quota of sixty minke whales is to be filled over three weeks, caught in Japanese waters, investigated and processed for consumption in a newly built shed on the edge of Ayukawa. I want to learn about the role of whaling in rebuilding Ayukawa, but I am continually hampered by my nationality.

'You are green peas?' my guesthouse owner asks when I present my passport at check-in. Her question, quaint in its mispronunciation, nonetheless carries an air of menace.

'Journalist,' I mumble, 'tsunami rebuilding.' She looks unconvinced.

My attempts to interview the manager of Ayukawa Hogei – the whaling company contracted to carry out the hunt – fail when he learns of my provenance. I'm told to stop killing kangaroos by one stooped woman at a service station when my interpreter, Lily, says I'm Australian. It is only when I ask Lily to refrain from mentioning my nationality that I am able to make any progress: the sushi chef who makes us lunch responds to my interest in whaling not with suspicion but by removing a manila folder from beneath the bar and showing me photos he took the week before of the first minke to be killed since the tsunami – and which, he tells me, I've just eaten.

It is the whalers who prove most elusive. I spend four days alone in Ayukawa spying on what I come to learn is a sleek operation. Upon catching a whale, the hunting boat must call base, because fifteen minutes before the vessel docks at the research station's jetty on the edge of town, a crane and a truck come to await its arrival. When the boat arrives, the minke is quickly hoisted into the waiting truck by the crane, driven the hundred metres to the research station and into a waiting garage, the doors of which are promptly slammed shut.

I think I'm growing paranoid the day I see a gumboot-clad whaling official pull out his mobile phone and make a call when I walk past the station in full view. But I feel vindicated when, later that afternoon, I take a long-range photo of the station and a whaling official there pulls a digital camera from his pocket, takes aim and shoots me back.

*

'Japan's tsunami seems to have succeeded,' trumpeted the *New York Times*, 'where years of boycotts, protests and high-seas chases by Western environmentalists had failed.'

'Whaling is finished,' explained Ayukawa's Shinobu Ankai to the *Times*' man in Tokyo, Martin Fackler, two weeks after the disaster had destroyed the town's whaling slaughterhouse, sunk its dock and scattered its fleet kilometres down the coast. 'There was Sea Shepherd,' Ankai lamented, 'and now this.'

But the truth is Ayukawa died long before both of them; the tsunami wasn't so much the final nail in the town's coffin as a passing pye-dog pissing on its grave.

When in 1906 the whaling company Toyo Hogei established a land station on this isolated spit of land, first settled by ten samurai seeking refuge from the civil wars of the sixteenth century, the fishing community of Ayukawa barely numbered 500. In the early twentieth century the Japanese government hired Norwegian expertise to develop a modern whaling industry; the same exposure that ensured Ayukawa's destruction in 2011 made it a perfect launchpad for whaling, the town quickly finding a niche as a producer of rice-paddy fertiliser made from crushed whalebones and entrails.

In 1925 the town's own coastal whaling company – Ayukawa Hogei – was established, and by the 1960s a community of 15,000 was enjoying the perks of a thriving industry. Ayukawa's old-timers (and they are all old-timers now) enjoyed a cinema, hotels, inns, even a brothel.

Down south, too, business was booming: at its height, in the summer of 1961–62, seven Japanese whaling fleets operated in the Antarctic, each with its own factory ship – as well as a total of eighty-six catcher boats, fourteen refrigerator ships, seven tankers and thirty-six freighters. That summer, 10,200 Japanese men – perhaps 1000 from Ayukawa – worked in the endless daylight at the bottom of the world. Here was a veritable armada, a different kind of navy.

But in 1976, when whaling quotas were reduced, a contracting industry forced the three Japanese companies licensed by Tokyo to work in Antarctica – Nihon Susian (Nissui), Taiyo and Kyokuyo – along with three coastal whalers to pool their resources and create Nihon Kyodo Hogei. The precursor of Kyodo Senpaku, it had government backing and, like its successor, wasn't so much a company as a commercial confederation of vessels and crews.

Instead of consolidation came contraction. When Nihon Kyodo Hogei first sailed south that summer, it did so with 1500 sailors, twenty catcher boats and three factory ships. From 1977 until the end of commercial whaling, by which time only minkes were allowed to be caught in the Antarctic, it had just one.

By 1979 Ayukawa's prostitutes still had a market, but their clients were already on the wrong side of history. That year Ayukawa's population had fallen to 9000, with diminishing stocks, tightened quotas and a zeitgeist of environmentalist awakening beginning to bite.

The IWC by this time was dominated by non-whaling countries, and with each annual meeting, the numbers were building to bring a moratorium into effect.

For communities like Ayukawa, it was a daunting prospect. Men here knew only one trade. In 1969 the Japanese whaling industry had employed 15,000 people; by 1979 it employed 1300. Most of those were involved in Antarctic whaling, with just eight vessels still working the Japan ground for a handful of struggling companies. One of them, Ayukawa's Nihon Hogei, had been operating at a loss for three years running, its quota now 600, one-fifth down from its allowable catch fifteen years earlier.

'If there's going to be a total ban next year,' its assistant manager Toshihiko Abe told the *Baltimore Sun* that November, 'then I think my family – all of us – will commit suicide.'

*

'And then, of course, the moratorium came in,' the priest of Kannon-ji temple tells me, 'and the few young workers remaining in Ayukawa left. This town became an aging town; more and more aging appeared.'

The priest is no spring chicken himself – seventy, at a guess – but he speaks of the aging population as if it were a plague of locusts that blew in overnight. And he's right to do so. Bereft of a future,

Ayukawa was frozen in time, longing for its halcyon days when the *ugga-ugga-ugga* of catcher boats arriving late at night would prompt people to shut their windows; now it's so rare that they don their dressing gowns and head down to the port to see what the boys have caught.

Kannon-ji sits among granite headstones and a garden of juvenile maples and cherries. Due to its position halfway up a small hill, the tsunami reached its third step but no further; the only damage the Buddhist temple sustained was a warped *shoji* sliding door, which now opens by itself on hot summer days.

The priest agrees to talk to me about Ayukawa's history – providing I come inside and pray. He looks unimpressed as I hop about, struggling with my boots for a moment, but his initial haughtiness melts into a wry smile when I finally prise them off to reveal a pair of odd socks.

The priest is chubby-cheeked, Michael Klim–bald and nearly as round as he is tall, with a loud Hawaiian shirt hanging loosely over his ample paunch. Kannon-ji, he tells me, is 380 years old and has long been a place of refuge for pilgrims on their way to and from the sacred island of Kinkazan, a short boat trip from Ayukawa.

It's a beautiful, peaceful place: floored with tatami mats, the temple smells of cedar beams and three centuries' worth of incense that has stained the ceiling above nicotine-brown. One wall is decorated with intricate cloisonné work; above it, a dragon takes flight.

The priest lost fourteen of his flock in the tsunami, he tells me blankly. He says there have been several tsunamis recorded here – perhaps twenty in the last 400 years – but as far as he knows, this was the first one that killed anyone.

Ayukawa's population currently stands at a few hundred; most locals, the priest says, chose to move to bigger towns following the tsunami. In 1986 the population plummeted too, from 4000 to half that. After the moratorium, whaling here was reduced to boutique status, the town pitching its history as a tourist attraction.

Whale Land, a kind of whaling theme park, opened in 1990. At its height it had hanging whale skeletons, whaling tools and even a 3D cinema. Lily, in her late thirties, tells me she remembers coming here on a school excursion from her home city of Sendai. They sold good ice-cream, she says.

The priest unfolds two plastic camping chairs – incongruous in the ancient surrounds – lights a stick of incense and beats his gong. I pray for those killed in Ayukawa when the wave rolled in, and those who were swept away and are likely never to be found; I pray for the whales dragged ashore here over the years, and for the whalers who hunted them offshore and further south. Finally, I pray for assistant manager Toshihiko Abe, a man who saw himself in 1979 as a victim of history, unable to adapt to a way of life the world no longer condoned. His worst fears wouldn't come true for another seven years, but what became of him I don't know. No one named Toshihiko-san, the priest tells me, has lived here in a very long time.

*

My mistaken belief that Ayukawa's residents would be prepared to judge me on what I have to say and not on my nation's anti-whaling reputation is partly a result of past experience: my friends in Iceland, Greenland and the Faroe Islands didn't let Australian condemnation of whaling (and sealing) prevent them from warmly receiving me into their homes.

But none of those countries has borne the brunt of international opposition to whaling quite like Japan. At the 1978 IWC meeting in London – the year before Abe threatened to take his own life – it was the Japanese delegation, not the Icelanders, Norwegians or Danes (representing Greenland), whom activists called 'murderers' and 'barbarians' before splashing them with red paint.

'Why did anti-whaling mobs splash dye only on the Japanese delegation?' Yuuzou Yamato, one of its members, later asked a Japanese journalist rhetorically. 'When they left the room, they splashed dye on the Japanese delegation who represented only one coloured whaling nation, without glancing at the seats of white whaling nations such as the USSR, Norway, Iceland, Spain. Obviously this was an expression of racism. It was for the same reason that the USA used atomic bombs only on Japan and had no intention of using them on white enemies in Europe.'

Throughout that decade, the United States had baffled the Japanese government by supporting the hunting of critically endangered bowhead whales by a handful of aboriginal communities to 'preserve the longstanding social customs of Alaska natives', while still opposing Japanese whaling.

And increasingly, it is Australia that is perceived to be at the vanguard of the attack. Bipartisan and overwhelming public support for a legal challenge to Japan's claims of scientific whaling under the ICRW and the fact that JARPA II is conducted in Australia's supposed sphere of influence are both explanations for Australia's near-exclusive focus on Japan's whaling industry.

I eventually get what I want in Ayukawa – a chat with a JARPN II insider – but only after conducting an experiment in national stereotyping that is inspired by my scruffy blond beard, which I notice one morning in the bathroom mirror. On my last afternoon before joining a team of tsunami clean-up volunteers, I react to the telltale signs of an incoming whaling boat – the truck and crane leaving the whaling station to meet it – not by watching the proceedings unfold from afar but by casually walking down to the jetty to meet it.

'What is your country?' a lanky man in jeans and a spray jacket standing beside the crane immediately asks in English. 'Norway,' I lie. 'I've come from Oslo to help with the tsunami clean-up, but I heard you guys are catching some whales so I wanted to see.'

What follows is a bizarre but enlightening five-minute conversation conducted in my best Scandinavian English accent. It turns out Shin is a Fisheries Agency employee in town to oversee the scientific whaling program. We talk whaling ('You Japanese catch minkes? Same as us!'), science (all he'll say about the hotly disputed worth of lethal research is that it's 'like when you chop down a tree and count the rings inside to determine the age – we conduct similar investigations') and even my presumed homeland ('You must visit in summer,' I urge him; 'the sun never sets!'). Presented with such an opportunity, I also can't resist gleaning Shin's views on Australians.

I say that I have read about 'troublemakers' clashing with Japanese whalers in the Southern Ocean and ask Shin whether this is also a problem in Japanese waters.

'Sometimes, but not so much,' he says.

'Because Antarctic whaling takes place close to Australia?'

'Exactly.'

My fun ends when, with the approaching whaling boat's silhouette in view, two detectives from the nearby city of Ishinomaki introduce themselves; my Norwegian disguise fails when they demand to see my identification.

I'm deliberately not carrying ID and curse myself for this decision; the police succeed in removing me from the scene as they accompany me to my guesthouse to see some. There I am accused of being a 'Sea Shepherd operative' and my (non-Norwegian) passport details are dictated to someone over the phone (presumably to check for previous piracy convictions). My backpack is searched and I'm made to show the detectives the photos on my SLR camera to prove that I haven't been taking any of the whaling station. (I have, but luckily they are hidden among shots of tsunami damage.)

I feel guilty using my tsunami volunteering registration form as a cover, but it proves my saviour. I claim that I am solely in Ayukawa to volunteer and that I'd lied about my nationality because I suspected Australians would not be popular in Japan's whaling heartland.

The two detectives inspect the form closely, talk in Japanese for a minute, then hand it back, along with my passport, backpack and camera. 'Thank you for volunteering,' one says as he and his colleague prepare to leave. 'It is unusual for Australians to help us.'

BIGGER FISH

STAMP COLLECTING

Semantics. That's what this legal dispute comes down to. Australia's case against Japan isn't about sustainability or refuelling too far south; it isn't about animal rights or sovereignty. It's a dispute over the interpretation of the scientific research exemption, found in Article VIII of the ICRW.

Australia contends that Japan has breached this exemption because its whaling program does not constitute scientific research. Japan seeks to convince the court that the 3633 Antarctic minke whales and eighteen fin whales it has killed under JARPA II do not breach Article VIII. What's on trial isn't so much Japan's Antarctic whaling program as the meaning of science.

The International Court of Justice sits in the Peace Palace, a handsome rose-brick Neo-Renaissance affair perched above 'Keep off the Grass' grass and a limp UN flag asleep at its post. With its towers and arches it looks like a palace, but it's barely a hundred years old, purpose-built in 1913 as the seat of arbitration for the Hague Conventions, which, along with the Geneva Conventions, set out the laws of modern warfare. Since 1946 the Peace Palace has been the United Nations' chief seat of arbitration for disputes between states.

Inside, halls floored with swirling marble mosaics are flanked by busts of famous pacifists: Gandhi, Mandela and Nehru; the

179

Scottish-American philanthropist Andrew Carnegie, the British liberal parliamentarian Randal Cremer and the Dutch jurist Bernard Loder. The chamber itself is surprisingly cramped; with its stained-glass windows, carved-wood walls and low-slung chandeliers, it reminds me of a church in a well-to-do French provincial town – except for the awful carpet, which looks like a rainbow Paddle Pop left on the dashboard five minutes too long (a present from Iran, I'm told).

Overseeing proceedings is Slovakia's Peter Tomka, the shiny-domed judge currently sitting in the ICJ president's chair; his fourteen fellow judges, all black smocks and white jabot bibs, have been dispatched from Mexico, Japan, France, New Zealand, Morocco, Russia, Brazil, Somalia, the United Kingdom, China, the United States, Italy, Uganda and India. Australia has appointed the ANU law school's Professor Hilary Charlesworth as an ad hoc judge for this case. Thoughtful, engaged and church-fête polite, she will prove a stark contrast to some of her colleagues. Certain judges remain mute throughout, while others are prone to bouts of narcolepsy or playing on their tablets, much to the mirth of the press corps safely ensconced in our glasshouse next door, where we watch the proceedings unfold on closed-circuit television.

This is the fourth time Australia has appeared at the ICJ but the first time anyone's noticed since Gough Whitlam took on the France of Valéry Giscard d'Estaing for testing nukes on Moruroa in 1974; the current attorney-general, Mark Dreyfus, will hope to have more success than Lionel Murphy, the losing agent in that case and the last Australian attorney-general to address the ICJ.

Even if the court rules Japan is in breach of Article VIII, it is unclear whether that will put an end to Antarctic whaling. Japan could simply leave the IWC and thus be absolved of its obligations under the ICRW. Maybe it'll brush off the court's decision like Israel did when the ICJ advised that its barrier along the West Bank was illegal. The UN Security Council does have the power to enforce the ICJ's decisions, but so far it never has.

No matter: the world's media is depicting this as the final judgment for Antarctic whaling. Space in the pressroom is at a premium, cables criss-crossing the parquet floor and hacks from twenty news organisations rubbing shoulders as they furiously churn out dispatches.

I'm next to Tony Press, an affable, apple-cheeked man on assignment for the *Conversation,* who introduces himself by asking, 'You take one shot or two?' as he walks to the cafeteria. His name sounds familiar, and my email search while he's buying us coffees reminds me why: a friend who teaches at the ANU recommended this Hobart-based Antarctic researcher as a 'street-smart (berg-bright?)' authority on Southern Ocean geopolitics. It quickly becomes apparent that, as the former head of the Australian Antarctic Division and Australia's delegate to the Antarctic Treaty from 1999 to 2008, Tony Press knows more about this issue than the lawyers he's reporting on.

Australia steadily builds its case over the next two days – 'weaving a basket', as Press puts it – that Japan, in the words of Australia's agent, Bill Campbell QC, 'seeks to cloak its ongoing commercial whaling in the lab-coat of science'.

The court is told how the details of JARPA and its successor, JARPA II – the crews, the ships, the waters, the timing, the species, the fact Japan hadn't previously shown an inclination for scientific whaling of this magnitude – suggest a continuation of Japan's commercial whaling industry 'retro-fitted' under the artifice of Article VIII. Some poor gofer in Canberra's even trawled through the Diet's records to find supporting evidence: 'After the moratorium commences, the path to ensure the continuation of whaling would be, for Southern Ocean whaling, to position it as a research whaling activity which has a scientific nature ... [and] the continuation of whaling ought to be planned for.' Australia claims that this quote from the head of the Fisheries Agency – two years after the moratorium was adopted and two years before it came into force – proves JARPA was not intended to be a permanent successor to Japan's Antarctic whaling industry so much as a quick fix before the moratorium could be overturned.

'The problem for Japan today, some thirty years later,' says Australia's solicitor-general, Justin Gleeson SC, 'is twofold: on the one hand, it has not achieved its goal of persuading other states to lift the moratorium; on the other hand, with limited exceptions, everything Japan hears from other contracting governments, and from the scientific community, is that its chosen technique is flawed both legally and by the measures of science.'

Australia calls two such members of the scientific community as expert witnesses. First up is Professor Marc Mangel, a mathematical biologist and fisheries management expert from the University of California, Santa Cruz. He's been asked to explain the essential characteristics of a program undertaken for purposes of scientific research, and to say if Japan's program contains them. Mangel looks nervous – a scientist more comfortable in the field, perhaps, than in the rarefied world of international law – and keeps adjusting the lapels on his pinstripe suit while he awaits instruction at the rostrum.

He's examined by Philippe Sands QC, who's debonair and very wry: 'Eighteen years of the JARPA program has offered nothing more than the information that Antarctic minke whales eat a great deal of krill … I knew that in 1972 when my biology teacher, Robin Jenks, told me that is what whales ate.'

Over the next half-hour, Sands helps Mangel tell the court that Japan's Antarctic whaling programs cannot be considered science because they do not meet the four criteria of scientific endeavour: a defined and achievable set of objectives, appropriate methods to achieve those objectives, strenuous peer review and a technique that does not adversely affect the subject being studied – killing a whale, Mangel argues, eliminates future opportunities to study the specimen.

Mangel is cross-examined by Vaughan Lowe QC, an avuncular Englishman who emits a calm air of reassurance. His approach of coaxing contradictions out of the professor is not as damaging as two questions that come from America's Judge Joan Donoghue, a biologist in another life.

Judge Donoghue first asks her compatriot's view on Australia's claim that 'for an activity to be genuinely motivated by an intent to conduct scientific research, it must not be for any other purpose or purposes': but isn't that the case with scientists employed by pharmaceutical companies ultimately driven by profits?

Mangel gives a short answer and a long answer, both of which add up to: of course, motivations can be mixed.

Judge Donoghue then neatly summarises Mangel's evidence that JARPA II's data collection isn't science because it's not testing a particular hypothesis. She raises the human genome project as an example of data collection – identifying all the genes in human DNA – with no discernible hypothesis, but which nevertheless appears to be 'science'.

Mangel seems snookered by this one. He concedes that the human genome project is collecting lots of data, and even applies the phrase Japan has used to define JARPA II – 'exploratory data analysis'. But as for a hypothesis, he thinks there are a few, like the location of genes that lead to a higher proclivity to cancer, for example. Mangel says he can get further details, should the court require; his lapel fidgeting has resumed.

Judge Kenneth Keith, a silver-haired Kiwi, wonders aloud whether 'that young man who got on the *Beagle*' was just beachcombing at first and slowly developed a hypothesis over time. Oh, and as an aside, he says, did we all know Charles Darwin and Abraham Lincoln were born on the same day?

*

After lunch Australia calls Dr Nick Gales, the chief scientist of the Australian Antarctic program. As a former colleague, Tony Press knows this pale, pensive man well and watches his responses to Justin Gleeson's examination with the mix of pride and apprehension of a boundary-riding parent at Saturday-morning sport.

Like Mangel, Gales tells the court that JARPA II isn't real science. But then the examination takes a turn from legality to morality. A photo of a harpooned whale is shown on screen, blood pouring into the Southern Ocean. I'd been wondering when this would happen.

Gleeson has Gales explain Japan's lethal method of harpoon grenade, taking the opportunity to display a second, more gruesome close-up: a mash of blood, blubber and the ruthless efficiency of industrial weaponry. Gales narrates the on-screen trauma: 'You can see, coming out from behind the minke whale's blowhole, the harpoon head, and it will be presumably bent as the rope comes through from the other side, so the whale is being pulled to the bow of the ship. About two-thirds of the whales are not killed instantly, so they are then shot from the bow of the vessel, or killed otherwise.'

Now for a lesson in how *real* scientific research on whales is done. Gales explains the Australian method of biopsy sampling, in which a projectile fired from a crossbow bounces off the target, collecting a plug 'the size of a little fingernail' from which DNA and other tissues can be extracted.

This is where Gleeson has been leading: 'Does the biopsy collection enable you to obtain the same information as you can by the harpoon grenade death of a whale?'

Gales gives him the answer he seeks: 'It certainly does. For genetics you only require a very tiny piece of tissue; additional tissue adds no advantage.'

Australia has tried its best to argue that unnecessarily killing your specimen is, above all, bad science, but Vaughan Lowe uses his cross-examination of Gales to fire the first courtroom shot in this culture war, nudging Gales to admit that a 'philosophical view of whether or not a whale should be killed should be kept to the business of the Commission', not its Scientific Committee. Even so, Australia soon steers its argument back to what it sees as decidedly dodgy methodology.

Because the thing is, Cambridge University's James Crawford explains as he sums up Australia's argument, science isn't stamp collecting. 'JARPA II is an activity which collects data on whales in the Southern Ocean without end or object.' Team Australia has just reduced Japan's research whalers to a bunch of philatelists.

US

Malcolm Fraser banned whaling because his little girl asked him to. In 1977, the prime minister's eleven-year-old daughter, Phoebe, came home from boarding school one Friday, skipped into the Lodge and told her papa she'd seen a program on the ABC about a ghastly whaling station in Albany. She asked him his opinion: didn't he think whaling was cruel and should be stopped? Within two years the station was closed, 'We love you, Phoebe' graffiti was fading from bus stops and Australia was pursuing an aggressive anti-whaling policy on the world stage.

At least, that's what the newspaper archives had told me.

'It's mostly nonsense,' says Fraser in his distinctive clipped baritone, before loudly slurping the morning's second cup of Earl Grey and clinking it back in its saucer. 'Phoebe was concerned about a lot of things, but whether she had asked me about it, I'm not sure. A delegation came to see me [to lobby for an end to Australian whaling], and I mentioned the fact that Phoebe was concerned and the delegation then went and spread it around ... The press, of course, ran with it: the idea of the prime minister's young child influencing policy!'

At eighty-three, Malcolm Fraser is having his teenage rebellion seventy years too late. Not known as a progressive when in office,

Fraser is now something of a well-groomed manic street preacher, spouting diatribes about our descent into moral turpitude from deep within his freshly pressed moleskins and fastidiously polished RM Williams boots. He's disgusted with the course our nation has taken – dog whistling to the electorate, economic growth at the expense of social cohesion, war mongering for political gain – and if you spend more than two minutes in his presence, he'll tell you as much.

Much bigger than I expected, Fraser is tall even by the standards of the Nutri-Grain generation. He looks every bit the Western District patrician as he sinks into his leather armchair, crosses his legs and holds his crockery up by his face as if he's Hamlet with Yorick's skull.

It's drizzling outside, and from the thirty-second floor of a Collins Street skyscraper, the Melbourne CBD is shrouded in mist. I've come to Fraser's city office – dominated by the stop-and-go coloured spines of Hansard records, a big Australian flag and a bigger desk – to discuss what was then a dramatic about-face in environmental policy.

When the twenty-ninth annual meeting of the IWC was held in Canberra in June 1977, it wasn't just diplomats who came to the party. In the late 1970s a worldwide moratorium on commercial whaling had become the cause célèbre of environmentalism, rooted in a need to conserve whale stocks, but also increasingly a question of morality as more was learned about the social, behavioural and intellectual capabilities of the great whales. The myth of the Super-whale was gaining traction.

In Canberra the IWC actually increased the quota for Australia's last whaling operation – the Cheynes Beach Whaling Company of Albany, Western Australia – from 624 sperm whales to 713, but the protests the diplomatic circus attracted raised awareness of an issue that had so far received little coverage in this country. Most Australians didn't even know they still had a whaling industry, and suddenly Greenpeace and the Whale and Dolphin Coalition were telling them that 400 kilometres from Perth, socially active, highly intelligent creatures were being shot via ninety-millimetre cannons with grenade-tipped harpoons that exploded upon impact. And for what? An oil whose price could no longer pay for the upkeep of the vessels that sought it.

In August the issue came to a head when activists clashed with whalers on- and offshore. Fraser wanted to act but was impeded by politics: Western Australia was at the time governed by the conservative premier Charles Court, a man who, the former prime minister tells me, 'didn't have a natural disposition towards environmental issues'. This is a diplomatic understatement: Court made Joh Bjelke-Petersen look like David Attenborough. Court said he had 'contempt' for the activists, while the *West Australian* was depicting the anti-whaling movement as another example of the eastern states meddling in WA affairs.

Back in Canberra, public pressure was mounting. When Fraser entertained Project Jonah, the delegation which would spread the Phoebe rumour, he was presented with over 145,000 signatures calling for an end to Australian whaling – one of seventy-eight petitions presented to parliament on the matter. To proceed in a way that he says 'wouldn't make an enemy of Charles Court', Fraser went to the December 1977 election promising an inquiry into whales and whaling, should he be re-elected. Once back in power, he charged Sydney Frost, a former chief justice in colonial New Guinea, with reporting on the industry.

Frost concluded that whaling was unnecessarily cruel and

offensive to Australian sensibilities; the legislation his findings spawned was the Whale Protection Act of 1980. It replaced the Whaling Act of 1960 and profoundly shifted the status of whales from a resource whose exploitation was encouraged by law to a protected species. Not only was the killing of whales in Australian waters outlawed, attracting fines of up to $100,000, but 'interference' of any kind, including 'harassing, chasing, herding, tagging, marking or branding ... or similar activities', was also banned. At the IWC, too, the prime minister accepted Frost's advice that Australia should push for a global moratorium.

I ask Fraser what happened in those twenty years, and if he thinks the Whale Protection Act reflected a newfound maturity in how Australians perceived their environment or was simply an emotional reaction to a greater awareness of what whaling entailed.

He thinks long and hard; I worry that I've lost him. Then he snaps to attention. 'Probably both. It was a progressive time: if you like, it was the end of the liberal period that began after the Second World War when a lot of good things were done, many worldwide. When I was in office it was still very much a liberal time internationally. Quite unlike today's world, which I think is a very different world.'

I sense our conversation is about to move far beyond whaling, but before it does, I rein Fraser back in and ask him why, if the Whale Protection Act was the result of a more liberal era, Australia since has not merely continued but dramatically increased its whale advocacy.

Australia, I point out, is now considered the leader of the anti-whaling bloc at the IWC. A 2010 poll conducted by UMR Research found that 94 per cent of Australians surveyed were opposed to Southern Ocean whaling and 82 per cent thought their government was doing too little to stop it; subsequent polls have suggested a similar level of support for Sea Shepherd within the Australian community. It was our government that decided to take Japan to court over the legality of JARPA II. Talking tough on whaling has become one of the few bipartisan environmental issues in Australian politics.

Fraser frowns and nods. 'In some ways we've got a strange environmental movement or a green movement in Australia,' he tells me. 'People care more about whales … than they do about refugees or asylum seekers. That's not necessarily a distinction which anyone should be proud of.'

*

Some years ago I joined a press junket to Brazil. On a flight between São Paulo and Cuiabá I was wedged between two travel writers from rival newspapers. Both are highly educated, worldly people; both are gay. Both have reported widely from Africa, a continent where in thirty-eight countries being homosexual can land you in manacles; somewhere over the camo-coloured Brazilian interior, both told me they would never visit Japan because of its Antarctic whaling program.

Why did those men deem a program run by a couple dozen suits in Tokyo worthy of a national boycott, but the draconian punishment meted out to those sharing their sexual orientation in Kenya or Uganda not prevent them from visiting the Maasai Mara and Lake Victoria? Why did a high-school acquaintance of mine take to the internet on 11 March 2011 to call the Japanese tsunami 'karma for killing all those whales'? Why does the mere arrival of migrating whales in our waters warrant news coverage, and why do their occasional strandings prompt communities to drop what they're doing and head to the beach – an inverse grindadráp whereby participants arm themselves with wet tea-towels instead of kitchen knives – to hold vigils and commandeer tractors from local farmers to try pushing them back out to sea?

Sea Shepherd, after all, is not representative of the Australian community. Most Australians are not, like Grug (and just about everyone else on the *Steve*), militant vegans who consider the killing of *any* animal morally indefensible; most Australians do not, like Squid, consider whales superior to humans; and most Australians would not, like Vera, think it fine to head to Yarralumla the next time Japan is commemorating the bombing of Hiroshima to accuse its ambassador of genocide.

Most Australians are not, like Elissa, particularly interested in upholding what they believe to be international law; they are not former whale researchers like Beck or animal rights activists like Gav; they are not, like Paul Watson, megalomaniac misanthropes; and they are not, like Percy, self-appointed whale bodyguards looking for a fight. So what gives?

It's a question I've been thinking about for a year now. It wouldn't need posing if Australia's environmental policy was consistent, but it is not: as of 2014 Australia ranks fifth-last on the Climate Change Performance Index – which assesses what the world's top fifty-eight emitters are doing to curb emissions – clears more native vegetation than any nation in the developed world and digs up coal as fast as China and India can buy it. In Anna Krien's account of the Tasmanian forestry wars, *Into the Woods*, she is repeatedly told by timber workers and industry spokesmen of their chief export market: 'Fuck the Japs.' 'The Sea Shepherd are my heroes,' one tells Krien. 'I'm right behind those guys. But leave us alone – we're sustainable.'

If whaling is no longer a conservation issue but one of 'compassion' towards our fellow 'sentient beings', then Malcolm Fraser raises a fine point: why do we welcome migrants from the Southern Ocean but detain those from the Indian Ocean? Is grey-skinned prey arriving from a hunting ground more worthy of refuge than brown-skinned dissidents fleeing a killing field? Are they acceptable because they stick to the 'humpback highway' rather than clogging up the M4? But then, is this issue even about whales anymore?

According to the WWF, up to 300,000 cetaceans (whales, dolphins and porpoises combined) die annually as result of entanglement in fishing nets, but we don't make a fuss about that. Hundreds more are thought to die from ship strikes. There are also the less tangible impacts of human development: the on-hold James Price Point LNG hub – unpopular in Broome but backed by WA premier Colin Barnett – was to be built smack-bang in the world's biggest humpback calving ground. And whales have far more to fear from our failure to curb climate change – ocean acidification and melting ice being but two killers of krill – than from Japan's harpoons.

The reception I received and the questions I was asked upon my return from Antarctica, just for sharing the same mess as Paul Watson, suggest that the Australian community regards Sea Shepherd with a mixture of admiration for its crewmembers' goal and jealousy at their commitment to pursue it. Sea Shepherd allows Australians a kind of vicarious outlawry that Hunter S. Thompson, writing about the Hells Angels in 1960s America, called 'a fascination, however reluctant, that borders on psychic masturbation'. But Australians cared about this issue before Sea Shepherd entered the fray.

Geography plays a part. Australia's population is concentrated on its east and southwest coasts – the same coasts that humpback and southern right whales visit on their migrations. Seeing whales, then – breaching, feeding, 'mucking about' – is not a foreign experience for many Australians; indeed, it is possible, even probable, that if you live in even the most urban pockets of these coasts you've seen them migrating.

They are thus a part of the outdoor furniture of our bronzed Aussie self-image – and increasingly so, as humpback numbers in our waters are currently growing by around 10 per cent annually, with perhaps 20,000 migrating up the east coast during the winter of 2014 and closer to 30,000 up the west (the latter thought to be the world's biggest population). That it is mainly humpback whales choosing to visit our coasts – a species blessed with charismatic characteristics that make anthropomorphising them easy – probably helps boost Australian views of 'whales' in general. I wonder how we'd view whales if it were only the less acrobatic species, like pilots or bowheads, visiting our waters?

But just as Squid hadn't seen a whale until he was saving them, Sydney author John Newton encountered his first leviathan only midway through writing *A Savage History*, his whale-loving chronicle of whale hunting. It was while reading Newton's book that I found a more compelling answer to the question of why we care so much about whales. It doesn't so much have to do with what we think of whales but what they make us think of ourselves.

Newton writes that Australia was the 'last English-speaking' country in the world to end commercial whaling. He could've told us we weren't the last country to hunt whales in the Southern Hemisphere (we pipped Peru and Chile to the post) or even in the neighbourhood (whales are still hunted off the Indonesian island of Lembata). But those lagging behind don't seem to count, because Britain, New Zealand, the United States and Canada all beat us.

Newton seems embarrassed: Australia is living up to its reputation as a colonial backwater, a culturally cringe-worthy nation of rednecks lagging behind the times. What is it to speak English? To take up the white man's burden, colour the map pink and spread light where once there was darkness? It's to be civilised. And civilised people don't kill whales.

Much is now made of the fact that in the Western societies of Australia, New Zealand, Canada and the United States, a happy transition has been made from whaling to whale watching. It's a powerful metaphor for how we have shifted our interactions with our surroundings in general – from exploiters to adulators. Moreover, it is presented as the rational one: Paul Watson frequently points out that, given their importance to the global tourism industry, whales are now worth more money alive than dead.

The evolution in the way we think about whales in this country presents a powerful symbol of the notion of progress. Whaling played a fundamental role in Australia's very foundation: it wasn't until 1833 – a full forty-five years after white settlement – that wool overtook whale oil as the largest-grossing export of the Australian colonies. If my grandparents' generation rode on the sheep's back, then their grandparents first clung to the whale's fluke.

Whalers, historian James Boyce tells us in *Van Diemen's Land*, were de facto colonists, explorers, ethnographers; they operated in parts of Australia that the Union Jack was yet to reach. They are the very embodiment of the myth that Australia is a nation of pioneers. Fast-forward 200 years, and the descendants of those whalers were correctly judged by the Rudd government to care enough about whales that spending at least $20 million to pursue Japan's Antarctic whaling program in the ICJ was not just uncontroversial, but a politically popular move. I'd wager that in plenty of countries such a decision – expensive, diplomatically risky, of minor conservation importance – would be questioned at least; here it was met with strong public support. For the *Daily Telegraph*, the legal action was 'historic'. This 'heartening' decision, the *Age* opined, 'not merely fulfils a long-standing commitment: it proves the government is prepared to get tough with Japan'. 'We do not believe whaling is required in the modern world,' the then environment minister, Malcolm Turnbull, said in 2007, the year Rudd was elected promising to take the whalers to court.

But then, I've seen this language before, in an email sent to Sid during the campaign and pinned on the *Steve*'s notice board:

Hi Sid and All,

Thank you for your news. It is so good knowing that you are down there in the Southern Ocean amongst the whales to protect them. You represent a change in human thinking, regard and respect for our fellow species – and so ourselves – which parallels other changes in recent centuries like the emancipation of slaves, education for all children and recognition that we are related to all other life on Earth (and were not made separately).

The great slaughter of the whales of the last three centuries is over and it is the Japanese whalers that sail against the course of human history while you go with the fair wind of empathy from all the future of human thinking. The world wants you down there and wishes you all success.

Yet you inevitably face a formidable and violent fleet of whalers intent on bloodshed and driven by both money and power. Stoking their boilers is the perverse idea, which some people never grow out of, that they are closer to supremacy over

nature if they kill other creatures bigger, faster or more mysterious than themselves, no matter how unthreatening, amiable
or technologically innocent these creatures may be.

I wish you great success and am proud to be working with
you. On this tiny, life-filled planet none of us is very far apart.
Though you are beyond our visual horizon, your presence and
life-saving work in the Antarctic is inspiring countless hearts
with its audacity it's [sic] morality and it's [sic] statement about
how we may secure the safety if [sic] the whales and, by extension, the future of all life on Earth.

We await your news,

Best wishes,

Bob Brown

Note that there's not one reference to conservation, the Southern
Ocean Sanctuary or international law. For Bob Brown there is only
one trajectory for humanity, and it is Sea Shepherd (and, by extension, its main supporter base: the Australian public) that holds the
course. A savage history has made way for a civilised future.

To help me sort through this 'civilised' thread of whale protection, I email Tom Griffiths, director of the Centre for Environmental History at the ANU and one of this country's foremost thinkers
on how our view of the environment has changed over time.

'I'm not sure that the first possible answer – familiarity with
charismatic creatures – is persuasive,' Griffiths replies. 'But the second one is much more convincing to me – that whales are a potent
symbol of our nation's ecological enlightenment, transformed from
first dominant economic resource to subjects of our salvation.
Many of the early whaling stations are now embraced within
national parks, another symbol of that same moral "progress".

There is something uncomplicatedly green and good for Australians in looking after whales.'

The social anthropologist Adrian Peace goes further, arguing that whales have become both metaphoric and metonymic of Australians' relationship with nature at large. For Peace, what is being expressed in 'looking after whales' – on the beach at 4am, on the high seas, in court at The Hague – is the belief that 'ours is a country which is "rational", "progressive", "informed" and "intelligent" in the way it thinks about Nature as symbolised by the whale. When that Nature comes under threat, ours is a society which is humane, responsive, and, in a word, civilised, in the way we unassumingly but with deep conviction go about our business.'

In an email to me, Peace suggests whale advocacy provides an anchor for an Australian identity cast adrift in a globalised world. 'It no longer makes sense to talk about an Australian middle class,' he writes. 'The relatively homogeneous middle class of old has become hugely differentiated, fragmented and diversified as a result of rising prosperity and full-scale commodification.

'For this reason, old icons and symbols [such as mateship] have lost their influence and appeal to these rising new classes. Their place has been taken by novel signs and symbols which are not directly tied to material conditions but are notably emotive in character, and those connected with environmental issues are most prominent of all.

'What's important about this ensemble of new symbols, which range from recycling to whale totemism, is that they can be made much of without the middle classes having to modify their (over/excess) consumption practices in the slightest. In fact, they can be conveniently used as a legitimation for increased consumption (more and newer household goods through to enviro-holidays, including whale watching), rather than cutting back across the board.'

Whaling, once the economic backbone of this country, has become that most trite of adjectives: 'un-Australian'.

*

Snug Cove is lifeless, but for a pair of cormorants preening themselves on a mast, when I arrive in the crepuscular spring morning. Four utes with footy-post aerials are parked in a row, presumably still to be retrieved after a big boys' night out. Three steps below them, at sea level, twenty-odd fishing boats and pleasure craft are tied up and deathly still; a prominent banner hangs off the stern of the one I'm boarding in an hour: 'See Whales'.

I've not been to Eden before. Four hundred and eighty kilometres south of Sydney, it seems at first your typical South Coast NSW town: a red-brick top pub and a red-brick bottom pub, Norfolk Island pines fronting a turquoise sea, iridescent rainbow lorikeets feasting on some nanna's grevillea. I've not been to Eden before but it feels like I have – precisely because I soon realise this isn't your typical South Coast NSW town at all: it's the Ayukawa of the Antipodes, or Taiji Down Under.

Anyone who thinks whales are no longer exploited in Australia hasn't been winked at by the cartoon Moby Dicks atop Eden Bedding and Furniture and the Eden Gateway Holiday Park; they haven't driven past Eden Public School with its whale-fluke logo or poked their head inside the Eden Art Gallery with its bilious New Age paintings of Hypercolor humpbacks; they haven't walked down Eden's high street in high spring, when rippling flags depict a breaching humpback and a three-word caption: 'Guess who's back'. Eden might now profit from whales in a different way from Japan's whaling towns, but it appropriates them identically. From the foot-paths to the football team, they are more than mascots; they are idols.

By 7.45am, fifty-five whale watchers have crammed onto the *Cat Balou*'s two decks, and skipper Gordon Butt is revving the 330-horsepower engine while wife Ros takes the mic. I'm joining a two-hour Saturday-morning whale-watching cruise on Twofold Bay, 'the third-deepest natural harbour in the Southern Hemisphere', Ros tells us over a pair of tinny speakers. As the only known place where humpback whales stop to feed on their southerly migration route, she continues, from mid September until late November, here and now is 'your best bet to witness the whales'.

Silver hills rise gently on the horizon as we gurgle out of Snug Cove and into Twofold Bay. The air is warm, and the mist that had enveloped the hinterland's bucolic dairy farms on the drive here is starting to burn away. The ocean is glassy and still; it's a beautiful day for gonzo anthropology.

The principal demographic on board is best described as daggy baby boomers with suncream-streaked faces and too much polar fleece; there are also a few young families with toddlers and three thirty-something girlfriends celebrating a birthday. Apart from a gaggle of excited Chinese tourists and one German backpacker, the cruise is an Australian affair.

I sit next to a friendly middle-aged couple from Sydney who tell me they've been seeing whales all week during their holiday on the Sapphire Coast: 'Even last night when we were having dinner at the RSL, we saw them out the window, just lolling about and that.' A serious man with a nasal voice and back-to-school dress shoes tells me he's been whale watching all over Australia but that Eden is the best. He's brought his own binoculars.

Ros cups her hands and starts calling the whales – 'Heeeeeeeere, whales!' Whether it works or not, within minutes someone's seen an exhalation and suddenly whales are appearing with the frequency of Peter FitzSimons popular histories: to port, to starboard, to aft, to stern. They're breaching, diving, feeding and 'spyhopping', which sees them pop their heads out of the water for an inquisitive look, like a fox terrier balancing on its hind legs for a doggy treat.

With each sighting come the now-familiar hoots and hollers; the clicks of cameras and animated applause reminiscent of Russians when their plane lands safely. The anthropomorphising comes on thick and fast.

'They're waving to us!'

'Here's mum to come check on the kids.'

'They're just so innocent.'

'What bloody show-offs!'

Even a cynic like me isn't always immune to the effects of charismatic megafauna: I find myself unexpectedly cooing at a calf covered in barnacles. The crustaceans look almost metallic, as if a steampunk submarine were emerging for air.

At one stage Gordon cuts the engine and the hydrophone is lowered over the edge to amplify any underwater sounds, but the sea is silent. When we finally hear the clicks and whistles of whale song, a mother asks her young son: 'Can you hear them saying hello to each other?'

'Enjoying your whales?' Ros asks me when Gordon finally fires the engine again. I think of Tokyo restaurateur Shintaro Sato asking me the same question and nearly choke on a crouton in my complimentary Cup-a-Soup.

By 9.30am we have seen perhaps fifteen whales, and a south-westerly wind is starting to whip up off the Tasman, making it hard to spot too many more. Above the spumes of froth slamming into Red Point, we are alerted to Boyd's Tower, a sandstone folly built for the nineteenth-century whaling magnate Ben Boyd as a private lighthouse, sporadically used as a watchtower by Eden's whalers. These days, judging by the bong I find there, it's used mostly by teenagers. 'Along with the nearby Davidson Whaling Station Historic Site,' crows Ros, 'the tower is now part of the Ben Boyd National Park.' Tom Griffiths later tells me: 'The killing platforms have become viewing platforms.'

On the way back to the wharf, a huge jellyfish surfaces to starboard. 'His name's Chris and he's from Maroochydore,' a man with long black hair scrunched into a peaked cap quips, and we all laugh.

But nobody laughs five minutes later when we pass around a laminated photo of 'Bladerunner', a humpback so-named because her fluke was run over by a propeller, leaving a distinct pattern of lacerations. We don't see Bladerunner today, but I'd read about her earlier that week in the *Canberra Times* ('Bladerunner's visit makes for exciting sequel').

'A lot of them have names,' says Ros, 'and they all have distinct personalities. Some of them have bad breath! Considering these whales were once hunted to the verge of extinction, it really is a privilege we can see them at all.'

*

Twenty minutes after we return to Snug Cove, I see many of the whale watchers again inside Eden's art deco Killer Whale Museum. It tells the story of the town's whaling industry, from its beginnings in 1828, when Thomas Raine established the first shore-based station on mainland Australia, until the 1930s, when overexploited stocks were already making bay whaling unprofitable.

At the industry's height in 1845, twenty-seven competing whale-boats operated out of Twofold Bay's eight whaling stations – stations competing with dozens more in Victoria, Van Diemen's Land and New Zealand. One humpback would yield, on average, 140 litres of oil worth £90; the average annual wage in 1830s New South Wales was £10. Between the late eighteenth century and 1963, perhaps 40,000 humpbacks were harpooned in Australian waters.

As the museum's name suggests, its centrepiece is a display on killer whales. In a remarkable story of cross-species collaboration, in the early twentieth century a pod of local orcas led by 'Old Tom' would allegedly drive passing baleen whales into Twofold Bay, encircle them, and alert the whalers onshore to the whales' presence with a series of tail slaps, breaches and acrobatics. Once the whalers had harpooned, killed and towed a baleen whale ashore, they would remove its tongue and lips and toss them to the orcas; it was an exchange of skills known as the 'law of the tongue'.

Under the hanging skeleton of Old Tom, a hand-painted plaque tells the story of these 'Killers of Eden', changing tone after it covers Old Tom's death to declare in black caps: 'In 1947 Australia, with sixteen other nations, signed an international whaling commission agreement placing complete bans on the taking of all endangered species to ensure that all may survive.'

That it was ultimately economic not conservational factors that killed Australian whaling doesn't rate a mention, but why spoil a good story? One equally rarely hears the fact that Cheynes Beach voluntarily closed its whaling operation because of waning profits more than a year before the Whale Protection Act came into force.

At this point the museum's signwriter plopped his or her paintbrush in the turps, picked up another, dipped it in jubilant royal blue and started a new paragraph. You can read the relief in their brushstrokes as they finished the museum's – and the country's – happy transformation: 'Australia is now an anti-whaling nation.'

PIRATES

By week two of the ICJ case, the public gallery has thinned out. The pressroom, too, is surprisingly deserted: apart from me, two Japanese reporters and Tony Press, the only regular attendee for the rest of the case is an unkempt Brazilian stringer for a wire service, who constantly curses the fact that French is still an official language of the United Nations, forcing him to wear too-tight headphones – 'They give me a fucking headache!' – each time President Tomka, some of the lawyers and a surprising number of the Japanese delegation address the court *en français*.

Luckily for him, the headphones aren't needed when Koji Tsuruoka, Japan's deputy foreign minister, starts his country's oral arguments, addressing the court in slow, deliberate English. This case, Tsuruoka emphasises, concerns the legality of JARPA II under international law, 'and not ethical values or the evaluation of good or bad science'. This assault on cultural imperialism will form the meat of Japan's defence: Tsuruoka reminds the court just who decimated the world's whale fishery in the first place, those black ships still lodged in the Japanese government's consciousness.

Tsuruoka, a thatch of greying hair swept across his serious face, is equally intent on resurrecting that old saw about Japan living in harmony with nature. 'Surrounded by sea,' he professes innocently,

'Japan would be the last to misuse whales as resources because we know we benefit from the fruits of the sea.'

This is the subplot to the debate over JARPA II's legality: according to the letter of the ICRW, whales are resources to exploit, not species to preserve. Australia, Tsuruoka asserts, is the one acting in bad faith by applying its moral values to a regulatory framework not designed for philosophical debate.

He quotes Malcolm Fraser in 1979, from one of those Hansards sitting on the former PM's Collins Street office shelf: 'The government upholds ... that Australia should pursue a policy of opposition to whaling ... both domestically and internationally through the International Whaling Commission and other organisations.'

'Why does Australia take such a position?' Tsuruoka asks. 'Are all cetaceans sacred and endangered? I can understand the emotional background to this position, but fail to understand how it can be translated to a legal or scientific position.'

After swaggering to the rostrum and adjusting his cowlick of oiled black hair, McGill University's Professor Payam Akhavan, a former UN prosecutor of Slobodan Milošević, says the reason Australia takes such a position is obvious: it's good politics. Australia's transition from whaling to anti-whaling came only after the much-publicised campaign to shut down Albany's Cheynes Beach Company had politicised it for the Fraser government. Sydney Frost's report, Akhavan says, had as its point of reference not sustainability but populism: that 'the killing of whales is wrong in the eyes of the Australian community' and that its continuation 'would outrage a significant proportion of the population'.

Akhavan emphasises Frost's explanation that Australians wanted to avoid inflicting 'pain and suffering ... irrespective of whether that being is a human or non-human animal'. This, he says, at a time when Australia was the world's biggest exporter of beef and involved in a widespread culling campaign of feral camels.

Frost's justification for this inconsistency is quoted by Akhavan as being that whales are unlike animals 'such as cattle, sheep and pigs that are traditionally bred for slaughter', or kangaroos, which are killed because they are 'a nuisance to farmers'. Reasonable Australians, Frost continued, 'would conclude that ... it is wrong to kill an animal of such special significance as the whale'. The report, Akhavan says, looking up from his own notes with a voice of disdain, 'even referred to whales as "sacred animals"'.

If Grug were in the public gallery, I suspect he would've yelled that *all* animals are sacred, before being ejected from the chamber. But it's the mentality of Grug's Australian colleague who told me 'the whale is not a food animal' that Akhavan is criticising.

'In this light,' Akhavan tells the court, 'the Frost Report recommended that "Australia should remain a member of the [IWC], which is the forum where its anti-whaling policy can best be pursued." In other words, Australia would remain in the IWC for the purpose of defeating its purpose.

'To borrow a phrase from the [Australian] agent's speech,' Akhavan says with a smirk, 'Australia seeks to cloak its political and cultural preferences "in the lab-coat of science". Having put an end to commercial whaling for the past thirty years through the moratorium, it now also seeks to end scientific whaling. It seeks to apply the Whaling Convention as if it were the Anti-Whaling Convention.'

Akhavan next launches a searing attack on what he depicts as Australia's two-pronged campaign to derail the IWC's remit and, through it, JARPA II's perfectly legal attempts to build a scientific case for a resumption of commercial whaling. While Australia's uncompromising delegation has hijacked the IWC at the negotiating table, he claims, at sea Canberra has 'outsourced Antarctic maritime enforcement' to *actual* pirates.

During Australia's first round of oral arguments, James Crawford had assiduously distanced the case from Sea Shepherd's campaigns, asserting Watson's crusade was 'of no relevance' and that, contrary to the ICR's and even the Scientific Committee's claims, the disparity between JARPA II's quota and take was not a reflection of Tommy's aim with a prop fouler, but – this being a commercial operation – a fall in demand for its product among Japanese consumers.

Akhavan instead paints a picture of collaboration on land and sea tantamount to state-sponsored terrorism. We hear how the very organisation whose methods have been condemned by the IWC, IMO, FBI and now Interpol – the very organisation that repeatedly prevents Japanese scientists from being able to study their desired sample size – is not just tolerated by the Australian government but is strongly influencing its policy.

The court is told how in 2009 Watson made an 'offer' to the Rudd government, stating publicly that 'if Australia or New Zealand … can agree to take legal action [against Japan], Sea Shepherd will agree to back off our aggressive tactics'. Rudd took Japan to court the next year.

Nor, Akhavan asserts, is this relationship partisan: he reads a letter from former PM John Howard's environment minister Ian Campbell, a member of Sea Shepherd's advisory board since 2008, in which he urges the president and environment minister of Costa Rica to reconsider their demand for Berlin to extradite Watson to San José during his period of German house arrest in 2012. 'I was proud to support Captain Watson when I was a cabinet minister in the national government of Australia,' wrote Campbell.

Akhavan's next line of attack is so familiar to me that he might have mined my notebooks for ammunition: 'A quick glance at the Sea Shepherd website demonstrates what is a private army used to wage war against Japanese research vessels on the high seas, using Australia as a base,' he says. The *Bob*'s apparent non-ramming of the *Nisshin* even gets a run: 'This sample photo ... demonstrates one such ship, named after the Hollywood celebrity Bob Barker, attacking Japanese research vessels in February of this year in Antarctic waters.

'Now, I would imagine,' continues Akhavan, 'that Sea Shepherd would be very disappointed at Professor Crawford's suggestion that they are of no relevance to Japan's reduced catch this year ... their website triumphantly states: "This was Japan's most disastrous whaling season ever. Congratulations to Sea Shepherd Australia for leading such a successful Antarctic whaling campaign." Just below, you will see a red tab inviting supporters to "Donate Now". Minimising Sea Shepherd's relevance as Professor Crawford has done is clearly unhelpful for their fundraising campaign.'

I'm surely not the only one in the Peace Palace amused by the irony that, by drawing attention to Sea Shepherd in an attempt to discredit Australia's legal challenge to JARPA II, Akhavan has succeeded only in giving Neptune's Navy a free plug. Paul Watson's been on Larry King, Kochie's couch and *South Park*, and now he's appeared on the big screen at the ICJ. Whichever Polynesian atoll or sympathetic Latin American president's broom cupboard he's currently hiding out in, I'm sure he's mightily pleased with himself.

*

With a bowtie round his neck, and his soccer-ball head topped by a comical combination of ginger eyebrows and white hair, Oslo

University's Professor Lars Walløe resembles nothing so much as a snowman. All that's missing is a pipe.

Walløe rebukes Professor Marc Mangel's assertion that real science requires a hypothesis (so the fact Gregor Mendel was growing peas in his convent's veggie garden precludes him from discovering genetics?), and refutes Gales' opinion that lethal sampling isn't necessary for gaining genetic information from whales: it's the only way to undertake morphometrics, a form of analysis that is crucial, he says, for determining the stock structure of Antarctic minke whales.

As for the findings of JARPA, dismissed by Gales as adding nothing new to the repository of scientific knowledge, Walløe contends that it was only upon reviewing the findings of JARPA that the Scientific Committee acknowledged the existence of two distinct stocks of Antarctic minke whales.

A decline in blubber thickness over the JARPA years, he says, was another important finding, as it indicates that a change in the Antarctic ecosystem is afoot. The importance of this finding, Walløe says, was accepted and acknowledged by the Scientific Committee – of which Walløe is a member – for three years, until in 2011 an Australian scientist used 'filibuster techniques' to reopen the finding's legitimacy.

On stomach content, too, Walløe rejects Gales' view that 'we know the Antarctic minke whales eat Antarctic krill almost exclusively'. That's not the point, says Walløe: the important finding is that over the JARPA years the content of the fore-stomach in Antarctic minkes was found to have declined.

Walløe concludes that by better understanding the Antarctic ecosystem, Japan will be able to create a more sustainable form of commercial whaling, should the moratorium be overturned.

Justin Gleeson SC has the look of a taunted bull that doesn't know whether to go for the matador, the press photographers or the brat throwing peanut husks at him from the front row. His eyes flit about the chamber, followed at a lag by his square head of close-cropped, woolly hair; his mouth is pulled tight like a drawbridge under siege. He takes a sip of water, pauses a beat, and channels his rage into a twenty-minute attack on the credibility of Japan's sole expert witness.

Gleeson questions Walløe's motives and independence, given his long history as a Norwegian delegate to the IWC, the fact that he has received one of the highest Japanese honours available to a foreigner, his collaboration with Japan's whale 'scientists' and with ICR staff on three papers about the number of stocks, blubber thickness and stomach contents – the same topics Walløe has high-lighted as JARPA's legacy to scientific discovery.

He cuts through Walløe's long-winded, mumbling answers to contest the Norwegian's views on the worth of JARPA's blubber thickness findings: 'Would you agree that, after twenty-six years of data from JARPA and JARPA II, neither the Commission nor the Scientific Committee has affirmed that investigations of blubber thickness are required for the conservation or management of whales or for any other critical research need?'

'I agree. It is not necessary for the management of whales or whaling.'

This is not the Japanese government's line. In the flame of Glee-son's blowtorch, the snowman is starting to melt.

Gleeson increases the heat: 'In light of the questions I have asked you this afternoon, would you wish to withdraw the claim that you are an independent witness?'

A murmur from the public gallery; grins and frantic typing in the press gallery.

'No, I would not. I think I am an independent witness in the sense that – much more so than, for instance, Dr Gales is an independent witness.'

Gleeson turns to the matter of sample size, and Walløe puts up less resistance now, admitting that even he doesn't fully understand how the minke quotas for JARPA II were reached. On the subject of fin and humpback sample sizes, Walløe stresses he was asked by Japan to focus on minke whales, but nonetheless agrees with Gleeson that the much smaller numbers suggest a twelve-year project, not a six-year one. He doesn't know why JARPA II would collect data for minkes on a six-year cycle while studying changes to the fin and humpback population over twelve years.

Gleeson frowns. I wonder if he knows that fin whales, apparently, make better eating than minkes.

Walløe goes on: 'I think, before you continue, that what I did not write in my Expert Statement, but what I was prepared to say, is that during the consultations I had with Japanese scientists ... I never liked the fin whale proposal because I think, and especially with eighteen whales caught, it is no information you can get from it.'

Gleeson looks as if he's won the meat tray at pub trivia: 'Thank you for that candid statement.'

All that's left of Professor Lars Walløe is a puddle on the carpet. Australia just acquired its third expert witness.

*

It's an irresistible game to guess which way the ICJ's judges are leaning from their questions. Justin Gleeson's stern interrogation of Lars Walløe prompts a flurry of queries from the bench – more than for Mangel and Gales combined.

Judge Greenwood asks the Norwegian whether there's a scientific rationale for the massive increase in sample size between JARPA and JARPA II; Walløe suspects it was because JARPA didn't reach its research objectives with a maximum quota of 440 minke whales.

Judge Keith wonders why the ICR doesn't collaborate with other research bodies operating in Antarctica, such as the multinational Convention on the Conservation of Antarctic Marine Living Resources or even Japan's own National Institute for Polar Research. A fair point, agrees Walløe.

Judge Charlesworth asks how lethal sampling ensures a representative sample of Antarctic minke whales and not, for example, just the slow ones. Walløe replies with something discursive about where the outer borders of the two Antarctic minke stocks are located.

But it is another question, asked of Australia this morning and to be answered next week, which I think could prove the most prescient. 'What injury, if any,' India's Judge Bhandari had inquired, 'has Australia suffered as a result of Japan's alleged breaches of the ICRW through JARPA II?'

Any reference to Japan's whaling in Australia's claimed sovereign territory in Antarctica has been conspicuously absent from Australia's arguments. A source close to the Australian legal team tells me this was deliberate, as Australia's claim over the territory has never been challenged and the government wasn't about to tempt anyone to try. If Australia is avoiding the implication that Japan is whaling in its sovereign waters, what tangible harm can it argue to have sustained? Can the court be expected to care if whaling hurts the feelings of Australians? The ICJ was set up as a seat of arbitration between contracting states, not to play the part of a headmaster acting on a dobber's tip.

THEM

It makes sense that for whales to assume a totemic status in Australian society – a defining and unifying representation of who we are and where we have come from – we need a foil, a whetstone on which to sharpen our self-definition. And in Japan, Australia is blessed with a very gritty whetstone.

For starters, Australians' stereotypical view of the Japanese emphasises our difference from them: they don't look like us (they're all the same!), they don't sound like us (日本語!), they don't eat like us (chopsticks!), they don't fantasise like us (vending machine panties!), they don't shit like us (heated toilet seats!); frankly, they may not even be human like us (their workers are never procrastinating online – they're too busy being 'salarymen', 'economic animals' or 'Japan Inc.').

But Antarctic whaling goes deeper, presenting a parable of everything that's wrong with People Like Them. Never mind that they hunt whales for another reason, the fact that the Japanese got into industrial whaling just as the West was beginning to deem it obsolete is proof of their backwardness. As a 2014 *Herald Sun* editorial put it: 'Whaling had a legitimate purpose in the nineteenth century, but not in the twenty-first. It is an unnecessary and bloody business and the Japanese whaling fleet should go home, never to return.'

Then there's the way they conduct themselves at the IWC. Not only do they not get the message that, in Bob Brown's words, 'the world' is against them (although of the 193 member states of the United Nations, less than half belong to the IWC, and half of those support Japanese whaling), they engage in vote-buying, tying aid to developing countries – many of which don't even have coastlines – in return for support in efforts to overturn the moratorium. That Western countries frequently engage in such diplomatic tactics doesn't rate a mention – Australia practises this realpolitik all the time, from roads-for-refugees in Papua New Guinea to schools-for-democracy in Fiji. Australia has also been accused by Japan of threatening the Solomon Islands with a withdrawal of trade concessions if it doesn't support Australia's position at the IWC.

Japan's motives, too, are consistent with the deceitful caricature of the East set out in Edward Saïd's seminal work of post-colonial studies, *Orientalism*: the 'science' of lethal research is so obviously a sham that it seems to have entered the Australian vernacular as a byword for bogus; in 2011, when Victorian mountain cattlemen protested the federal government's block on grazing in the Alpine National Park, arguing that the practice is a way of keeping bushfire fuel in check, the then federal environment minister, Tony Burke, likened it to Japanese 'scientific' whaling.

Opponents of JARPA II often claim that the whale meat which ends up on Japanese tables (or at least in warehouse freezers) precludes the program's 'scientific' pretensions. They obviously haven't read the fine print of the ICRW, which allows 'any whales taken under these special permits' to be processed.

Even Japan's claims to be upholding a tradition have a spurious historical basis. 'How absurd has the argument become,' Tony Burke tweeted in early 2013, 'if Japan is now arguing that it has a traditional cultural practice of travelling from one side of the planet to the other to kill whales in a whale sanctuary.'

But the pickled plum on top of the bento box is that the same nation that shoots whales in Antarctica today, the same nation that Paul Watson claims shot *him* during *Whale Wars*, shot my grandpa – and the grandpas of many other Australians – during World War II.

The particularly *foreign* nature of the foreigners involved here – off the cultural Richter scale, a diametrically opposite view of nature, a wartime enemy – makes their demonisation not just an easy but an integral part of Australia's whale advocacy. The way the Australian media covers this debate is a case in point.

In 2009, Wakayama University environmental studies professor Kumi Kato studied over 380 items (films, TV and radio reports, home movies) at the National Film and Sound Archive in Canberra to examine how nature is represented in the Australian media, as epitomised by our interactions with whales. Her study aimed to 'examine the formation of the "anti-whaling" idea, in which the media is considered to play a significant role'.

Starting with the 1911 film *Whale Slaughter* and ending with contemporary news clips of naval jousts between Sea Shepherd and the ICR's fleet, the clips chart a familiar path: the transition from the pragmatic relationship between exploiter and exploited, through the signing of the ICRW and the rise of environmentalism to the contemporary global conservation ethos, in which the killing of whales has no place for those 'trying to save the planet'.

Kato divides the evolution of whale discourse in the Australian media into five distinct periods. From 1911 to 1946, the stories were about the Antarctic expeditions, adventuring into the unknown to engage in grand-scale operations. From 1947 until the early 1960s, the narrative changed to the economic development of this new industry: 'brave men' and 'mighty whales'. The 1960s and '70s brought with them the rise of environmentalism, which heralded the emergence, by the 1980s, of the anti-whaling discourse and whale tourism as an industry.

It is the current period which is most enlightening as to why we still care about this issue. Since the start of this century, Kato argues, what began as a movement to stop whaling and evolved into one that was anti-whaling has become nothing less than a *war* for whales. While Greenpeace first stressed out Tameo Ryono by zipping in front of his catcher boat with banners that read 'Illegal Whaling' and 'Research Bloody Research', Sea Shepherd has upped the ante significantly, priding itself on intervening instead of protesting, and bragging about the eleven whalers it has allegedly sunk, starting with the *Sierra*.

It's chum for the press pack, and Kato saw fighting words everywhere she looked: 'Japan is far from *beaten* ... Japanese representatives *declared defiantly* that they *would not back off* on commercial whaling ... Japan's determination to *grind out victory* in a long-term campaign ... they would be *back in greater force* next year ... at the heart of Japan's *strategy* is its counting of small, impoverished nations' (Kato's emphasis).

I'm guilty of it too: the subtitle of this book refers to the 'whale wars'; everyone loves a bit of biff.

Since every war needs goodies and baddies, according to Kato, the battlelines were quickly drawn: 'The conflicts have led to mutual accusations: "illegal whalers" and "aggressive activists", or more recently "terrorists" [according to the ICR], provide video to prove the other's wrongdoing. The words used here are "accusation, distrust, blame, criticism, harassment and hostility"; it is about *them – the whale killers* against *us – the whale savers*.'

216

Kato, by the way, is no lackey of the Japanese government: she speaks English like the Queenslander she once was, considers Bob Brown a mate and drives around Wakayama City in a van with a 'No Nuke in Japan' sticker on the back.

For Kato, the principal collateral damage of this whaling 'war' is the whales themselves: 'What is most striking is that as the *whale war* intensifies,' she writes, 'the discussion of *whales* decreases.'

Adrian Peace has kept a close eye on the Australian print media's coverage of the issue. The inventory of insults Peace has uncovered could easily be applied to the Srebrenica genocide: the Japanese whalers are said to 'butcher', 'massacre' and 'torture' the 'gentle' and 'defenceless' whales. Sea Shepherd crewmembers, for their part, were labelled 'brave' 'eco-warriors', their campaigns over-whelmingly praised for attempting to 'stop the whale slaughter' and for their combative approach to an 'increasing menace'.

The coverage of the tumultuous summer of 2009–10 was par-ticularly revealing – and it wasn't Pete Bethune, boarding the *Sho-nan Maru 2* with a knife, who was painted as an aggressor. Early in that 'killing season', when the ICR conducted aerial surveillance in a bid to locate Sea Shepherd (as Sea Shepherd does with its helicop-ters to find the whalers), the *Herald Sun* called them 'spy flights' stoking 'sea warfare'. When the 'small' and 'defenceless' *Ady Gil* then collided with the *Shonan*, the same paper condemned the 'ram raid on the high seas'.

Peace concluded: 'the dominant message is unambiguous: the Japanese are a barbaric and cruel lot, just as they were back in World War II. In true Orientalist fashion, they are deceitful in claiming to be engaged in scientific research; they are unreliable in providing data on their catches; they buy the support of bank-rupt Third World nations; above all, they are cruel and callous in the way they go about their whaling business.'

This perfect storm for sensationalist journalism also serves as a pat on the back: 'On the one hand, contemporary Australian identity is being constituted in relation to the whale as a non-human cultural Other,' Peace writes; 'on the other hand it is being constituted vis-à-vis the Japanese as a human yet profoundly flawed Other.'

Australia has built its monument to whales on a foundation of demonising Japan. And Sea Shepherd knows it.

*

It took me less than twenty-four hours on board the *Steve* to find evidence of the attitudes I'd suspected I would encounter. It was during my welcome-aboard tour: we were in the dive locker, andd Beck was telling us about the scuba gear used for at-sea repair jobs. But I wasn't listening – I was distracted by something I'd noticed on a piece of chipboard leaning against the wall written in small, angry handwriting:

Today we rammed filthy fuckin' Jap whaling pricks – we nearly died and the crew just laughed – slightly annoying
Dan 02/06/09

A few evenings later I spoke to an Aussie deckhand on the forward deck of the *Steve* about Sea Shepherd's booming popularity among the Australian public. We were still drifting off New Zealand: the North Island's highest peak, Mount Ruapehu, was silhouetted in amber haze.

'I think the whole pirate thing resonates with a lot of people,' he said. 'The kids especially love the Jolly Roger.'

But then I told him about the graffiti. He initially got defensive: 'That came from the Red Room [where the *Whale Wars* crew sleep]; it wasn't us!' But then the deckhand frowned. We were the only ones on deck, but he lowered his voice and assumed an air of gravity. 'I think, unfortunately, a lot of the popularity does have to do with racism, though. I used to volunteer onshore; Sea Shepherd does beach clean-ups and has stalls at sustainability events. Over and over people would come up to us and say things like: "I love you guys because of what the fucken Japs get away with down there." I remember once a woman said to me: 'You guys must have plenty of Jap jokes, eh!" It's a real shame to think that's where a proportion of our support comes from.'

I asked him if he had any racist crewmates. 'Nah, no way, there's no place for that on the *Steve*.'

But unfortunately there was. The majority of the *Steve*'s crew was not racist – or, at least, not that I saw. Percy thought the Japanese were a 'bunch of motherfuckers', but I suspect he'd have said the same of the Icelanders, the Faroese or the Greenlanders.

Then there was Squid. He deserves some slack: a depressed, grief-stricken man who told me that Sea Shepherd had become his surrogate family. But that's no excuse to repeatedly call the whalers 'slopey-eyed cunts', which was brought to my attention by a concerned crewmember. When I nervously confronted Squid about it one day on the tawdry '70s couch of my cabin – this is the guy who wanted to knock my block off for eating kanga bangas, remember – he grew nervous himself and gave me that hackneyed excuse of racists the world over: 'I'm just havin' a laff!'

Vera's racism was both rabid and farcical. She refused to eat *Chinese* food because of Japan's Antarctic whaling program, and once, when Alex, the sound mixer for *Whale Wars*, said 'Sayonara' to me as he left the comms room, she looked up from her PC and chastised him for using 'that' language.

But these crewmembers were aberrations: most of the crew had 'enlisted' (to use another warlike word) because they opposed the Japanese whaling fleet, not the Japanese people.

Arthur told me he was so worried about appearing racist that he nearly didn't join Sea Shepherd. Uncle Bruce, a former business-man who has worked in Tokyo more times than he can remember, was as glowing about Japanese society as he was damning of his own: 'Japan is a scrupulous nation: they know that the rest of the world doesn't like what they're doing, but they are prepared to take it on the chin. They ask permission from the IWC to do this, and they proceed only when it's granted. I mean, if these were Australian fishermen they probably wouldn't even do the paperwork! They'd probably just come in and steal as much as they could.'

Grug, Uncle Bruce, Beck, Sid, Tod and several others told me during the campaign how much it frustrated them when they were pitted against 'the Japanese' in the media. Which makes it all the more baffling how they could miss – or ignore – the warmongering that surrounds them.

When I asked Paul Watson whether his organisation was racist, he flippantly rejected the question as 'silly', denying even that his supporters were racist. I guess he doesn't count Brigitte Bardot as a supporter: she's been fined so many times under France's anti-hate laws for her public Islamophobia that the last time she fronted court, the prosecutor in Paris said she was weary of charging Bar-dot with racial hatred offences. 'Now my country, France, my homeland, my land,' Bardot once penned in Le Figaro, 'is with the blessing of successive governments again invaded by a foreign, especially Muslim, overpopulation to which we pay allegiance.'

But Watson's too clever to resort to outright racism; Sea Shepherd's approach is calculated and nuanced. World War II rhetoric is inserted into the debate to create the sense of a continuous narrative, the Battle of the Southern Ocean depicted as the last stand before those Australian Yen that Tokyo have ready and waiting become legal tender.

'We have Japanese crew, for Chrissakes!' I imagine Watson would say. True: there's one on the *Sam*, and a handful working in Taiji. I wonder what those crewmembers make of this 2007 post by him, still on Sea Shepherd Australia's website: 'The Japanese say that whaling is a matter of national pride. What kind of sick perverse culture can take pride in the cruel and bloody slaughter of whales and dolphins? Oh yes, I almost forgot, the same culture responsible for the Rape of Nanking and the beheading of Australian, American, Canadian and Dutch soldiers and civilians.'

Or this one, from the year before: 'Japan has always closely identified with blood and slaughter. From the decapitations by the Samurai upon innocent peasants to the suicidal insanity of the Kamikaze, violence and self destruction have been a part of Japanese culture.'

Or this one, delivered in the lead-up to Anzac Day 2010: 'Captain Bethune was not brought back to Japan as a criminal. He was brought back as a prisoner on the ship that had so viciously attacked him and when that ship arrived it was greeted with a nationalist rally of cheering and jeering Japanese right-wingers in the same manner as they cheered the marching of POWs down the Kokoda Trail or through the streets of Tokyo in 1942. This was the first time since the Pacific War with Japan that an ANZAC soldier (Pete is a veteran) [Watson was wrong; he isn't] was transported back to Japan from the Southern Ocean after the sinking of his ship, and the first time that a prisoner was greeted with such jingoistic hatred. They treated him as a prisoner of war and that is exactly what he is.'

There's no doubt Watson is a military nerd; a replica sword hangs from the wall of his cabin, and the after-lunch vacuum before crew begrudgingly took their plates to the scullery and got back to work was often filled with soporific Watson monologues about the American Civil War, or why Mussolini was a technically a fascist, not an anti-Semite.

But there was only one war in mind for the designers of Sea Shepherd's 2011–12 Antarctic campaign, Operation Divine Wind (the literal translation of *kamikaze*), its logo incorporating the Rising Sun flag – a flag used only for military purposes. And in case you didn't catch which way that divine wind is blowing, 2009–10's jingoistic Operation Waltzing Matilda had a boxing kangaroo wearing a piratical eye-patch.

'Australians are the most passionate whale defenders on the planet,' wrote Watson in the press release announcing that campaign. 'Operation Waltzing Matilda will reflect our gratitude to Australia for the incredible support we have received from the people of this wonderful nation since 2005. The *Steve Irwin* will depart in December from Western Australia with the majority of the crew being Australians.'

Further down in the same press release is this remarkably candid admission of World War II jingoism: 'Kylie Herd, a Sea Shepherd crewmember from Perth attending the IWC Conference in Madeira, said, "Our logo this year is modelled on the art that adorned the fighter planes of the legendary Flying Tigers who fought the Japanese Imperial forces in China. The colors of the Aboriginal and Australian flags have been incorporated into the design with the pirate kangaroo holding Neptune's trident of justice. We intend to waltz down to the Southern Ocean to dance dangerously with the Japanese whaling fleet and we intend to unroll a Matilda full of defensive tactics for the whales against the Japanese whale poachers.'

Grug denies that this is dog whistling to the Australian moral low ground, and he's right. It's not dog whistling; it's standing on the balcony of the Emery Point lighthouse and blowing a conch to signal that the Japs have been spotted over the Timor Sea flying in kamikaze formation towards Port Darwin.

*

Australians don't care about whales; we care about *our* whales. Japan, of course, isn't the only country that hunts whales. According to the IWC, in 2012, the year I stepped on board the *Steve*, Norway killed 464 whales to Japan's 424. If we stick to endangered fin whales – justification alone for Sea Shepherd's campaigns in Antarctica, according to Elissa ('fin whales *are* endangered') – in 2013, by my count, Japan, with a self-appointed quota of fifty, killed zero to Iceland's 134. Yet I suspect you didn't know that. In Adrian Peace's analysis of the Australian media's whaling coverage, on the few occasions Scandinavian whalers warranted a mention they were depicted as hardy and tough, hewing a living from a harsh landscape.

We might find it harder to demonise the Icelanders – people like us – if they were the ones hunting whales in Antarctica. I once ribbed my Icelandic friend Signý about how Icelanders get off scot-free for killing and trading in endangered fin whales, while the Japanese get taken to court for squishing cockroaches of the sea. 'It's because everybody loves Iceland', she said with a shrug. 'We're a nice little country that doesn't hurt anyone. We knit beautiful sweaters, gave the world Sigur Rós and elect openly gay prime ministers [well, one and counting: Jóhanna Sigurðardóttir].'

Peace argues it would be hard for Australians to point pitchforks at Reykjavík even without our love of Sigur Rós: 'Demonising the Japanese has long been the other side of the coin to worshipping the whale. But Icelanders look like us and talk like us, their science is much the same as ours (including the science which sets whale quotas), as are their political processes. Turning our gaze northwards to Iceland's whaling economy will require realignment of our moral compass.'

Racial prejudice aside, the curious thing about Australians' preoccupation with Japan's Antarctic whaling program is that, contrary to popular belief, the hunt occurs far from Australia. The northernmost point of JARPA II's 'sample zone' is still approximately 650 kilometres south of Macquarie Island, itself 1300 kilometres southeast of the Tasmanian 'mainland'.

The hunt often occurs within the territorial waters of the Australian Antarctic Territory (AAT), the largest slice of the Antarctic pavlova claimed by any nation. The AAT is frequently invoked as 'Australian waters' by Sea Shepherd, but it's not as if Kyodo Senpaku is harpooning whales off the St Kilda pier. Under the terms of the Antarctic Treaty System, the framework that has governed the frozen continent since 1961, sovereignty claims are neither recognised, disputed or established. Only four countries – Norway, New Zealand, Great Britain and France – see Australia's patch of ice as Australia's.

And yet for Sea Shepherd, the possessiveness is pervasive. In his interview with 7.30's Leigh Sales on 26 February 2013, Bob Brown said, 'Tokyo's taken over our backyard, our whales, our international whale sanctuary and is thumbing its nose at our laws'. As well as ignoring the political reality of Antarctica and being spectacularly hypocritical about Sea Shepherd's 'biocentric' philosophy, this is legally incorrect: Antarctic minke whales – a migratory species that travels thousands of kilometres – are, like all swimming species, by law considered *ferae naturae,* or wild and unowned until captured. They don't belong to anyone.

In his email to me, Tom Griffiths had written: 'Are whales "Antarctic" in our minds? And is Antarctica another world, free of the usual politics, a place apart, but in some peculiar ways *our* place to defend and protect?'

A few weeks later I have breakfast at the ANU with Tom and two of his Antarctic-minded PhD students, Alessandro Antonello and Diane Erceg, to ask their views on how Australians think about Antarctica. We all agree that the AAT, as a formally defined territory, probably doesn't rate much – if at all – in the Australian consciousness; Diane, who has worked as a tour guide on Antarctic cruises, thinks if Australians have heard about Australia's claim at all it is 'from stories they hear from friends of friends who went down for a winter as a scientist or a sparky'.

But equally there is consensus that Antarctica is considered Australia's backyard. Is this, I ask, because Australia doesn't have a land border? The South Pole is as close to Canberra as is Singapore, but while our north is cluttered with frontiers – islands, peoples, stories and histories – our southern extremity is less clearly defined.

The obvious comparison, I suggest, is Canada: a people largely limpeted to the US border but a *nation* stretching to the end of the Earth. In that nation's collective myth-making, the north is more an idea than a place: at the very margins of the pioneering lumberjack's – let alone modern-day Ottawa's – reach. Out of sight, but not of mind. Is the south the same for us?

We are the Great Southern Land, but where does our southern border exactly start and end – if not on paper, then in our minds? Alessandro points out that Australia is the only country that considers the Southern Ocean to begin at its southern edge: New Zealand, South Africa, Chile and – to a lesser extent – Argentina may also have southern coastlines, but they border other oceans. 'The broad point here,' he says, 'is that, in Australia, reference to the Southern Ocean in the news or by an environmental organisation can play off Australians' sense that the Southern Ocean begins in the Bight and goes all the way to the ice.'

And linking the Bight to the ice on their migrations, bringing the feats of Mawson to our beachside barbeques, are whales.

THE GREAT ANTARCTIC
MOONING INCIDENT

When attorney-general Mark Dreyfus makes his first appearance before the ICJ, he's jovial, gratified and rooster-chested, as if he's speaking as the father of the bride, not the first law officer of the nation. Delicately at first, then cloyingly, he reassures the Japanese delegation that, whatever the ultimate decision of the court, Australia's case won't just have no detrimental impact on diplomatic relations, it will even 'mark a step forward in what is a close bilateral relationship'. What effect Canberra taking Tokyo to the ICJ will have on their relationship is an intriguing question, but the idea of it being a positive one seems a fanciful piece of political spin.

'Did anybody from the Japanese side say that?' Masayuki Komatsu later snaps when I tell him Dreyfus maintained the case wouldn't harm Japanese–Australian relations. A close Japan watcher tells me: 'Make no mistake about this, from the people I've spoken to within the foreign ministry, the Japanese government was very unhappy about it. There was basically an agreement that Japan and Australia would agree to disagree at the IWC and not let it spill over into the bilateral relationship.'

Dreyfus addresses Japan's accusation that Australia has 'out-sourced Antarctic maritime enforcement to Sea Shepherd' by retorting that, bereft of a legal argument, Japan has resorted to playing the man. The accusation is 'wholly untrue, and ridiculous', he says, citing frequent government calls for both parties in the whale wars to exercise restraint. He notes that Sea Shepherd vessels and crew are able to visit Australian ports, as is any person or organisation. That may even include Paul Watson; when we docked at Williamstown in March, Dreyfus told parliament the Australian government had no plans to arrest Watson, had he been with us.

That Japan has played the cultural imperialist card, Dreyfus asserts, shows they don't have much of a hand. He slams Payam Akhavan's analysis of Australia's motive for the lawsuit – a civilising mission rooted in a populist opposition to whaling – and claims instead that the case 'is of great importance to the Australian people and the Australian government', because of the virtues of 'upholding the rule of law at the international level and the positive effect that has on international relations'.

But if that's the case, what about Australia's obligation to the UN Convention relating to the Status of Refugees? Or the United Nations' concern about the suspension of the Racial Discrimination Act brought on by the Northern Territory Intervention? Or the Iraq War, when Australians allowed John Howard to follow Tony Blair and George W. Bush down a legally dubious rabbit hole?

When I later ask the attorney-general why this case is in our national interest, his answer is no more convincing: 'I think that Australians are very conscious of the need to conserve whales; they're very conscious of the fact that humanity hunted whale species, many of them almost to extinction, in the last century, and that we want to do everything that we can as a nation to preserve this species. I can't perhaps explain to you beyond saying that there is an appreciation of these magnificent creatures; the popularity of whale watching tells us a lot about the interest that Australians have in whale species.' Is that not, as Japan claims, a civilising mission rooted in populist opposition to whaling?

The ICRW's overriding goal, Dreyfus argues, is not stuck in 1946, as Japan claims, but has evolved to reflect modern sensibilities, as 'evidenced by the continuing shift in the IWC's focus to non-consumptive uses of whales, such as whale watching, as noted in Australia's Memorial'. And Australia says that a breach of the ICRW itself is sufficient to cause 'injury' to Australia, which answers Judge Bhandari's earlier question. Australia's counsel Laurence Boisson de Chazournes later explains that the preamble to the convention specifies that conservation and recovery of whales is of common interest to the 'nations of the world'. 'In view of their shared values', then, by contravening the convention, Japan is causing injury not just to Australia, but every convention party.

Against this framework, Australia's team uses the beleaguered Professor Lars Walløe's evidence to point out what Justin Gleeson calls 'a rather gaping hole at the heart of JARPA II: the lack of a scientific justification for the number and species of whales to be taken'. This is not just a gaping hole at the heart of JARPA II – it could well be the stake that stops it beating at all.

*

Tony Press takes me to dinner when he learns I've been supplementing the daily special in the ICJ's cafeteria with bread rolls pilfered from my youth hostel's breakfast buffet. He's a scientist but his demeanour is more like a trade unionist's: he's full of ripping yarns from his decade in charge of the Australian Antarctic Division and another decade and a half before that working in government as he plies me with those portly glass goblets the Dutch serve their beers in.

I'm told of hapless environment ministers and gone-loco-over-winter base scientists; which members of the Australian legal team he suspects will be 'getting on the sauce' at The Hague; and the tale of 'The Great Antarctic Mooning Incident', in which, during a chance high-seas encounter with the Japanese whaling fleet a few years back, an Australian scientist stepped onto the deck of the division's icebreaker, *Aurora Australis*, turned his back to the bridge of a passing vessel and lowered his breeches. The incident earned Australia a diplomatic dressing-down but, so the story goes, the offending cheeks were quietly sought out for congratulations by a member of parliament upon their return to Hobart.

Tony won't tell me his personal view on Japan's Antarctic whaling program but says he agrees with some things the Japanese counsel has said about Australia's interpretation of the ICRW being beyond the treaty's 1946 remit. He also tells me he has spoken to a few people from the Australian team who've said they aren't fazed by Japan's arguments so far.

We're sitting outside on the footpath, eating soggy hamburgers in between sips from our goblets. Cyclists on heavy frames clunk past on the cobblestones. At one stage a delivery van cuts one off, earning its driver a clenched fist on his bonnet.

Press agrees with my scepticism that Japan is whaling with one eye on a future Antarctic carve-up and guffaws at the suggestion Australia just cares about whales to protect its own interests in the frozen continent – he's long been a proponent for greater government engagement there. And he's not the only one: following a 2011 Lowy Institute report urging the Australian government to take a more assertive approach to its Antarctic stewardship, in 2013 the Australian Strategic Policy Institute released its own report imploring the Abbott government to invest more in Antarctica. 'We run our Antarctic program on the smell of an oily rag,' the Institute's deputy director, Anthony Bergin, said at the time. 'For 2013–14, its overall budget is $169 million, an 8 per cent cut from 2012–13.'

A little later in our conversation, Press raises an index finger, leans in and speaks *sotto voce*, three signs I've learned to interpret over the past three weeks as meaning he's about to divulge something interesting: 'One night a few years ago [in Hobart] – after too many sakes, of course – my Japanese colleagues told me their pollies were very close to pulling out from Antarctica for good after the tsunami.'

The disaster, the scientists told Press, presented an acceptable, face-saving exit for their pariah program. Northeast Honshu's coastal communities had been devastated, requiring the state to pool its resources for years to come: research whaling didn't figure in this national rebuilding narrative, and nor would its voters expect it to. Indeed, when the tsunami struck on 11 March 2011, the *Nisshin* raced from the Southern Ocean to the Tohoku littoral, where it helped distribute emergency aid.

'So what happened?'

Press relaxes back into his wicker chair. His voice springs back to life. 'They say Watson came out harder than ever after the tsunami and backed them into a corner. They say their politicians felt they had no choice but to keep going down there.'

When I get back to my hostel I open my laptop and bring up that poem Paul Watson wrote the day of the tsunami.

Tsunami
Neptune's voice rolled like thunder thru the sky
Angrily he smote the deep seabed floor
From the shore echoed mankind's mournful cry

... The sea rose up and struck fast for the shore
From out of the East with the rising sun
The sea's fearful wrath burst upon the land
With little time to prepare or to run
Against a power no human can stand

Watson has vehemently denied that the poem implies karmic retribution for Japan's whale and dolphin hunters. In response to a wave of criticism, he penned an op-ed in the *Huffington Post* three days later: 'This earthquake struck Japan purely on the basis of geography and geology ... What has happened in Japan is horrific and how we respond to it reveals the integrity of our hearts.'

Tony Press hadn't heard of Watson's tsunami poem, nor had anybody I raised it with in Japan. But whatever you make of its meaning, its timing was spectacularly tactless – it was a lesson, as one online commenter pointed out, in what the Japanese call *kiyomanai*: 'can't read the feeling'.

THEM

According to its website, today's Eden Whale Festival is 'Australia's premier whale celebration'. In half an hour there's going to be a street parade; the artisanal market, ocean cruises, and kiddies' treasure hunt got underway this morning. The whole thing, the site boasts, culminates tonight with the 'Whale Song Gig' before a curtain-drawing firework display. I'll have to take their word for it – I'm at the Taiji Whale Festival, which runs on the same weekend.

In the dusty gravel car park hosting Japan's premier whale-eating celebration, perhaps 500 locals peruse a horseshoe of stalls selling chicken satay skewers, octopus balls and, of course, the star of the show, whales: on the barbie, in cans, in deep-fried nuggets, in broth and in jerky.

A temporary stage has been erected, and throughout the day traditional drumming and dances will be performed in homage to Taiji's net-whaling history. Of more interest to the kids are the eight dolphin-hunting vessels, two of which fly the Rising Sun flag – it seems Sea Shepherd isn't the only one beating the drums of war – giving ten-minute pleasure cruises out past the heads and around a small island lighthouse. We head out in convoy – Rising Suns taut in the breeze and seawater sloshing over the shallow gunwales – past five floating pontoons holding dolphins. When we round the

233

island and make for Taiji, a group of fishermen under the light-house waves to us; the skipper on my boat takes off his baseball cap and waves back.

Onshore, I'm alerted to a tent where women with hankies on their heads are serving JARPA II whale meat from a giant pot. I ask a teenage boy in patronisingly slow English if he likes eating Antarctic minkes, but I'm not sure whether he understands me. In any case, his reply is pertinent: 'It's free.' As it should be. All I can think is that Kyodo Senpaku must be trying to make space at the bottom of its freezers for the influx of meat at the end of whaling season that they won't be able to sell. Submerged in bowls of broth and skeins of udon noodles, the strips of meat are the colour of Hugo Chávez's forehead after he'd lain in state for three days – and probably as tough. I fish out a couple of enoki mushrooms and chuck the rest in the bin. Several people before me have done the same. What started life swimming around the Southern Ocean now looks destined to end up as chum for the sharks of the North Pacific.

As I pass the ICR's tent, I see a sign fluttering like a knight's standard. It translates as 'Research whaling: go get 'em, boys!' If there exists a more succinct admission of what Japan's Antarctic whaling program has become, I can't imagine it.

*

To recap, Japan continues to defy Australia either:

a) Because it is conducting scientific whaling; or

b) Because it is conducting 'scientific whaling' (nudge, wink).

The problem is that we look for a reason that's rational. But there's another choice so obvious it seems to have been dismissed:

c) Because it's good politics.

Populism has rarely been based on rationality.

Junichi Sato recoils when I tell him about the festival – the Rising Sun flags, the binned research meat, the jingoistic ICR slogan. 'Nowadays, it really is all about nationalism,' the executive director of Greenpeace Japan tells me at his Tokyo office. 'So I don't want to call it scientific whaling or even commercial whaling; it's more like *patriotic* whaling. It doesn't really matter how much money they lose, it's just a matter of continuing, or not being willing to stop.'

Sato, an attentive man with a thin face and defiant tuft of Astro Boy hair, knows only too well the place of Antarctic whaling in Japanese nationalism. Along with colleague Toru Suzuki, he forms the 'Tokyo Two' – anti-whaling activists who in 2008 went under-cover to track and intercept a box labelled 'cardboard' that was unloaded from the *Nisshin Maru*. They'd been tipped off by a whaling whistleblower that the twenty-three kilograms of Antarc-tic whale meat the package actually contained had been embezzled by Fisheries Agency staff before it could reach the ICR, and that black marketeering was rife inside the whaling program.

Sato and Suzuki reported the incident to the police and held a press conference with their loot to publicly embarrass the Fisheries Agency. A month later the Tokyo public prosecutor's office dropped its embezzlement investigation – and charged the Tokyo Two with theft and trespass. They pleaded not guilty to both charges on grounds of acting in the public interest; they were eventually con-victed and sentenced to one year in jail, suspended for three years.

Before that, Sato and Suzuki were held without charge for twenty-three days and allege they were tied to chairs, questioned without lawyers and routinely interrogated for up to twelve hours at a time – allegations echoed by a UN human rights working group on arbitrary detention and Amnesty International. Toru

Suzuki claims his interrogators compared him to the Aum Shinrikyo cult, perpetrators of the 1995 sarin gas attack on the Tokyo subway that left thirteen commuters dead. Both men were labelled unpatriotic by many of their compatriots. 'Even by my parents!' Sato exclaims.

But it is the Fisheries Agency's more recent attitude towards the incident that Sato thinks indicates a shift in its stance on research whaling. In late 2010 – two years after it had denied corruption within its ranks and a police investigation had cleared its whalers of any wrongdoing – the agency made an unprovoked apology, publicly admitting that five officials were being reprimanded for receiving more than $3000 worth of meat at the end of the 2007–08 Antarctic season. 'I deeply apologise for this act in which officials took whale meat,' Fisheries Agency spokesman Toyohiko Ota said at a press conference. 'It's an act for which we will lose credibility. We will take prevention measures so it will never happen again.' Looking distinctly chastised, Ota bowed – slowly – before the cameras.

While this was not a confession of embezzlement as such, and it's a fraction of the meat alleged to have been flogged on the black market – 'One crew member would take home 500 to 600 kilograms [of whale meat] as if it's normal,' one whistleblower told ABC's Mark Willacy – it was nonetheless a surprising development for the Tokyo Two.

'I thought it was a kind of changing moment,' Sato explains, hands tightly clasped on the table between us. 'In the past, if [JARPA II] was criticised, the Fisheries Agency would never apologise, right? From that point I thought maybe some people from inside the Fisheries Agency, they were not really interested in continuing whaling, and *maybe* some parts of the Fisheries Agency are actually against [it].'

Sato believes the Fisheries Agency is privately sick of being made to wear the research-whaling dunce hat at international negotiations on matters of *actual* food security and economic importance to Japan – most notably the conservation of the world's tuna fishery. He thinks the admission of corruption may have been a way of starting a face-saving retreat from the Southern Ocean.

Soon after the apology and the promise that those responsible were being reprimanded, the management of the Fisheries Agency changed. What had been a top tier stacked with pro-whaling executives was being replaced; Masanori Miyahara, suspected by Sato to be against Antarctic whaling, is now its deputy director-general.

'I can feel that he was really frustrated because of the pressure coming from the whaling issue,' says Sato, 'because then that's basically preventing him from negotiating in a good manner with other countries on the tuna negotiations.'

Sato has provided a neat segue to my next question: what does he think of the widely held theory that the Fisheries Agency doesn't want to give in on whaling for fear of it having a domino effect on the killing of other species?

'I think that was the case before.' But nowadays, Sato says, given that much of the tuna fishing is done by Chinese, Taiwanese and European vessels, 'the Fisheries Agency is now on the side of the conservationists, because they need to make sure that the smaller numbers of Japanese [vessels] can take good tuna to sell it to Japan.'

The Fisheries Agency is now on the side of the conservationists: it's a startling assertion from a conservationist who has spent his career campaigning against the environmental profligacy of the Fisheries Agency. But it also makes sense.

Up until a decade ago Japan was the bullyboy of tuna fishing, accused by Australia and New Zealand, at a UN Convention on the

Law of the Sea tribunal in 2000, of encroaching on their quotas for southern bluefin using a familiar argument: a loophole that allowed 'research' fishing in excess of Japan's allocated annual share of 6065 tonnes. That tribunal ruled it didn't have jurisdiction on the matter; however, a 2006 report by the Commission for the Conservation of Southern Bluefin found Japan had illegally caught $6 billion worth of tuna in the previous twenty years, this time because of under-reported catches. The report speculated that if Japan had stuck to its quota, the stock would be presently five times larger. And that's just for southern bluefin.

But now there's a bigger kid on the block. Taiwan has become the principal fisher of tuna in the Pacific, a ground accounting for one-third of the global tuna catch and an industry worth $1.9 billion a year. According to Greenpeace, between 2007 and 2012 the total volume of new Taiwanese purse seiners being put out to sea was five times that of Japan, fourteen times that of China and thirty-eight times that of South Korea.

'So Japan really needs to focus,' says Sato, 'saying to Taiwanese vessels, you know, "Please don't overfish." To some extent Japan really wants some of the conservation manners in place.'

There are signs this is already happening. In July 2013, when the twenty-five member states of the Commission for the Conservation of Antarctic Marine Living Resources met in Bremerhaven to discuss the proposal of the world's largest marine park in the Ross Sea, it was Russia and Ukraine – not Japan – that scuttled the plan, inconsistent with the popular belief *chez* Sea Shepherd that Tokyo is somehow sneaking its way into Antarctic fisheries by very loudly, very publicly whaling there.

So what's stopping the Fisheries Agency from pulling the plug on JARPA II and concentrating its efforts on tuna management?

Sato smiles at my naivety. 'Nationalism is huge in this country. It's the politicians – *they* are demanding [the] Fisheries Agency to continue. That's why they are giving loans to the ICR and Kyodo Senpaku that they really don't need to pay back.'

'Because it's politically popular?'

That wry smile vanishes; Sato nods and slowly takes his hands off the table. 'In Japan, I think whales and whaling are totally different things. People love whales; people love to go dolphin watching. But when you say *whaling*, then people have a totally different idea – it's nothing about conservation and so on, it's more about Japanese culture. It's not just whaling but other issues which relates to the culture – or is supposed to be about the culture – then people tend to be quite conservative. When people outside of Japan try to criticise it, automatically, people will defend it.'

One half of the Tokyo Two is filling in the blanks before my eyes. 'When politicians in this country want to avoid criticism,' he continues, 'they say "tradition". For Japanese politicians it is kind of a magical word.'

*

'Go get 'em, boys!' The slogan reminds me of *Team America*, the puppet piss-take of Bush-era military interventionism brought to you by the creators of *Whale Whores* ('America: fuck, yeah!'). But this is no piss-take.

I've read that in the early '90s, when the Clinton administration was criticising Norway's commercial whaling industry, the locals responded by holding a giant public whale barbeque – on the Fourth of July. Nobody I spoke to at the Taiji Whale Festival was aware that at the precise moment they were harpooning majestic giants of the deep-fryer with toothpicks, Aussie kids dressed as crêpe-paper humpbacks were sweating their way up Eden's main street, 8000 kilometres to the south. It was probably just a coincidence.

What they were all aware of was when the Taiji festival started: 1986. Taiji had 300 years to publicly celebrate Wada Kakuemon's invention, but it chose to start in the year the moratorium on commercial whaling came into force.

Japan, a hermit kingdom for over 200 years, and a country which – in my great-grandfather's lifetime – summarily executed foreigners shipwrecked on its coast, has never needed encouragement to reflect on its differences from others. 'It is almost an article of faith among Japanese that their culture is unique,' writes the Dutch journalist Karel van Wolferen. 'Not in the way that all cultures are unique, but somehow uniquely unique, ultimately different from all others.' Kumi Kato agrees: 'I think Japanese people definitely love to play that up, the myth that they are mysterious and impossible for outsiders to understand.' They even have a word for it: *nihonjinron* ('theory of Japanese cultural specificity').

Whaling is proof of nihonjinron. It's a practice that – if you read the Australian papers – only Japan does. Never mind that relatively few Japanese people are involved in the practice or that it is historically a parochial tradition, the restructuring of whaling as a state enterprise since the IWC moratorium has turned this once local issue into a national one. The 'boys' from the ICR are representing Japan on the world stage, and whaling seems to have been embraced as a national symbol only when it was challenged by outsiders.

Successive Japanese IWC commissioners have argued that their whalers are unfairly singled out: why are they not allowed to hunt non-endangered minkes in their own waters when Alaskan Inupiat are allowed to hunt endangered bowheads? Why can't the four towns of Taiji, Abashiri, Wadaura and Ayukawa be allowed to hunt whales for cultural reasons when a handful of far-eastern Russian towns can hunt gray whales because they are aboriginal?

The answer, they suggest, is Western racism, a claim that easily gains traction in a society where most people are baffled at how anyone could view a whale differently from a pig or a cow. The anti-whaling movement, then, is seen as a vehicle for broader criticism of their way of life ('cultural imperialism') or even jealousy over their success: 'The more economic progress Japan achieves,' wrote historian Shichibei Yamamoto in 1986, 'the more the whaling issue escalates.'

This singling out of Japan may actually strengthen the pro-whaling cause and prolong the myth of a pan-prefecture 'whale-eating tradition'; perversely, by focusing its sights on one of many whaling nations, the anti-whaling movement serves to reinforce notions of Japanese exceptionalism that unify the nation.

The environmental anthropologist Arne Kalland argued that eating whale has become a defining feature of Japanese identity, not because every Japanese person does it, but because outsiders reject it. 'The anti-whaling campaigns,' he wrote, 'have turned whale meat into a symbol for Japanese culture, and eating whale meat has acquired a new meaning: it has become a ritual act through which the partakers express their belonging to the Japanese tribe, not only to the local community as before.' Kalland wrote that back in 1998, when some people other than centenarians and Taiji tightarses looking for a free lunch actually ate the by-product of scientific whaling. Junichi Sato didn't fail to remind me that the popularity of whale meat is probably now at its lowest level since World War II.

Yet the popularity of the Antarctic whaling program seems stronger than ever. Successive newspaper polls inside Japan show widespread, cross-generational support for research whaling.

When in December 2012 Shinzo Abe became the first Japanese prime minister since 1948 to be returned to office after a stint in the political wilderness, the Parliamentary League for the Promotion of Whaling became synonymous with the cabinet, with its high-profile members including the PM himself. The vast majority of the league's nearly 100 members represent electorates with no ties, past or present, to whaling. And, as Sato pointed out, the fact that JARPA II now enjoys the benefit of national subsidies removes any pretence that the program be expected to pay for itself.

During my visit to Rakuno Gakuen University, I follow Jun Morikawa's advice and ask five students – aged between nineteen and twenty-four – their views on whaling. None of them likes whale meat: Natsuka, a cherub-faced 23-year-old, with ribbons in her hair and a SARS mask over her mouth, tells me that ten years ago her junior high school attempted to serve the meat as a special treat on the last day of term. 'I refused to eat it,' Natsuka says. 'When I think of whales I don't think of food.' She tells me her twenty-five classmates also refused to eat it, and it was never served to them again. By contrast, she says her grandpa (aged eighty-three) likes to eat whale meat, but her mum and dad (forty-eight and fifty) only sometimes do.

But here's the thing. I also ask the group if they think Japan should stop whaling. Not one kid thinks they should. When I ask why, Natsuka concentrates intensely, waiting until she's found the right words before she says them. 'I don't like Sea Shepherd,' she tells me. 'They are … extremely aggressive.' A 2009 survey of 529 Japanese youth aged between fifteen and twenty-six, conducted by the University of Tasmania's Julia Bowett and Pete Hay, exposed the same distinction. Their findings squared with their anecdotal evidence that 'many Japanese students residing in both Japan and

Australia have stated that the hostility shown to Japan by anti-whaling nations and environmental groups has pushed them towards an acceptance of whaling'. Repeatedly, survey respondents admitted to a lack of interest in eating whale themselves, despite seeing Japan 'as a "victim" of western cultural imperialism, precisely the view generated by the GOJ [Government of Japan] and Japanese media'.

Perhaps it's not whaling itself that matters but the act of resistance it represents. The reaction of Jun Morikawa's students, the drunken revelation of Tony Press's colleagues, the ICR sign at the Taiji Whale Festival, the hostility towards Australians in Ayukawa: all suggest that an attack on whaling is interpreted as an attack on Japan itself. Toshihiko Abe, the suicidal whaler from Ayukawa, has become the embodiment of the nation: an average bloke just trying to live his life; a Japanese incarnation of *The Castle*'s Darryl Kerrigan. Japan isn't pro-whaling. It's anti-anti-whaling.

HIGH TIDE

It's the last week of a four-year case to resolve a quarter-century dispute. Under a sky slashed by contrails, my boots clap along their now familiar commute: over tram tracks and along canals; left at the Javanese restaurant with the faded soccer posters and through the mall with the pouting chavs; right at the roundabout commemorating Waterloo and across the bridge linking the city centre to the diplomatic quarter, seagulls below bobbing amid discarded French fries and cigarette butts.

I'm early for court and first in the pressroom. Fifteen sets of headphones are neatly arranged on the one central table; the TV shows a frozen ICJ logo, Lady Justice on top of the world. I dreamily watch a stand of chestnut trees outside swaying in seeming slow-motion, like seagrass underwater.

'Hello.' A security guard is standing in the doorway. I haven't seen him before.

'Hello ...'

'This is my first day here – do you know if those guys from TV are here?'

'Which guys from TV? There was a guy from TVNZ here last week but I'm not sure if he'll be in today.'

'No, no. I mean those guys who have their own show and make war on Japanese ships!'

*

It's a closed session. The rumour being spread by a Dutch freelancer is that there's been a security breach, but when I ask the court's PR guy what's going on, he replies only with sarcasm that there's 'not enough legroom' today. Like a goalkeeper alone at his net, Payam Akhavan stands before an empty public gallery to critique last week's proceedings.

'It would not be an exaggeration,' he exaggerates, 'to say that Australia's case now hangs by a thread.' His courtroom counterparts, Akhavan claims, have spent much time pointing out that the scientific community is divided on the merit of JARPA II. Big deal, he says: Article VIII merely requires the program to have 'scientific purpose'. The question before the court, continues Akhavan, is not whether Japan could improve its scientific research, but whether its research is 'commercial whaling in disguise'.

Akhavan says Japan has had to defend itself against 'baseless accusations' of bad faith and defiance against collective regulation by the IWC. He counters that if Australia had neither abruptly rejected the IWC's Proposed Consensus Decision in 2010 nor brought this case – in other words, had Australia expressed the slightest willingness to compromise – this dispute would likely already have been resolved.

The Proposed Consensus Decision that Akhavan is referring to was backed by Greenpeace, the WWF and some anti-whaling nations, including its sponsor, the United States. Japan would phase out its Southern Ocean 'scientific' whaling over a ten-year period in return for limited commercial quotas in its own waters. Iceland and Norway would also be assigned commercial quotas by the IWC instead of unilaterally setting them. It was controversial in that it allowed limited commercial whaling in the Southern Ocean

Sanctuary, but the deal's proponents saw it as a pragmatic way to break the IWC's deadlock while ultimately reducing whale kills, doing away with the controversy of 'research' whaling and bringing Norway, Japan and Iceland back under the tent of multilateralism.

For Australia, the ideological regression it represented was insupportable. 'We believe that whales are worth more alive than dead,' then environment minister Peter Garrett said. After having initially granted Japan a November deadline to end JARPA II before he pursued litigation, Kevin Rudd unexpectedly announced Japan would be taken to the ICJ six months earlier – in the month before the compromise deal would be debated at the IWC. 'We knew he had his finger on the trigger,' a source who worked at the Department of Prime Minister and Cabinet at the time told me. 'We just didn't know when he was going to pull it.'

When the IWC met, the deal, two years in the making, fell apart. Japan questioned the timing of Australia's decision to bring forward its litigation; former New Zealand prime minister Geoffrey Palmer, the deal's chief negotiator, who had earlier praised Japan's willingness to compromise, cautioned his government against joining in the winner-takes-all gamble with their counterparts across the ditch.

Akhavan's reference to Australia's unwillingness to compromise reminds me of something Tony Press told me weeks earlier. I'd wondered aloud how hard Australia had tried to resolve this dispute behind closed doors before bringing it to court; he told me to ask Peter Bridgewater, Australia's IWC commissioner for most of the 1990s. As Akhavan moves on to the irony that Australia is only able to accuse Japan of commercial whaling in disguise because Tokyo has not left the IWC and started unilateral commercial whaling, I flip through my diary to where I'd made a note to contact Peter Bridgewater. I underline it.

*

The press are all back on the last day to file their case-is-adjourned pieces to camera in front of the ICJ's rosebed and fluttering UN flag: the ABC, the BBC, SBS; Reuters, AAP and a dozen Japanese journos dressed in a uniform of ill-fitting shirts, and ties that look as if they were birthday presents from mothers-in-law.

Standing at the rostrum, Koji Tsuruoka looks tired. His voice cracks and wavers; I'm sure his hair wasn't this grey four weeks ago. In stilted French, Japan's deputy foreign minister outlines the esteem in which his nation holds international law and thanks the court for the opportunity to clarify the nature of JARPA II in such a venerable institution.

But then his speech changes to English, and with it comes a menacing tone.

He repeats a maxim from his opening speech: '*Pacta sunt servanda*: what you have agreed, you are bound to observe. What you have not agreed, however, does not bind you.' After taking the court through the meaning and importance of multilateralism, he finishes with a shot across Australia's bow: 'But what will happen to stable multilateral frameworks when ... one morning suddenly you find your state bound by a policy of the majority, and the only way out is to leave such an organisation? Japan, a country that places importance on the rule of law, trusts that the outcome of this case will uphold stable multilateralism.'

Did he just say that if Japan loses this thing, they are going to shrug their shoulders and unilaterally resume commercial whaling? When I ask Tsuruoka ten minutes later, in the press scrum outside, if Japan is preparing to leave the IWC, he plays a dead bat: 'The Japanese government does not predict what the court could say. We will wait for a decision that the court themselves have the authority of supplying to us. Second-guessing what they could say is not a proper role for Japan to play at this time.'

In the courtroom, when Tsuruoka finishes, President Tomka peers down his nose to declare the oral proceedings complete. The court will now retire for deliberation.

I slip off my headphones and turn to my right. 'So, you got a tip for me, Tony?'

'A tip for your book? Shit, no – you'd have to have Paul Watson's ego to call this one!'

US

What does one wear to a coffee date with an ultra nationalist? I play it safe: sky-blue business shirt (unbuttoned to the sternum to maximise chest-hair exposure and, ergo, machismo), khaki pants (hopefully that toothpaste stain will be mistaken for a war correspondent's wound), Rossi boots (polished enough that he won't think I'm a radical extremist but not so much that he thinks I'm a pinko lefty). And though it's only 3pm, beer seems the wise choice. When my ultra nationalist arrives he's dressed like the Purple Wiggle. He orders an iced coffee.

Here's my hypothesis: We need Them, and They need Us. Because when I ask Atsushi Nakahira – resplendent in mauve skivvy, matching bumbag and indigo sneakers – if he likes eating whale, he doesn't even bother to lie for the liberal Western press.

'It's not bad,' he shrugs, tapping a cigarette from its pack and lighting up. 'If you want to eat it, fine. But there's better things to eat right now: American beef, Australian beef, chicken, pork ... If there was nothing to eat, like after the war, then maybe ... But at the moment there's no reason to eat it.'

Hardly a glowing endorsement from a self-proclaimed patriot; for Nakahira-san, whale meat belongs in your World War III bunker on the same shelf as Chase's Spam cache. It's that well-done goanna to Crocodile Dundee's can of baked beans – you can eat it, but it tastes like shit.

We're in an empty café in Shingu, an industrial town of low-rise grottiness half an hour's drive up the coast from Taiji. It's a week after Halloween but cardboard jack-o'-lanterns still hang off the potted palm tree behind Nakahira, who's a 54-year-old council worker with big brown eyes and mysteriously white teeth for some-one about to smoke four cigarettes in forty-five minutes.

My fixer had neglected to mention the children's-entertainer get-up when he told me, 'This guy is a badass.' But he did tell me that, along with his small band of minutemen (their business card trans-lates as 'We fight for the children'), Nakahira has earned a reputa-tion for making life hell for Sea Shepherd's Cove Guardians: blocking their cars with his own, yelling at them in the street, disrupting them from filming dolphin hunters heading out to sea and filming them himself. He is one of the people who makes life hell for Masaru Zukeran, the cop charged with keeping the two sides apart.

But my hypothesis proves to be overly simplistic. When I ask Nakahira if his beef with Sea Shepherd is motivated by foreigners meddling in Japanese affairs, he's equally indifferent. 'No, that's fine,' he says, shrugging once more, the cigarette now precariously hanging from his bottom lip like Dan Aykroyd's character in *Ghostbusters*. 'This is a democratic country. As long as they don't break the law, it's okay.'

Does he have a hatred for the individual activists, then?

'Scott West [the Cove Guardians' leader] is a serious guy, a man's man, I have a lot of respect for him ...'

Now I'm confused. He confronts Sea Shepherd but he respects them and respects their right to stop the Taiji dolphin hunt?

'The thing that made him most angry is that movie, *The Cove*,' interjects my interpreter, Jay, letting my interviewee smoke in peace for a while. Two years after it was filmed, *The Cove* was shown at the 2009 Tokyo International Film Festival. Nakahira sees the decision by the Tokyo government to green-light the screening as tacit approval of its content. He thinks the Taiji townsfolk shouldn't have even let it get that far. 'He keeps using this word to describe them,' says Jay. 'I don't know what the word means – "*hikyo*" – he says people in Japan these days are always "hikyo", especially the ones from Taiji …'

When Nakahira realised nobody else was going to stop *The Cove* premiere, he tried to do it – and subsequently spent three weeks in prison without charge.

'The worst thing about Japanese people is that they never say anything,' Nakahira says, after having a good chuckle about his arrest. 'They just swallow it: hikyo, hikyo, hikyo …'

Does he wish Japanese people were stronger then?

'*Soo desu!*' ('You got it!')

Like before the war? I venture cautiously.

'*Sooooooooooooo desu!* After the war,' he elaborates, 'we gave up. We're too weak now; we just kowtow to white people … it's really embarrassing, all this hikyo … America crushed the spirit of the Japanese: now it's just money, money, money …'

I think I get it: he wants Japan to be *like* Sea Shepherd. 'And before the war?'

'We had confidence. We were proud to say we were Japanese. We had the heart to say we were Japanese …'

I point out that this is exactly how Japan behaves at the IWC.

'You're right; it's good. We have a strong opinion there; we don't waffle. It costs us a lot – paying off all those little countries, but I think it's worth it.'

When Atsushi Nakahira eventually leaves – in a hatchback with a baby seat – Jay and I look up that word.

Hikyo: Cowardice. Submissiveness. Meekness. Servility.

*

Since returning to the Japanese premiership in December 2012, Shinzo Abe has made a good fist of annoying just about everyone in the neighbourhood. His first move of external aggression was a mere domestic formality: announcing his cabinet. Fourteen of Japan's nineteen ministers belong to the Parliamentary League for Going to Worship Together at Yasukuni, a group that, despite its play school–sounding name, pays its respects to war criminals executed and interred at Tokyo's controversial Yakusuni shrine. 'To describe the new government as "conservative",' opined the *Economist* upon the allocation of ministerial portfolios, 'hardly captures its true character. This is a cabinet of radical nationalists.'

Abe seemed to be making a statement: hikyo no more. Soon after he was re-elected, the new prime minister told the Diet: 'we will deal sternly with any case where there is an intrusion into [Japanese] territorial waters or any other intrusion.' To ram home his message, he posed for photos inside a tank decked out in combat fatigues – the first Japanese leader in uniform since the war.

Under the conditions of its 1947 US-drafted constitution, Japan surrendered its right to maintain air, sea or land forces. Instead, the Self-Defence Forces (SDF) were created in the 1950s as a kind of reservist police force, only allowed to act if Japan was first attacked. But with 230,000 active personnel (they're not called soldiers), a bulging weapons box and even a non-combative role in the Iraq War, the SDF is increasingly looking more like a chained tiger. Abe wants to set it free.

The scion of a hardline nationalist family, Abe has never hidden his desire for Japan to move on from its postwar penance and take a more assertive approach to international relations. 'There's a growing view among younger Japanese that they're sick of apologising for the sins of their grandfathers and that Japan should now be able to defend itself like everyone else,' Michael Heazle of Griffith University's Asia Institute tells me over the phone.

Heazle calls Abe a nationalist, but only in the sense that he wants to secure his nation in line with the contemporary realties of post–Cold War Asia. Heazle is quick to dampen the sensationalist journalist in me: 'To think that Japan is suddenly going to go back to what it was in the 1930s is absurd,' he says. 'This is a mature liberal democracy.'

And whether the man with the barn-owl face and perpetually tousled hair would even commit Japan to combat is another matter entirely, but for now the prospect of a militarily stronger Japan is proving an electoral boon. In a country that tends to go through prime ministers like toothbrushes, Abe's popularity was 70 per cent after a year in the job; since his party gained control of the upper house in July 2013, he now looks safe until at least 2016.

If Shinzo Abe is looking for baddies – real and imagined – in order to get his hands on a real army, it makes me wonder: does he regard Sea Shepherd as a headache, or a year-end bonus?

*

'The main reason I am getting involved in this issue is I am a patriot,' Shun Fujiki tells me in Americanised English when we meet in a suburban Tokyo *izakaya*. 'It's the same as China: I don't feel we can be friends with China – a commie is a commie.'

A commie is a commie? What is this, M*A*S*H?

I've progressed to a dinner date with a right-wing nationalist, but if Atsushi Nakahira wasn't quite what I expected, Shun Fujiki is everything and more.

A dumpy man with the face of a pugilist who decided to hang up his gloves one fight too late, Fujiki is a wealthy entrepreuner in the amplifier export business. In Shun Fujiki's Weltanschauung, commies are commies, Russians aren't to be trusted (former commies), North Koreans are commies (and thus commies), South Koreans are 'born swindlers', and the 900,000 Koreans from both ends of the peninsula living in Japan are all leaching off the system – or breaking into your house/car/wife. But it's another enemy of the state that's increasingly taking up his time.

'I've found a lot of similarities between the whaling issue and some other issues for exploiting Japan,' he explains over soba and steins, with a backdrop of tinkling piano music. 'I got involved with this issue because I got involved with comfort woman issue – have you ever heard [of] that?'

I reluctantly nod.

'We call it victimhood business,' he continues, leaning into me like he's revealing some kind of elixir. 'There is, you know, absolutely no victims, but some woman is making as victim and then there is guys trying to support asking for donations! That's why I had thought [of the] similarities on these issues – not just these two issues, but a lot of other issues.'

'What are some more?'

'The Nanking Massacre.'

I immediately regret asking that question and return the conversation to whaling before Fujiki can tip his bucket of whitewash over me.

Sea Shepherd, he tells me, is part of a wider effort by canny entrepreneurs – states and citizens – to take advantage of Japan's postwar passivity for their own gain. 'Basically, Paul Watson is a smart guy; he exploits those suckers around the world, right? So they are just emotional wrecks, so they just care for animals like the whales and the dolphins – dolphins looks like a smiling face, you know. That's why he can get the money from the suckers.'

His views are almost identical to Nakahira's: it's not foreign interference that's the problem but the fact that Japanese people are too timid to resist it. 'As a nation of Japan, the people are very quiet. I don't believe that they fought with [against] the Allies in the World War Second [sic],' he says. The whaling itself is secondary to the defiance it represents: 'I don't care if the whale meat is available in the market or not – I don't eat so often. But we don't criticise the kangaroo hunting – we understand it's culture, it's tradition'.

He thinks Japan needs to start sticking up for itself before it's too late: 'If we behave like this now in Japan we will be defeated again, because the people are careless or defenceless.'

Shun Fujiki is in favour of Japan remilitarising to ensure deterrence through armament – 'passive, not active' – and he's in favour of public displays of patriotism. He has a small plastic Rising Sun flag on his briefcase and flies big nylon versions at rallies with Zaitokukai, a 10,000-strong nationalist group that calls for the expulsion of Japan's Korean community.

He tells me that this summer he's organised rallies in Tokyo, Osaka, Nagasaki and on his native island of Kyushu to 'educate Japanese on the whaling issue'. By 'whaling issue' he means both Taiji's dolphin drives and Antarctic whaling: they are marches to protest Sea Shepherd rather than to celebrate whaling and dolphin hunting.

Fujiki fires up an aging laptop and navigates to the YouTube page for Tony Morano, aka 'Propaganda Buster', his American friend who helped organise the rallies and who shares Fujiki's antipathy for postmodern pirates. There are hundreds of poorly researched diatribes, mostly about Sea Shepherd but also on what Morano calls 'the commies in China' and 'the Korean comfort women comedians'.

I later interview Morano on Skype in an effort to glean how a white, retired telco middle-manager from Houston came to espouse the political convictions of Japan's wartime emperor, Hirohito. He tells me he's a patriot not of Japan but America: because Paul Watson has a US passport as well as a Canadian one, Morano wants the world to know that Sea Shepherd doesn't act in the name of all Americans. How that justifies historical revisionism in the name of imperial Japan is beyond me.

Getting increasingly drunk in an increasingly empty izakaya, Fujiki and I watch one of Morano's episodes, filmed a few months earlier in Taiji itself. In it the Propaganda Buster, a squib of a man with a slack bottom lip and Elmer Fudd's voice, teeters along a sea-wall where three young Sea Shepherds are filming the harbour. They show remarkable self-restraint as Morano starts berating them, Fujiki playing the role of a Hollywood lackey, hovering behind his master and oafishly echoing every putdown.

It's juvenile in the extreme and I'm tempted to dismiss these videos as the ramblings of a lunatic fringe – most have barely 2000 or 3000 views, and several comments point out that rather than bust propaganda, Morano propagates it. But later I watch versions of the same videos with Japanese subtitles added by Shun Fujiki: the most popular one has 458,616 views. Not exactly Nek Minnit, but Japanese people are watching this stuff, and if YouTube thumbs-ups are currency for legitimacy in this day and age, they support it.

The last train for downtown Tokyo left hours ago, so Shun Fujiki offers to drive me back. I close my eyes and pull my seatbelt taut to form a pillow; even through my eyelids, the flicker of lights tells me we are passing underneath train tracks, wildly strung above the city like those wire-and-bead roller coasters in the corner of every doctor's waiting room.

'You know, Sam, in Australia you have a lot of immigrants from the South Korea too: they are trying to be a prostitute. Right, Sam?'

I don't even grace that remark with a reply. I'm sick of people who deal in absolute dichotomies: eco-warriors or poachers; scientists or eco-terrorists; floating steaks or minds-in-the-water; patriots or prostitutes. I find the whale wars interesting because in them I see shades of grey: legally, ethically, environmentally, politically. But so many people just see a chequerboard of right and wrong; a point by which they can fix their moral compass.

I don't believe you can make sense of the human experience by compartmentalising everyone into neat boxes. Think you're more compassionate than Shun Fujiki because your gummy bears weren't made from last year's Melbourne Cup winner? He tells me he spent US$100,000 from his own pocket on tsunami rebuilding and spent most weekends in 2011 up north volunteering. After I interview him, I read an article about him flying to America in mid 2013 to donate US$13,000 to tornado-hit Oklahoma as a mark of gratitude for America's fundraising for the disaster in Tohoku.

On the flipside, I find it hard to accept that Shun really thinks Paul Watson's just in Sea Shepherd for the money. Watson's a brilliant businessman, undoubtedly, but living at sea with a bunch of unwashed kids for the best part of thirty years seems a strange way to fritter away your fortune. The day I met him, he told me he'd be prepared to die for a whale. Nothing in his behaviour during the ensuing three months gave me reason to doubt the sincerity of that statement.

It's past 2am when Fujiki drops me at Asakusabashi station. On the street a homeless man is pushing a lasagne of flattened cardboard boxes in a supermarket trolley; I notice that two businessmen staggering out of a bar haven't even loosened their ties. When I round the corner and see the neon sign of my youth hostel, I realise I don't have the code to get inside. I'm cold, drunk and beyond tired, but I'm not yet drunk enough to resign myself to the fact I'll be sleeping rough tonight. To soften the pillow of the pavement and rid my mind of whale huggers and whale hunters, I scull two super-sized beers from a vending machine and toast the fact that here, unlike on the *Steve*, at least I'm allowed to drink.

*

Atsushi Ishii estimates that the tipping point of demand and supply for the JARPA II whale-meat by-product was in 2006. 'The demand in whale meat is so tiny,' he explains, 'that from then it could even not sustain the operation of the scientific whaling crews.'

'As older people started to die?'

'Yes.'

'The ones who were nostalgic about eating whale meat after the war?'

'Uh-huh.'

Ishii is the political scientist who argued that Japan's belligerence at the IWC was aimed at undermining, not achieving, the resumption of commercial whaling. 'And now the situation has changed,' he tells me in the cafeteria of Sendai's Tohoku University. 'The Fisheries Agency, in their mind, they want to pull out from the Antarctic. Because every scientific research cruise to the Antarctic will bring you ¥1 billion [$11.2 million] deficit, in the budget. That's really not sustainable.'

Like Greenpeace Japan's Junichi Sato, he's convinced that while the Fisheries Agency now wants to end research whaling, the politicians – especially the ideological warriors in the current government – are overruling them: 'If it becomes a fight against Sea Shepherd, then it's not really a technical issue for the Fisheries Agency; it's really a political issue.' Like Sato, he thinks Japan's weak media enables the ICR to manipulate footage of Sea Shepherd to strengthen public support for the program.

'So are you saying that Sea Shepherd is merely prolonging—'

'Yes.' Ishii is so confident in his answer he doesn't even hear out my question.

'That what they are doing is counter-productive?'

'Yes. Absolutely. I would imagine that if Sea Shepherd didn't exist at all from 2006, then the whole problem would have disappeared two or three years ago.'

'Because it would allow the Japanese government to retreat without losing face?'

'Uh-huh.'

It's speculation, of course, but it's an opinion I've heard repeated over and again during my time in Japan. Jun Morikawa thought the ICR and Sea Shepherd 'were like the yin and the yang – they need each other'; Simon Wearne says Taiji has been pumped up by the injection of government money Sea Shepherd triggers; Professor Kasuya thought nationalism gave widespread support to the program. Junko Sakuma, an investigative journalist I met in Tokyo, believes the whaling fleet is happy to have the scapegoat of Sea Shepherd as an excuse not to fill its quota – a quota it knows will never be sold anyway.

Ishii nods as he sees me processing what he's said. 'Nowadays they are not so aggressive,' he eventually says. 'So that is a sign that, in their mind, they want to pull out from the Antarctic.' I think of the *Steve*'s bridge, full of activists wearing beanies that say 'Stand by to ram' while whingeing about being nudged; I think of a Catalonian deckhand who told me the captain of the *Nisshin Maru* was 'obviously' trying to kill us, because 'anyone who can kill a whale can kill a human'.

I ask Ishii: 'Is the ICR happy to have the excuse of Sea Shepherd as a reason why their hunt is cut short to minimise losses?'

He nods.

Ishii's views are based on close analysis of the whale wars and the intimate understanding of Japanese society and culture that only belonging to it can bring. An application of his counterfactual analysis suggests he's right. For Japan's Antarctic whaling program to be commercial whaling in disguise, as the Australian government alleges, it must be profitable – which it was during the years of JARPA and the early stages of its successor, but is no longer.

To prove that JARPA II's aim is to show there are enough whales for commercial whaling to resume, as Japan alleges, requires two conditions: that the IWC is concerned there aren't enough minke whales in the Antarctic, and that resuming commercial whaling would be viable on the Japanese market. Neither of these has been met. If the aim is to keep the emphasis on whales instead of fish, the world's environmental police would need to be currently too busy trying to shut down whaling to focus on fishing. Japan's recent focus on conserving tuna stocks and the fact that NGOs already have the resources to intervene against both Japan's fishing and whaling suggest that this isn't the principal reason behind JARPA II's longevity. And for Ishii, Japan's insistence on research whaling actually *increases* the risk of a domino effect, because the tainted reputation of JARPA II's 'science' carries over to global perceptions of the nation's fisheries science – a point Junichi Sato echoed.

The only possible reason left is to pander to right-wing nationalists like Shun Fujiki and Atsushi Nakahira – and left-wing potential voters like Jun Morikawa's students (in Japan, even the Communists oppose Sea Shepherd). Does sticking it to Sea Shepherd have support within the electorate? Yes. Does Japan have a compliant media to spout the government line? Yes. Does it have an audience who don't understand why Australians consider whales special because they have an inherently different view of nature? Yes. But the principal prerequisite of anti-anti-whaling – the necessary condition on which everything else rests – is anti-whaling itself.

*

In 2008 Greenpeace changed its strategy. No longer would it dispatch activists to Antarctica to confront the whalers at sea; instead, it would pursue a low-key effort to reduce the market by creating an anti-whaling groundswell within Japan. In an interview with the *Huffington Post* in 2011, Greenpeace UK executive director John Sauven said, 'We have to say each to their own tactics. We think strategically to fight our battles and we feel that we are winning the battle against whaling by talking to the Japanese themselves. Sea Shepherd are confronting Japanese people aggressively and it is exacerbating nationalism, and actually making it more difficult.'

Paul Watson responded on the Sea Shepherd website two days later: 'What do you mean "we" John? The battle is in the Southern Ocean Whale Sanctuary not in your offices … Sea Shepherd has prevented the slaughter of nearly 3000 whales while Greenpeacers were sitting and eating whale meat with the Japanese to demon-strate so-called sensitivity to Japanese culture.'

Looking beyond the cynical but pragmatic reality that Green-peace and Sea Shepherd are rival NGOs competing for the same donations, the crux of Watson's response is that the only way to dis-mantle Japanese whaling is to smash it – although he is conspicu-ously quiet on Sauven's point about nationalism. I agree with him that Greenpeace isn't stopping Antarctic whaling: when I asked Junichi Sato what Greenpeace had to show for this period of groundswell-building, he mumbled something unconvincing about shopkeepers becoming aware of the outside world's distaste for whaling.

But in order to devise a strategy to stop Japanese whaling, its motive must first be understood. Sea Shepherd aims to sink JARPA II economically by physically stopping it from killing whales, but with the effective nationalisation of the whaling program, money appears to have become irrelevant.

Whether Sea Shepherd likes it or not – 'Culture is the product of an irrational being,' Squid once told me – the organisation is itself the product of a particular culture. Civil disobedience has a long history of enacting change in North America, whether by tipping tea into Boston Harbour or by refusing to give up your seat on a bus. In Japan, a country with no such culture, civil diso-bedience is frowned upon by the populace as immature, and met by the authorities with the full force of the law – just ask the Tokyo Two.

'The anti-whaling movement must recognise that it is them that created the situation, not the Japanese,' Atsushi Ishii says. He has an air of finality, knocking a knuckle against the table to emphasise his point. 'Of course the Japanese government has been good at advertising that this is anti-Japanese and so on, but they [the anti-whaling movement] have made the situation.'

'So what's to be done?'

'I'm always saying that if you just want to exercise your democratic rights and seize the high moral ground, then please go ahead, but if you want to stop whaling, you should do nothing.'

'*Nothing*?'

'Nothing.'

And therein lies the potential problem with direct action: what if 'doing something' for the sake of it is worse than doing nothing at all?

Sea Shepherd spent over $5 million during Operation Zero Tolerance and restricted Japanese whalers to 103 whales. But the victory was pyrrhic if Ishii's analysis is correct.

There's no objective reason to justify the Japanese government's whaling policy, Jun Morikawa told me. Perhaps the anti-whalers should pull the nationalistic rug from under Tokyo's feet and play them at their own game. They want to overturn the moratorium? Go right ahead: the free-market economy would bury this industry. If the Japanese whaling fleet was suddenly bereft of the state sponsorship that the research exemption provides, what private investor in their right mind would go to Antarctica to hunt whales? Depoliticised, one of the longest-running controversies in environmentalism would end.

'The irony is that if the moratorium was lifted in the early '90s like it was supposed to be,' says Michael Heazle, 'Japan would've likely pulled out of the Antarctic years ago.'

Instead, the Australian government took Japan to the highest court in the world for its most politicised case in years.

EPILOGUE

31 March 2014. It's 10am at The Hague and 7pm at the farm where I wrote this book and am now trying to follow the ICJ's ruling on live stream. The NBN is yet to roll out and up these hills; President Peter Tomka has been frozen on my laptop for two minutes now, his oversized white bib splitting the screen.

Night falls amid the rat-a-tat-tat of a restless flycatcher and the chorus of frogs; the live stream flickers to life. Tomka confirms that the Article VIII exemption allows for the 'killing, taking, and treating of whales' in accordance with that article's provisions. Theoretically, then, lethal whaling for scientific research is permissible in Antarctica. First blood to Japan. The feed dies for another two minutes.

I put up with the patchy feed for twenty minutes, until my pocket starts trilling with text messages.

The ICJ has ordered Japan to stop its Antarctic whaling program.

Tomka states that the court need not pass judgment on the scientific merit or importance of the program's objectives to determine its legality. What instead counts is whether such a program is 'for purposes of scientific research'. The court has concluded, twelve judges to four, that Japan's whaling program does not have scientific motives. Tomka's team sees no evidence of feasibility studies on non-lethal means, nor into the possibility of Japan achieving its goals through a decreased lethal take and an increased non-lethal sample size.

The court notes JARPA II was launched before the Scientific Committee's final review of JARPA, further supporting its view that the program is 'not driven by strictly scientific considerations' – a view strengthened by the scant analysis and justification provided for setting the overall sample size. Ironically, by not taking humpbacks and barely any fins, JARPA II is further condemned: the court cites a glaring disparity between the proposed and actual take. Tomka lists three additional aspects of the program that cast doubt on its research claims: its limitless timeframe, its limited scientific output and its lack of collaboration with other Southern Ocean research projects.

It's a more decisive judgment than even the most strident anti-whaler can have legitimately have hoped for.

I contact Japan's PR representative, Noriyuki Shikata, for a response. 'Japan will abide by the court's ruling and uphold its obligation under international law,' he says, before ruling out leaving the IWC.

Will the quota for the North Pacific whaling program be increased to make up the shortfall?

'We consider them separate issues. Today's ruling concerned special permit whaling in the Southern Ocean; Japan maintains committed to analysing and conserving whale stocks in the North Pacific.'

Is this the end of Antarctic whaling or will Japan simply design another Southern Ocean program – a JARPA III – that complies with the ICJ's decision?

'Our delegation will closely consider the findings of the court before making a decision on future developments.'

If that's a caveat, it doesn't deter the Australian public's sense of victory: complementing the text messages from people I haven't heard from in months are media reports and tweets about 'our' whales finally being 'saved'.

The Sunday after the ruling, a montage on the ABC's *Insiders* includes footage of the *Steve*'s crew gathered around a laptop in the mess as they watch their hopes realised. After the ruling, the cameraman turns to the whiteboard in the scullery, which was filled with many flowery motivational messages when I was on board all those months ago. Tonight there is just one.

'We Won.'

*

Is it possible to win a culture war? The longevity of this dispute attests neither to a desire for whale meat in Japan nor to the strength of the environmental and animal rights lobby in Australia; that Tokyo insisted on continuing its program for so long in the face of sustained high-seas confrontation and massive financial losses, and that Canberra cared enough about it to pursue litigation, attests to the totemisation of the same symbol by two nation-states – and a prominent NGO – for mutually exclusive purposes.

Why whales? Because they make Australia look green and they make Japan look Japanese. As long as the stakes are that high, each side is likely to push for nothing less than total victory.

'I think that's part of the problem,' says Peter Bridgewater, Australian commissioner to the IWC from 1990–97 and its chairman from 1995–97. 'There is no winner takes all in this – and there never can be because you're dealing within a legal regime. And rightly or wrongly, the regime is about the regulation of the whaling industry. The fact that there isn't one anymore – and, seriously, nobody wants one, not even Japan – doesn't take away from the fact that that's what the convention is for.'

I've finally tracked Bridgewater down on the Isle of Man, of all places, and we Skype one month after the ruling. Japan has said it will table a new Southern Ocean whaling program, one that complies with the ICJ's findings, at September's IWC meeting, with the hope of resuming lethal sampling in Antarctica in late 2015. In the meantime, its whalers will stick to non-lethal 'observation'. The celebratory mood of the Australian public has given way to the sobering reality that the ruling was against JARPA II, not Antarctic whaling.

Bridgewater expected nothing less. 'The legal basis for Article VIII is now very clear,' he tells me. 'It always was clear, in my view, but having gone through the ICJ wringer, it's clear that it's perfectly possible for states to undertake scientific research. They then did the obvious thing, which is look at this particular problem that's been raised [JARPA II], and they took it to pieces. I don't think anything has necessarily gone away.'

It's refreshing to be talking to a diplomat instead of an activist or a politician, and I ask Bridgewater if the continued stand-off could've been avoided if, while he was Australia's whaling commissioner, the anti-whaling bloc had accepted Japanese overtures for the towns of Taiji, Ayukawa, Abashiri and Wadaura to be granted a similar status to the aboriginal subsistence whalers of Alaska in return for an end to Antarctic whaling.

'Oh, absolutely. The arguments they put forward were logically unchallengeable.' (Bridgewater doesn't share Greenpeace's concerns over the two stocks.) 'But the IWC does not work on logic. It ought to. It pretends to work on science, and actually acts on emotion.'

In Bridgewater's view, the only likely breakthrough is going to happen if Australia and Japan agree to talk in a closed room 'with no keys', each bringing a concession to the table so that a consensus may be achieved. 'And I'm not sure how you can do that,' he admits, 'because the Australian population particularly would not be able to understand why, after being told for twenty years that whales were in danger and they're all going to die and what have you, they are in fact increasing at quite strong rates and if Japan wants to take some whales to feed a population then that's fine.'

As for the Japanese public, Bridgewater thinks they continue to be confused because they see no conservation issue, nor any emotional one, 'because not everybody wants to cuddle the animal like we do'. I agree, and think it's a confusion that is capitalised on by Japan's government every time it portrays the anti-whaling movement as a xenophobic attack on Japan's way of life.

When fisheries minister Yoshimasa Hayashi announces Japan intends to resume lethal 'research' in Antarctica, he does so at a whale-meat tasting event in Tokyo. 'As for unlawful acts of violence committed by anti-whaling organisations,' Hayashi says, as behind him a Rising Sun envelops a stylised minke and whaling vessel, 'we will study counter-measures in line with a new research program from the standpoint of ensuring the safety of the research fleet, researchers and crew members.' Silhouetted in the sun's nationalistic bosom, the ship looks more like a naval destroyer than a catcher boat.

*

Paul Watson is right to say we're eating the oceans alive. According to the United Nations Environment Program (UNEP), up to 80 per cent of the world's primary catch species are being 'exploited beyond or close to their harvest capacity'. A much cited 2006 study published in the journal *Science* warns that at the current rate, the species we consume today will have disappeared by 2048 –

a process of incremental downsizing which the British author Callum Roberts calls our 'collective amnesia'.

Amid this backdrop, the great whales of Antarctica are a welcome aberration. Since being pushed to the brink during the first half of the twentieth century, most baleen species have bounced back in three decades of limited whaling. That some are recovering more slowly than others – the blue and the fin, for example – is because they are collateral damage to broader environmental problems. Blue whales have not been hunted there since the Soviets were cooking the books in the early '70s, and, on average, two fin whales a year were taken during the lifetime of JARPA II.

From an environmental perspective, then, saving the Antarctic's whales from Japan's whalers is about as pressing a concern in 2014 as addressing East Germany's acid rain.

So why does Sea Shepherd, a 'conservation society', emphasise this issue ahead of conserving the Pacific's sharks or the Mediterranean's bluefin tuna? In 2011, Sea Shepherd boasted of spending US$9.2 million on its campaigns, of which US$4.2 million was spent on the Antarctic anti-whaling efforts; just US$1178 was spent helping sea-life affected by the 2010 explosion of the *Deepwater Horizon* oil rig, which spewed 4.9 million barrels of oil into the Gulf of Mexico – history's biggest accidental maritime oil spill.

'Where was Greenpeace,' wondered Tim Flannery in the *Monthly*, 'when the last baiji succumbed? The baiji, a dolphin found only in China's Yangtze River, is the only member of the whale family to have been driven to extinction by humans.' That Flannery needed to add that second sentence is as telling as the point he makes in the first.

Where was Sea Shepherd when Greenpeace *was* publicising arguably the most pressing maritime concern of our time – Arctic oil exploration – when its icebreaker *Arctic Sunrise* was boarded and seized by the Russian Coast Guard in September 2013?

I don't doubt that Sea Shepherd's priorities reflect the public's demand: Grug told me that the day in 2009 when Sea Shepherd released footage from the *Steve*'s helicopter of a minke being harpooned remains the most lucrative in the organisation's history.

'I think it's human nature that you're not going to find a concordance between what people care about and what perhaps most needs our attention,' Flannery tells me a day after the ICJ's ruling. 'So people are always going to care about whales and dolphins more than they care about krill and climate change.' In the lead-up to debating a possible compromise deal, Peter Bridgewater tells me, the IWC secretariat approached Greenpeace and the WWF – then the two biggest anti-whaling NGOs – to gauge their reactions to a possible resumption of limited commercial whaling. 'And their view was, "Actually, there are so many more important issues than whaling [that] we'd really like to spend less resources and less effort on it, but at the moment we can't because the public attention is focused on it."'

With the United Nations' court now on Australia's side, Uncle Bruce doubts the symbolic pull of whales can prompt broader environmental change. 'Because the tide of consumerism and individualism in this country is stronger than the one to protect the environment; in among all the celebrating over the ICJ ruling, I didn't hear anyone say, "Now we can stop the government from allowing tankers through the Great Barrier Reef," or "Now for old-growth logging." Australians care more about their flatscreen TVs and private schools for their kids.'

Twenty minutes after that conversation I'm stopped at traffic lights when my phone chimes with an incoming text message. 'Hi

Sam. Just thought of something that may support your societal observation: Australia is very low in terms of enthusiasm vs money raised. The last campaign was essentially funded by SS Germany. Bruce.'

ACKNOWLEDGMENTS

This book was possible only because I was allowed to run away to sea. I thank the Sea Shepherd Conservation Society for letting me report on Operation Zero Tolerance from the vantage point of the *Steve Irwin*, and, especially, the crew and associates of the *Steve* for sharing their time and stories with me. A few people warrant special mention. Grug, Alex, Giacomo, Elissa, Hillary, Beck, Chase and Mike: irrespective of the job I was there to do and the job you were there to do, it was, in Squid's words, 'fookin' great stoof'.

In Japan, Jun Morikawa deserves singling out for opening so many *shoji* sliding doors – as do Simon Wearne and Kumi Kato. Ryoko Sugio was an accomplice in many of my nefarious schemes in and around Tokyo. Thanks for your interpreting, friendship and tolerance for questions that broke all social mores.

Back home, Tom Griffiths has been a wise source of counsel on this subject since I met him in brilliant sunshine in Copenhagen – and then met him again a few weeks later in a blizzard in Nuuk. Billy Griffiths, another survivor of that snowstorm, enthusiastically read – and constructively critiqued – the manuscript. At *Griffith REVIEW*, thank you, Julianne Schultz, for publishing the piece of reportage that grew into this book. Lying about my identity to the cops is the best career move I've yet made.

At Black Inc., I am profoundly grateful to my publisher and

editor, Chris Feik, for taking a punt on an untested (and, when I first met him, unwashed) writer. I've tried my best to repay the enormous faith you've shown in me. To my Track Changes confidante, Nikola Lusk, thanks for your edits, encouragement and banter. And to Julian Welch, thanks for de-fouling the prop before we docked.

My mum and dad, Jane and David Vincent, were kind enough to let me move back to the family farm to write full-time – even if they occasionally interrupted me to ask me to help turn on the siphon or chase calves out of a plantation. Thanks to the twins, Lucy and Sarah Vincent, for keeping my ego in check, and to my biggest sister, Eve Vincent, for politely pushing me past the periphery. You're the best writer I know.

And so I get to the bit I've been looking forward to the most. A writer I like once said he needed his friends to keep him mercifully unemployed. Centrelink's got nothing on my gang. Writing *Blood and Guts* is the most selfish thing I've ever done, but you LoT sure as hell haven't made me feel guilty. Thanks for letting me live on the jib, keeping me posted on RHCHM's movements and playing *Junkie or Hipster?* Uptown *and* Downtown. Harry Watson, Nick Stubbs, Cassie Simakoff-Ellims, Shellaine Godbold, Harriet Lee Robinson, Caitlyn Brooks, Sam Burns, Joey Burns, Helen Daley, Alex Boynes, Shannan Langford Salisbury, Claire Stacey, Dave Johnston, Lance Gurney, (and because I'm a nostalgic soul) Isabel FitzGerald, Gabrielle Clay Lauder, Matt O'Rourke, Benji Hubbard, Eliya Nikki Cohen, Clare Thackway, Greg Hodge, Claire de Luca, Luke Menzies, Elle ('Farken') Boyd and Jane Wilson: you're not paying for your drinks until 2016.

www.ingramcontent.com/pod-product-compliance
Lightning Source LLC
Chambersburg PA
CBHW050340270326
41926CB00016B/3537